The Augustan Defence
of Satire

The Augustan Defence
of Satire

—

P. K. ELKIN

OXFORD
AT THE CLARENDON PRESS
1973

Oxford University Press, Ely House, London W. 1

GLASGOW   NEW YORK   TORONTO   MELBOURNE   WELLINGTON
CAPE TOWN   IBADAN   NAIROBI   DAR ES SALAAM   LUSAKA   ADDIS ABABA
DELHI   BOMBAY   CALCUTTA   MADRAS   KARACHI   LAHORE   DACCA
KUALA LUMPUR   SINGAPORE   HONG KONG   TOKYO

*Printed in Great Britain
at the University Press, Oxford
by Vivian Ridler
Printer to the University*

Preface

SATIRE has been a lively field of inquiry during the last couple
of decades. Particular satirical works and satirists, and the
general principles of satire, have been the subject of a number of impressive critical studies. 'Augustan' satirical works
and 'Augustan' satirists, especially, have been most carefully
examined—naturally enough, for they still represent the height
of achievement in English satire. Notwithstanding this spate
of scholarly inquiry, however, no comprehensive account has
yet been given of the *critical view* of satire held by Dryden,
Swift, Pope, Johnson, and their contemporaries. Yet it should
go without saying that the critical opinions of an age which
was predominantly satirical in temper, and which by common
consent succeeded in making satire its own, cannot help but
increase our understanding not only of its own writings but
also of satire generally. What were 'Augustan' writers' and
critics' views of the aims of satire, and of the effects which it
should or could have? What did they regard as its distinctive
features and principles? Its necessary limitations? Did they
look on it as a genre or, as we should today, rather as a temper
of writing? How highly did they rate it—as compared, for
example, with comedy, and tragedy? How 'personal' did they
consider it should be in its references? It is to answer these and
other questions of the same sort that the present book has been
written.

The opinions of the age have been gathered from poems and
prose writings, from essays and books on satire and individual
satirists, from prefaces and dedications of satirical works, and
from letters written by satirists and critics to one another
and to their friends. The criticism of satire expressed in plays and
in writings about plays, has been left somewhat to one side,
chiefly in order to avoid involvement in questions which, while
they might bear on the principles of satire, are in essence peculiar to the late seventeenth- and eighteenth-century theatre—the

controversy regarding the alleged immorality of Restoration comedy is an obvious instance. Nevertheless, comments from plays, and from critical writings on plays, have been used whenever they serve to illustrate particularly well some aspect of satiric theory or contemporary critical opinion.

One minor problem has been to find a comprehensive term for critics and satirists from Dryden to Johnson. I have decided on 'Augustan', although I agree with J. W. Johnson's argument in 'The Meaning of "Augustan" ' (*JHI* xix [1958], 507–22) that the term should, strictly speaking, be reserved for the first four decades of the eighteenth century, and also although the use of 'Augustan' in connection with English writers of the late seventeenth and eighteenth centuries means that it cannot be applied to the true Augustans, who have to be called 'Roman' or 'classical' instead. Short of resorting to numerals or a code-name, however, which would be unacceptable for other reasons, there does not appear to be a satisfactory alternative.

Except where sound modern editions of writers' works are available, first editions have been preferred—first 'collected' editions in the case of journals such as *The Tatler*. Quotations are faithful to their originals, which means that sometimes obvious misprints have been preserved, for example in quotations from a badly printed first edition such as Corbyn Morris's *An Essay Towards Fixing the True Standards of Wit, Humour, Raillery, Satire, and Ridicule* (1744). All quotations from Pope's poems are from the Twickenham edition; and all quotations from Boileau's poems are from Albert Cahen's edition of the *Satires* (Paris, 1932). The 1742 English translation of Joseph Trapp's *Praelectiones Poeticae* (1711–15) has been used instead of the original. Quotations from Horace and Juvenal are from the standard Oxford editions.

My thanks are due to Miss Mary Lascelles for her wise and generous counsel, to Miss Nina Burgis, Mrs. Sandra Tomlins, and Mrs. Margaret Massey for assistance in preparing the typescript, and to my wife Patricia for her help and support in all stages of the writing of this book.

P. K. E.

Contents

Abbreviations

Works cited

Boileau's *Satires*	Nicolas Boileau-Despréaux, *Satires*, ed. Albert Cahen (Paris, 1932).
Brown (1745)	John Brown, *An Essay on Satire* (1745).
Brown (1751)	John Brown, 'Essay on Ridicule', *Essays on the Characteristics of the Earl of Shaftesbury* (1751)
Corbyn Morris	[Corbyn Morris], *An Essay Towards Fixing the True Standards of Wit, Humour, Raillery, Satire and Ridicule* (1744).
Dacier	André Dacier, 'Préface sur les satires d'Horace', *Œuvres d'Horace* (1681–9), vi (1687).
Dryden's *Essays*	John Dryden, 'Discourse concerning the Original and Progress of Satire', *Essays*, ed. W. P. Ker (2 vols., Oxford, 1900).
Dryden's *Poems*	*The Poems of John Dryden*, ed. J. Kinsley (4 vols., Oxford, 1958).
Dryden's *Works*	*The Works of John Dryden*, ed. Walter Scott (18 vols., 1808).
Harte	Walter Harte. *An Essay on Satire, Particularly on the Dunciad* (1730).
Pope's *Correspondence*	Alexander Pope, *Correspondence*, ed. G. Sherburn (5 vols., Oxford, 1956).
Pope's *Poems*	*The Poems of Alexander Pope*, Twickenham edn., ed. J. Butt and others (6 vols., 1954–63).
Rapin	René Rapin, *Reflections on Aristotle's Treatise of Poesie*, trans. Thomas Rymer (1674).
Swift's *Correspondence*	Jonathan Swift, *Correspondence*, ed. H. Williams (5 vols., 1963–5).
Swift's *Poems*	*The Poems of Jonathan Swift*, ed. H. Williams (3 vols., Oxford, 1937; 2nd edn., 1958).
Swift's *Prose Works*	*The Prose Works of Jonathan Swift*, ed. H. Davis (14 vols., Oxford, 1939–63).
Trapp	*Lectures on Poetry*, trans. W. Clarke and W. Bowyer (1742), from *Praelectiones Poeticae* (1711–15).

Periodicals cited

AJP	*The American Journal of Philology*
CP	*Classical Philology*
E & S	*Essays and Studies published by the English Association*
ELH	*A Journal of English Literary History*
HLQ	*The Huntington Library Quarterly*
JEGP	*Journal of English and Germanic Philology*
JHI	*Journal of the History of Ideas*
MLN	*Modern Language Notes*
MLR	*Modern Language Review*
MP	*Modern Philology*
N & Q	*Notes and Queries*
PMLA	*Publications of the Modern Language Association of America*
PQ	*Philological Quarterly*
RES	*Review of English Studies*
SP	*Studies in Philology*

1. The Need for a Defence

CRITICISM of satire in the great age of English satire was rarely conducted at a high theoretical level. It was occasional, incidental, expedient, adventitious, and defensive—perhaps, above all, defensive. Like the satire itself, it frequently constituted part of the political and social cross-fire of the period. Satirists attacked their personal and public enemies, and one another, and critics attacked or defended satirists; and all in turn defended themselves. That was bound to happen. As satire is hostile by nature, it inevitably arouses hostility, with the result that the more active it is, the more it is attacked and the more it needs defending. In the late seventeenth and eighteenth centuries, satirists were constantly being called to account. They could expect every satire they published to arouse a storm of protest: attacks on their characters, questionings of their motives, and aspersions on their literary capabilities. Every satire that reached its mark was likely to breed counter-satires, anonymous and pseudonymous letters, and critical commentaries for and against. It is no wonder that a number of critics questioned the value not only of contemporary satire, but also of the mode itself. There was probably not a single Augustan writer who did not, at one time or another, warn against the dangers and ills resulting from its misuse. The satirists and their critical allies, therefore, were put on the defensive: they found that they not only had to guard their own literary reputations, but also to justify their using satire at all. They found themselves having to explain its noble aims, its classical standing, its singular efficacy as an instrument of social and moral reform, and its general usefulness to religion, government, and the law. Moreover, they found themselves having also to explain, or explain away, their motives, and to present a picture of the satirist as an innocent and tender-hearted victim of misunderstanding, not the trouble maker he was often accused of being. The result is a considerable body of theoretical opinion on the nature and function of satire. There are essays specifically entitled 'essays on satire', such as Mulgrave's (1679), Walter Harte's (1730), John Brown's (1745), and Charles Abbott's (1786); other essays on aspects of satire (contemporary satire, usually) which are without specific titles, for example Addison's celebrated attack on *ad hominem* satire in *The Spectator*, No. 23;[1] and brief commentaries on the history and nature of satire in such general works of literary criticism as Gildon's *The Laws of Poetry* (1721).[2] In addition, attitudes to satire and opinions of its various aspects are to be found in poems like Pope's *Epilogue to the Satires* and Churchill's *Epistle to William Hogarth*; in critical writings on English satirists such as Johnson's *Lives* of Dryden, Swift, and Pope, and Joseph Warton's *Essay on the Genius and Writings of Pope* (1756); in essays and books on topics like raillery, ridicule, humour, and wit, which are closely related to satire;[3] and in dedications and prefaces to translations of Horace, Juvenal, Persius, and Boileau.[4] Finally, there are also the numerous comments on satire made by satirists and their friends in their correspondence.

All in all, then, much was written on satire in the late seventeenth and eighteenth centuries. (Pope's comments alone, in advertisements, prefaces, footnotes, letters, and poems, would fill a book.) It would be a mistake, however, to expect this formidable volume of critical writing to yield a 'theory' of satire, using 'theory' in the sense of a consistent and coherent body of opinion. Perhaps, indeed, it is better to avoid the term, and to speak instead of Augustan 'opinions' or 'views' of satire. For at the outset it must be recognized that late seventeenth- and eighteenth-century writers normally only wrote about satire for

[1] 27 March 1711. Other examples are to be found in Steele's *Tatler*, No. 242, 26 October 1710, Swift's *Intelligencer*, No. 3, 25 May 1728, and Joseph Warton's *Adventurer*, No. 133, 12 February 1754.

[2] See also Rapin's *Reflections on Aristotle's Treatise of Poesie*, trans. Thomas Rymer (1674); Trapp's *Praelectiones Poeticae* (Oxford, 1711–15); and Newbery's *The Art of Poetry on a New Plan* (1762).

[3] e.g. Corbyn Morris, *An Essay Towards Fixing the True Standards of Wit, Humour, Raillery, Satire, and Ridicule* (1744).

[4] e.g. Barten Holyday's Preface to *D. J. Juvenal and A. Persius Flaccus Translated* (Oxford, 1673); André Dacier's 'Préface sur les satires d'Horace', *Œuvres d'Horace* (Paris, 1681–9); Dryden's Dedication of *The Satires of Decimus Junius Juvenalis* (1693); and N. Rowe's 'Some Account of Boileau's Writings, and This Translation', prefixed to *Boileau's Lutrin*, trans. John Ozell (1708).

much the same reasons as they wrote satire itself—that is to say, for personal reasons, to clear themselves of charges that had been made against them, to protect themselves and to retaliate, or simply to settle scores new and old. For example, when Pope found that his *Epistle to Burlington* had raised a furore, he wrote a long letter to John Gay,[5] defending the poem and reflecting broadly on satire. Mulgrave's *Essay on Satyre* (1679) provides an excellent example of a critical piece written for the purpose of settling scores. It was Dryden who had to pay in Rose Alley for its effectiveness. Although on such occasions writers sometimes followed the advocate's practice of proclaiming general principles, they were more likely to be making a special plea than stating their settled convictions. They found the principles handy sticks with which to beat off their assailants. Swift, for instance, in his *Vindication of Mr. Gay, and The Beggar's Opera*,[6] appealed to the widely held belief of his day in the corrective powers of satire, although it is evident from his writings as a whole that he did not really share this belief at all.[7]

The Augustans came to satire as their major mode of expression without fully realizing that they were doing so—almost against their will. It was epic poetry which they wished to write, and it was to epic poetry, not to satire, that they built their critical monuments—Le Bossu's *Traité du poème épique* (trans. W. J., 1695), for instance. In this connection it is worth noting that the single most important critical work on satire written during the period, Dryden's *Discourse on the Original and Progress of Satire*, contains a large preliminary section on the epic, on epic machinery especially, and includes a statement of its author's ambition to compose an epic on King Arthur.[8]

Furthermore, Dryden's essay illustrates as well as anything else written during the period the occasional and haphazard nature of Augustan criticism of satire, although allowances have to be made for Dryden's habitual methods of critical writing. The essay is both rambling and derivative. Possibly because of its great historical significance, and because it bears the stamp of Dryden's distinctive style in every sentence, the fact that a substantial part of it is simply a translation of André Dacier's

---

[5] [William Cleland] to Gay [16 December 1731], Pope's *Correspondence*, iii. 254–7.
[6] *The Intelligencer*, No. 3, 25 May 1728.
[7] See pp. 86–8 below.
[8] Dryden's *Essays*, ii. 26–38.

'Préface sur les satires d'Horace' (1687)[9] is usually passed over or understated. Dryden is engaged by the subject certainly: whenever he disagrees with one of his authorities, Casaubon, Heinsius, Rigault, or Dacier, he does so openly and with his customary spiritedness; and he gives in some detail towards the end of the essay his prescription for modern satire. But he has none the less felt it sufficient for the large sections on the etymology and the origins of satire merely to give a free translation of Dacier's Préface together with a few marginal comments of his own. He uses the same allusions and quotations (from Livy, Quintilian, Virgil, Horace, Diomedes, Ennius, Scaliger, and Heinsius), though in a number of instances he liberally expands the quotations.

Of those essays on satire, then, which were composed during the great age of English satire, the only one by a writer whom we should now recognize as among the leading literary figures of the age was derivative, loosely constructed, and in large part not on satire at all. The other leading Augustans commented on satire only in passing, though in a few instances their comments were sufficiently systematic and extensive to make them essays on aspects of satire, even if they were not so called. *The Spectator*, No. 23, for example, is virtually an essay on the abuse of personal satire, *The Tatler*, No. 242[10] is an essay on the advantages of gentle satire, and Pope's letter to Arbuthnot, 26 July 1734,[11] an essay on the moral function of satire and the uselessness of general satire. But aside from these and a few similar instances, comments on satire by leading Augustans were merely incidental. For example Dr. Johnson, though he was an imitator of Juvenal, as well as the biographer-critic of Dryden, Swift, and Pope, never had occasion to write specifically on satire. He devised a genealogy for it in the eighteenth-century style of genealogies in *The Rambler*, No. 22; he defined it in his *Dictionary*; he remarked on the ephemerality of personal satire in a footnote on Holofernes;[12] he condemned 'general lampooners of

---

[9] See Amanda M. Ellis, 'Horace's Influence on Dryden', *PQ* iv (1925), 39–60.

[10] It should be noted that *The Tatler*, No. 242, became the standard eighteenth-century essay on satire. It was used in Newbery's *The Art of Poetry on a New Plan* (1762), ii. 101–2, and in the *Encyclopaedia Britannica*, 2nd edn., viii (1781), 6328–30 (also in 3rd, 4th, 5th, and 6th edns.).

[11] Pope's *Correspondence*, iii. 420.

[12] *The Plays of William Shakespeare* (1765), ii. 155.

mankind' in *The Idler*, No. 45 (24 February 1759); he ridiculed the application of the term 'satire' to Dorset's 'little personal invectives' in his *Life of Dorset*;[13] he remarked that strong personal feeling 'can add great force to general principles' in his *Life of Dryden*;[14] he commended the service to public taste performed by *The Dunciad* in his *Life of Pope*;[15] and, in the same biography, he expressed his revulsion at Swift's and Pope's preoccupation with sordid subject-matter.[16] But that is about all he left by way of specific commentary on the general principles of satire. For further hints as to his views we have to turn to Boswell and Mrs. Piozzi, and to his critical judgements of satirists and their writings in *The Lives of the English Poets*.

For the Augustans satire was too familiar and too useful to become the subject of disinterested speculation. It was part of the hurly-burly of their lives: from the mid seventeenth century it had become increasingly a favourite weapon for both public controversy and private slander.[17] According to one estimate, more than 3,000 satirical pieces from the period 1660–78 still survive in print, in addition to approximately 2,500 in manuscript.[18] 'Political' is the tag commonly attached to these satires; but it can be misleading. There is nothing 'political', in our sense of the term, in many of the poems printed under the title *Poems on Affairs of State* between 1697 and 1733. As politics was more intimate in the seventeenth and eighteenth centuries than it is today, and as it was conducted very largely in terms of personalities rather than principles, many of the poems are merely satirical commentaries on the doings of the day, on disreputable happenings in high places, and on facets of the lives of public figures which in a less 'Curious and Censuring Age'[19] would have been kept private.

From 1655 on [comments G. de F. Lord], every aspect of public affairs in England was subjected to the satirist's increasingly minute and bitter scrutiny. . . . Not a drunken frolic, nor a brawl at court, nor

---

[13] *The Lives of the English Poets* (Dublin, 1779–81), i. 452.
[14] Ibid. i. 349.   [15] Ibid. ii. 428.   [16] Ibid.
[17] See C. V. Wedgwood, *Poetry and Politics under the Stuarts* (Cambridge, 1960), p. 2.
[18] *Poems on Affairs of State: Augustan Satirical Verse 1660–1714*, vol. i (1660–78), ed. G. de F. Lord (New Haven, 1963), p. xxvi.
[19] Sir William Temple, 'Of Poetry', *Miscellanea*, The Second Part (1690), p. 3.

a bribe in Parliament, not an instance of cowardice or chicanery in the navy, nor one of hypocrisy or bigotry in the Church escaped satirical notice.[20] When it was this sort of satire they had in mind, critics were unlikely to turn their attention to first principles. They were far more likely to enter directly into the controversies raised by the satirists, to strike back with counter-satires, or, if they happened to be involved personally, to conduct *ad hominem* campaigns against their opponents—John Dennis's critical writings supply examples of all three of these preoccupations.

There is, however, another side to the picture. Besides being familiar with satire as political propaganda and social commentary, the Augustans knew it also as literature. The classical poets they most admired—Horace and Juvenal—were satirists; so too was the French neo-classical poet, Boileau. Moreover, Boileau had demonstrated that a modern poet could write satire of as high a quality as any produced in the past. The English neo-classical satirists could claim to be following in a distinguished tradition, and allow themselves a considerable degree of latitude in expatiating on the exalted nature of their aims. In particular, in defending their own works or their Muse, they could fall back on the traditional justification of satire on the grounds of its moral function—its exceptional usefulness as an instrument of correction and reform. The ways in which they elaborated this traditional defence will be described later; in the present introductory chapter it is appropriate rather to explore their reasons (unstated as well as stated) for adopting it. These reasons are, after all, crucial: they explain not only why the critical defence of satire in the seventeenth and eighteenth centuries took the shape it did, but also why satire inevitably became the paramount mode of expression for more than a century.

That the defenders of satire should have sought to justify it principally on the ground that it can help to set things in order, and bring wrongdoers into line, will surprise no one who is reasonably familiar with English history of the late seventeenth century, that is of the formative years of the Augustan age.[21] Englishmen who remembered the 'late times of *Civil War*, and

---

[20] *Poems on Affairs of State*, I. xliii.
[21] See especially P. S. Wood, 'Native Elements in English Neo-Classicism', *MP* xxiv (1926), 201–8.

confusion',[22] longed above all for stable government and a settled, peaceful life. They felt they could discern beyond the realities of the present and the immediate past the ideal of a society founded on permanent principles of order, and infused with the radiance and grandeur of the heroic world of antiquity, though without the embarrassing imperfections of that world, such as its moral lapses and fantastic superstitions. Their outlook in short was ethical and didactic rather than historical: it was focused less on men's motives than on their deeds and the effects of those deeds, less on the processes of social change for their own sake than on significant patterns of events. Hence they regarded individuals primarily as types, and church, state, and society as subject to established authority. They had suffered long enough, so they believed, from singularity, excess, and caprice, from the 'lawless salvage Libertie'[23] of the Puritan interregnum. So Charles II was welcomed back to England specifically 'for the moderating of Extremities, the Reconciling of Differences, and the satisfying of all Interests';[24] and Dryden, joining in the general hallelujah of joy and hope at the Restoration, proclaimed the end of factions and party strife—

    . . . the hateful names of Parties cease
    And factious Souls are wearied into peace.[25]

The turning was from the singular to the usual or common: from 'private Optiks'[26] to common sense, from the whims of individuals to a single objective standard—the ultimate compromise, the golden mean. Accordingly, the reconstructed monarchy was a compromise between the extremes 'Of pop'lar sway and arbitrary reign'; and the Church of England was a compromise between the Roman Catholic Church and the dissenting sects, between centralized church government and absolute authority on the one side, and private judgement and decentralized church government on the other side. In these circumstances the arch-villain was a Satanic individualist, such as Dryden's Achitophel, plotting to overthrow the established government and form a new government with his fellow rebels; or at a more ordinary, social level he was the Overdoer, as

---

[22] Thomas Sprat, *History of the Royal Society* (1667), p. 152.
[23] 'Astræa Redux', Dryden's *Poems*, i. 17.
[24] *The Earl of Manchester's Speech to His Majesty* . . . *At his Arrival at Whitehall. The 29th. of May, 1660* (1660).   [25] *Poems*, i. 24.
[26] Sir William Davenant, *Poem, to the King's Most Sacred Majesty* (1663).

Samuel Butler called him, the man always wrong because always immoderate. Extremes in anything were out of fashion—in dress and manners, even in mistresses and parties. 'Their speech & habits they cannot indure should be like their Neighbours',[27] Richard Head observed sarcastically of the dissenters; Matthew Prior praised 'Jinny the Just' for her complementary qualities— 'She cutt even between the Coquette, and the Prude';[28] and Dryden claimed that he and his friends, like poets in the age of Augustus, were careful to avoid extremes on their 'Genial Nights'—'our discourse is neither too serious, nor too light . . . the raillery neither too sharp upon the present, nor too censorious on the absent; and the Cups onely such as will raise the Conversation of the Night, without disturbing the business of the Morrow'.[29] So universal indeed did the principle of moderation seem to the Augustans that they were able to attribute it even to the English climate, and even to the Almighty Himself:

Our *Trimmer* therefore inspired by this Divine Vertue, thinks fit to conclude with these Assertions, That our Climate is a *Trimmer*, between that part of the World where men are Roasted, and the other where they are Frozen; That our Church is a *Trimmer*, between a Phrenzy of Platonick Visions, and the Lethargick Ignorance of Popish Dreams; That our Laws are *Trimmers*, between the Excess of unbounded Power, and the Extravagance of Liberty not enough restrained; That true Vertue hath ever been thought a *Trimmer*, and to have its dwelling in the middle between the two Extreams; That even God Almighty is divided between his two great Attributes, his Mercy and his Justice.[30]

Halifax and the other writers just quoted were of course describing an ideal. Many writers, like Sir William Temple, were well aware of the extremes of English national life, and of the idiosyncrasies of the English character, and at times indeed regarded them with pride.[31] None the less it remains true that a yearning for the middle way was both fervent and widespread in the

[27] *Proteus Redivivus* (1675), p. 236.
[28] *The Literary Works of Matthew Prior*, ed. H. Bunker Wright and Monroe K. Spears (Oxford, 1959), i. 302, line 51.
[29] Dedication of *The Assignation, or Love in a Nunnery* (1673), Dryden's *Works*, iv. 351.
[30] [George Savile, Marquis of Halifax], *The Character of a Trimmer* (1688), pp. 42–3.
[31] See Temple, *Miscellanea*, ii. 55; also references in Clara Marburg, *Sir William Temple* (New Haven, 1932), p. 91; and P. S. Wood, 'The Opposition to Neo-Classicism in England between 1660 and 1700', *PMLA* xliii (1928), 183.

formative years of the Augustan age; and living in an age whose goals were order, stability, and compromise, instead of experiment, revolution, and individualism, writers aimed less to inspire and arouse than to correct. One senses this especially in their essays, whether on literary topics, polite conversation, or life in the city or the country. They loved to lay down rules, draw morals, cite precedents, and give warnings. It is no wonder then that they were able to put forward the traditional defence of satire on the grounds of its moral function with especial conviction. They believed that when it was properly employed, satire was doing something for society which was urgently necessary, something which any right-thinking, practically minded citizen might well look upon as his duty. Moreover, they were for the most part, as a result of their faith in reason, perfectly convinced that it was something which could be done.

Augustan satire was firmly rooted in the comforting conviction of the age that men are free and responsible beings, who can set about improving themselves and their society by the exercise of reason—of those higher powers of will, understanding, and mind, which make civilization possible.[32] Had not this conviction been widely held (for naturally there were some currents of opinion, such as the 'ruling passion' theory, which conflicted with it), satire could not have flourished as it did. Such faith in free will and the efficacy of reason made men unusually eager to increase knowledge and to raise themselves and society to a more highly civilized level; and, with notable exceptions, like Swift and Mandeville, it made them extraordinarily confident of their ability to achieve such a goal. But it did much more than this, for it opened up an ideal world against which the real world could be measured and found wanting. If, on the *cogito ergo sum* principle, man is ideally that part of himself which reasons, then the discrepancy between his ideal and his real self is dishearteningly wide. Furthermore, as Basil Willey has expressed it, 'The temper which views all things in their theory rather than in their historical setting must also see little, as it gazes upon human institutions, but failure and futility, and as it contemplates human actions, little but departures from the rational norm.'[33]

[32] See, for example, Benjamin Whichcote, *The Work of Reason* (1660), *passim.*   [33] *The Seventeenth-Century Background* (1934), p. 91.

In the awareness of this discrepancy between the rational and the actual, both the necessity for satire and its function were readily apparent. The Augustans were able simultaneously to look down with scorn on human actions and institutions and solemnly to propound the corrective function of satire. This latter notion, as has already been observed, provided them with the basis of their defence of satire, and enabled them to hail it as an instrument of virtue and justice, of the divine will—a 'sacred Weapon'. As might be expected, however, the loftier the statements on satire became, the vaguer they became also. Sometimes one can hardly be sure whether it is satire, or literature, or morality itself, which is being defended. Consequently, before proceeding to give a detailed account of Augustan poets' and critics' views on satire, it is necessary to determine as exactly as possible what they understood by the term.

2. The Meaning of 'Satire'

'ANYTHING sharp or severe, is called a Satyr', stated *Cocker's English Dictionary* (1704). This definition would seem to be so vague as hardly to be a definition at all. Yet, if anything, the meaning of 'satire' in the late seventeenth and eighteenth centuries was even vaguer than that definition allows, for in addition to being used to describe almost anything written or spoken of a 'sharp or severe' turn, it was applied to light mockery too. In most dictionaries (Johnson's included) it was given the reasonably specific literary definition, 'invective poem'; but in common usage it was associated with all sorts and types of writing: epistles, diatribes, encomia, squibs, lampoons, puffs, essays, fables, dialogues, plays, travel-books, romances, rehearsals, footnotes, advertisements, critiques, and histories. This is really to say that it was no longer applied mainly to a particular form—namely, verse satire on the Roman model—as it had been in the sixteenth century, but instead to the informing spirit of all or part of a literary work or conversation. Hence Pope's comment to Swift: 'You call your satires, Libels; I would rather call my satires, Epistles.'[1] It could indeed be used to refer to almost anything that smacked of censure and was delivered in a mocking, ironical, derisive, censorious, abusive, or jesting manner. In one context it might mean light-hearted mockery, banter, or raillery; in another, malicious slander or libel; in another, denunciation of follies or vices; and in yet another, a vengeful, personal attack on an enemy's infirmities or weaknesses. It could be used to mean ridicule, censure, sharp rebuke, or malicious wit; or to designate a literary work, or the kind of literature, which consists predominantly of ridicule and censure, or the author of that kind of literature.[2] In short, during the Augustan

---

1 2[0] April 1733, Pope's *Correspondence*, iii. 366. For comments on the gradual expansion of the meaning of 'satire', see David Worcester, *The Art of Satire* (Harvard, 1940), p. 1; and for comments on its vagueness in the eighteenth century, see Ian Jack, *Augustan Satire* (Oxford, 1952), p. 146.
2 For this note, see pp. 202–3 below.

age, 'satire' served a bewildering variety of purposes: it was used freely and often carelessly, sometimes capriciously; at other times deliberately, and with malice or flattery aforethought, according to the needs of the moment. Once in a while someone (Steele, for instance, in *The Tatler*, No. 242) would attempt to say what 'true satire' really is; but, as is usually the case with words that have to be monitored by 'true' or 'genuine', 'satire' went on being used as vaguely and variably as before. Moreover, to complicate matters, as John Brown remarked, different classes and social groups had different ideas as to what was ridiculous, humorous, witty, or the like: 'What is high Humour at *Wapping*, is rejected as nauseous in the *City*: What is delicate Raillery in *the City*, grows *coarse* and *intolerable* as you approach *St. James's*. . . .'[3] Sometimes 'satire' was more or less deliberately confused with similar terms, as in such phrases as 'raillery and satire', 'satire and ridicule', 'libel and satire', and 'comedy and satire': the author in each case wanted to bring the associations of one word to bear on the other word. For example, by coupling 'True raillery and satire' in his essay on that topic in *The Tatler*, No. 242, Steele aimed to bring 'satire' into line with 'raillery', to confer on it the delicacy and light-heartedness of 'raillery', as he understood this term and wanted it understood by others. Similarly, in *The Spectator*, No. 23, by coupling 'lampoons' and 'satires'—'Lampoons and Satyrs, that are written with Wit and Spirit, are like poison'd Darts . . .'—Addison was doing his best to give 'satire' a bad name.[4] Then again, sometimes 'satire' was simply included in a list of items or ingredients, where its meaning cannot be clearly distinguished from that of the other terms in the list:

. . . *Gallantry, Raillery, Humour, Satire, Ridicule, Sarcasms*, or other Subjects, are generally blended with WIT. . . .[5]

To be more serious, new fashions, follies, and vices, make new monitors necessary in every age. An author may be considered as a merciful substitute to the legislature; he acts not by punishing crimes, but preventing them; however virtuous the present age,

³ Brown (1751), pp. 53–4.
⁴ Cf. John Tillotson, *Works* (1728), i. 397: 'The Wit of Man doth more naturally vent it self in *Satire* and Censure, than in Praise and *Panegyrick*.'
⁵ Corbyn Morris, p. 3.

there may be still growing employment for ridicule, or reproof, for persuasion, or satire.[6]

At other times careful attempts were made to distinguish 'satire' from the terms with which it was most commonly confused. It is its relationships with these terms—comedy, raillery, ridicule, libel, slander, and lampoon—that we shall now briefly examine.

(a) 'Comedy' and 'satire'

The common practice in the seventeenth and eighteenth centuries of using 'comedy' in much the same sense as 'satire' is confusing to modern readers. We are inclined to assume that there is a radical distinction between the two modes, even while admitting that they are sometimes so closely interwoven in the one work (Don Quixote for example) that it is difficult to say where one ends and the other begins. We distinguish them mainly in terms of effects: comedy, we say, encourages us to laugh freely—it has a liberating effect—for it enlarges our sense of the possibilities of life; whereas satire allows us only responsible laughter, for no matter how gay and sparkling its surface, it is always fundamentally judicial—its distinctive effect is that of intensifying our awareness of norms, conventions, traditions, and established standards.[7]

Now late seventeenth- and eighteenth-century critics did on occasion differentiate between 'comedy' and 'satire'. For example, 'comedy' was sometimes used to designate a certain kind of stage-play—one that gives a realistic depiction of low life—and 'satire' to refer to the element of ridicule or censure it contained.[8] Swift notes this broad distinction in one part of his defence of The Beggar's Opera and then proceeds to elaborate it.

[6] Oliver Goldsmith, An Enquiry into the Present State of Polite Learning in Europe (1759), Collected Works of Oliver Goldsmith, ed. Arthur Friedman (5 vols., Oxford, 1966), i. 314–15.

[7] See James Sutherland, English Satire (Cambridge, 1958), pp. 2–4; and Maynard Mack, 'The Muse of Satire', Yale Review, xl (1951), p. 85.

[8] I am sensible that Callow was so like the Life, that the Rot me Sparks openly declar'd their dissatisfaction at the Satyr: but 'tis a sign it hit them, when they complain of the wound. 'Tis a base and ill-natur'd, as well as ignorant Age of Chriticism, when the Vertues of a Play shall be Arraigned as Defects; for if these Gentlemen understood either the Original, or end of Comedy, they wou'd never quarrel with the Satyr of it, since from its beginning 'twas design'd to correct Vice, and Folly, by exposing them.
(Charles Gildon, A Letter to Mr. D'Urfey, Occasioned by his Play Called the Marriage-Hater Match'd (1692), sig. a 1r.)

The 'satire' in *The Beggar's Opera*, Swift implies, begins where the comic realism ends: it is the result of a pointed reference to a world beyond the realistically depicted world of the 'comedy', and of an explicit moral judgement of both worlds. The 'satire' is a fourth dimension, as it were, of the 'comedy'.

> In this happy Performance of Mr. GAY's, all the Characters are just, and none of them carried beyond Nature, or hardly beyond Practice. It discovers the whole System of that Common-Wealth, or that *Imperium in Imperio* of Iniquity, established among us, by which neither our Lives, nor our Properties are secure, either in the High-ways, or in publick Assemblies, or even in our own Houses. It shews the miserable Lives and the constant Fate of those abandoned Wretches; for how little they sell their Lives and Souls; betrayed by their *Whores*, their *Comrades*, and the *Receivers* and *Purchasers* of these Thefts and Robberies. This *Comedy* contains likewise a *Satyr*, which although it doth by no Means affect the present Age, yet might have been useful in the former, and may possibly be so in Ages to come: I mean where the Author takes Occasion of comparing those *common Robbers of the Publick*, and their several Stratagems of betraying, undermining and hanging each other, to the several Arts of *Politicians* in Times of Corruption.[9]

Furthermore, a difference in tone between 'comedy' and 'satire' was widely recognized, 'satire' being regarded as more severe. Thus 'satirical' (usually spelt 'satyrical') appeared in the dictionaries as 'severe, sharp, biting, censorious, bitter, scoffing, or reproving'; and 'comical' as 'jocose, merry, diverting, witty, humorous, pleasant, agreeable, or facetious'.[10]

Nevertheless, while it is true that Augustan critics at times distinguished between 'comedy' and 'satire', they tended, when discussing their broad purposes, to run the two together. Rapin, for example, declared that the end of comedy is 'to shew on the Stage the faults of particulars, in order to amend the faults of the Publick, and to correct the people through a fear of being rendr'd ridiculous' and that of satire 'to instruct the People by discrediting Vice'.[11] In short, Rapin sees 'comedy' and 'satire' as having much the same aims; but he limits the sphere of 'comedy' to the stage. Especially when they were justifying comedy,

---

[9] *The Intelligencer*, No. 3.

[10] See for example: [Thomas Blount], *Glossographia Anglicana Nova* (1707); B. N. Defoe, *A Compleat English Dictionary* (1735); or E[dward] P[hillips], *The New World of English Words* (1658).

[11] Rapin, pp. 124–5, 137.

Augustan critics spoke of it as though it were satire; or, to put the same point another way, they sought to justify comedy on the grounds of what we should call its 'satirical' aim and content. 'Comedy proposes for its object', wrote Hugh Blair, 'neither the great sufferings nor the great crimes of men; but their follies and slighter vices, those parts of their character, which raise in beholders a sense of impropriety, which expose them to be censured, and laughed at by others, or which render them troublesome in civil society.' He goes on to say: 'This general idea of Comedy, as a satyrical exhibition of the improprieties and follies of mankind, is an idea very moral and useful.'[12] In the opinion of many critics throughout the period the prime object of comedy was to depreciate vice by making it ridiculous. Indeed, in Jeremy Collier's view, as he made clear in the very first sentence of his celebrated attack on the contemporary stage, this was the object of all drama.[13]

(b) 'Raillery' and 'satire'

In late seventeenth- and early eighteenth-century dictionaries 'raillery' was defined as 'jesting, sporting, scoffing or merriment'.[14] The word was borrowed from the French to describe a conversational mode, which became highly fashionable in the latter part of the seventeenth century, and which was idealized in the first half of the eighteenth century, especially in essays and books on 'polite conversation'. With its associations of ease, subtlety, moderation, and refinement, it is one of the key words of the Augustan age. It was to be distinguished especially from 'railing', which meant scolding or upbraiding, or using angry or abusive language. In the late seventeenth century, 'railing' continued to be practised and approved. John Oldham railed at the 'Printer that exposed him by Printing a piece of his grossly Mangled and Faulty', and in that poem and one of his prefaces sought to justify rough, hard-hitting satire.[15] As Augustan

---

[12] Lectures on Rhetoric and Belles Lettres (1783), ii. 528.

[13] A Short View of the Immorality and Profaneness of the English Stage (1698). For further comments on the corrective function of comedy, see Sir Richard Blackmore, Preface to Prince Arthur (1695), first unsigned gathering [2v], and Thomas Cooke, A Prologue to Comic Poetry (1753), p. 7.

[14] See P[hillips], The New World of English Words; E[lisha] Coles, An English Dictionary (1676); and Edward Cocker, Cocker's English Dictionary (1704). And see also Norman Knox, The Word IRONY and its Context, 1500–1755 (Duke Univ., N.C., 1961), especially pp. 189–208.

[15] See The Poems of John Oldham, ed. Bonamy Dobrée (1960), pp. 7, 12.

vaiues became more securely established, however, 'railing' was relegated to the barbarous past: it was regarded as the weapon of malcontents and overdoers. The true Augustan thought it better 'to rally' a man than 'to rail' at him, better that is 'to reprove [him] for a fault in a merry way'[16] than to berate him severely and directly. So Horace was often preferred to Juvenal, because he 'rallies, but ne'er rails'.[17] 'To rally', indeed, did not necessarily carry with it any notion of reproof: it could mean merely 'to banter, joke, sport, or play with words',[18] to entertain or divert without giving offence. 'Men of Wit, who understand Raillery, are always on the Laughter-side . . . ', observed Bellegarde, and he warned that 'if you criticize the Follies or Infirmities of others, you offend them. . . . '[19] 'Were I to define Raillery,' Arthur Murphy stated, 'I should call it a delicate Exertion of Pleasantry upon the Foibles or the slight Inadvertences, which disclose themselves in the Actions of Men.'[20] Fielding emphasized the lightness and harmlessness of 'true raillery' in a lengthy descrip-tion he gave of it in *An Essay on Conversation* (1752). He said that it consists in 'playing on peccadillos', in making mild fun of a person's minor faults and foibles, or 'in pleasantly re-present-ing real good qualities in a false light of shame, and bantering them at ill ones', or 'in ridiculing men for vices and faults which they are known to be free from'.[21] Fielding here analyses the most widely approved meaning of 'raillery' in the eighteenth century. In the late seventeenth century, however, it was some-times used to refer to clumsy as well as skilful jesting. Thus Roger L'Estrange remarked on the existence of 'two sorts of *Raillery*, or Mirth; the one is *Course, Petulant, Criminal* and *Foul*; the other, *Cleanly, Gracious, Ingenious*, and *Face-tious* . . . '.[22] Late seventeenth- and early eighteenth-century writers on polite behaviour and conversation drew attention to these 'two sorts of *Raillery*' in order to damn that which was 'gross' and to praise that which was 'fine' or 'delicate'. A more subtle distinction was made between 'fine' or 'delicate' raillery

[16] Thomas Dyche, *A New English Dictionary* (1740).
[17] Harte, p. 16.
[18] Dyche, *A New English Dictionary*.
[19] J. B. M. de Bellegarde, *Reflexions upon Ridicule* (1706), pp. 70–1.
[20] *Gray's-Inn Journal*, No. 26, 23 March 1754.
[21] *Works*, ed. Sir Leslie Stephen (1882), vi. 325.
[22] *Tully's Offices* (1681), p. 51.

on the one hand, and 'sharp' raillery on the other. 'Sharp' raillery was held to be no less skilful than 'fine' raillery but to differ
from it in its capacity to offend and hurt; it could be employed
deliberately for the purpose of wounding. It should be noted too
that 'railing' did not, at least in the late seventeenth century,
necessarily carry with it suggestions of crudity and clumsiness.
Indeed in the following comment Dryden commends the skill of
Juvenal's 'railing' as against the unsureness of Horace's 'rally-
ing':

> Juvenal has railed more wittily than Horace has rallied. Horace
> means to make his readers laugh, but he is not sure of his experi-
> ment. Juvenal always intends to move your indignation, and he
> always brings about his purpose.[23]

These inconsistencies and confusions notwithstanding, the distinction between 'raillery' and 'railing' was vitally important in
the Augustan age, especially during the late seventeenth and
early eighteenth centuries, that is during that part of the age in
which the values of subtlety and refinement were being most
strenuously advocated. It was probably in order to sharpen the
distinction that writers often used 'rallery' in place of 'raillery',
for 'raillery' could be mistaken for the noun form of 'to rail' and
so be confused with 'railing'. The ability 'to rally' a friend, an
opponent, or a circle of acquaintances, became in the eighteenth
century one of the marks of a gentleman. Railing was rejected
as crude, ill natured, uncivilized. As for satire, it had to change
its rough ways or be rejected too. It had to become more like
'raillery', or even indeed become 'raillery'. So Dryden used the
phrase 'fine raillery' to describe the new ideal of satirical writing
and his own Zimri portrait;[24] and Joseph Warton, over half a
century later, referred to the 'fine-turned RAILLERY' of *The Rape
of the Lock*.[25] 'Raillery', however, belonged properly to conversation; 'satire', for all its unpleasant associations, was tradi-
tionally the literary term. What it needed to do, therefore,
in order to gain favour, was to acquire a new image and a new
set of associations. To highlight the change which was demanded, and largely achieved, we may contrast the string of
unflattering epithets considered appropriate to 'satire' by the

[23] Dryden's *Essays*, ii. 95.
[24] Ibid., pp. 92–3.
[25] Joseph Warton (1756), p. 248.

seventeenth-century lexicographer Joshua Poole with William
Whitehead's idealized description of eighteenth-century satirists
composing their satires:

> *Satyre.* Girding, biting, snarling, scourging, jerking, lashing,
> smarting, sharp, tart, rough, invective, censorious, currish, snappish,
> captious, barking, brawling, carping, fanged, sharp-tooth'd, quipping,
> jeering, flouting, sullen, rigid, impartial, whipping, thorny, pricking,
> stinging, sharp-fang'd, injurious, reproachful, libellous, harsh,
> rough-hewne, odious, approbrious, contumelious, defaming, calum-
> nious.[26]

> We, like *Menander*, more discreetly dare,
> And well-bred Satire wears a milder Air.
> Still Vice we brand, or titled Fools disgrace,
> But dress in Fable's Guise the borrow'd Face.
> Or as the Bee, thro' Nature's wild Retreats,
> Drinks the moist Fragrance from th'unconscious Sweets,
> To injure none, we lightly range the Ball,
> And glean from diff'rent Knaves the copious Gall;
> Extract, compound, with all a Chymist's Skill,
> And claim the motley Characters who will.[27]

Yet, even well on into the eighteenth century, 'satire' continued
to have overtones of harshness and severity. In most dictionaries
it was defined principally by its severity. One may say that this
was the first line of distinction between 'satire' and such related
terms as 'comedy', 'ridicule', and 'raillery'—and the dictionaries
fell back on it, typically defining 'satire' as 'a poem in which the
vices and follies of all sorts of persons are sharply censured and
published in the most glaring colours to make them appear the
more hateful'.[28] It is precisely on the grounds of its comparative
severity that Corbyn Morris, writing not at the beginning but
towards the end of the period, distinguishes 'satire' from 'raillery'. In his view 'raillery' is a gentle attack on *'slight* Foibles
and Oddities' whereas 'satire' is 'a witty and severe Attack' on
vices and habits which are really harmful, and whereas the intention of 'raillery' is to provoke uncritical laughter, the intention of 'satire' is to arouse detestation of vice. The sharper the

---

[26] *The English Parnassus: or, a Helpe to English Poesie* (1657).

[27] *An Essay on Ridicule* (1743), p. 15.

[28] Lewis Morery, *The Great Historical, Geographical and Poetical Dictionary*, trans. 'by several Learned Men' (1694).

sting, Morris concludes, the more excellent the 'satire', its 'Intention being entirely to root out and destroy the Vice'.[29]

Satire was still regarded by some eighteenth-century critics then as essentially different from raillery. In their eyes satire belonged properly to the tough-minded practical reformer, whereas raillery could be safely employed by good-humoured gentlemen and well-mannered young ladies. 'There ought also to be a great Distance between Raillery and Satire', says Arabella in *The Female Quixote*,

> so that one may never be mistaken for the other: Raillery ought indeed to surprise, and sensibly touch, those to whom it is directed; but I would not have the Wounds it makes, either deep or lasting: Let those who feel it, be hurt like Persons, who, gathering Roses, are pricked by the Thorns, and find a sweet Smell to make amends.[30]

(c) 'Ridicule' and 'satire'

Although 'ridicule' was sometimes used synonymously with 'raillery' and 'satire', it tended mostly to come somewhere between the two, being regarded as sharper than the one, less severe than the other. It was used more widely as noun than verb, and most commonly to mean 'the practice of making persons or things the object of banter, mockery, or derision'. That was what Temple meant by it when he complained of ridicule corrupting modern poetry, and what Shaftesbury meant when he recommended ridicule as an effective counter to enthusiasm. But whereas Temple would have placed the emphasis on 'derision', Shaftesbury would have placed it on 'banter'. The shadings between 'banter' and 'derision' are frequently difficult to determine. Clearly the general tendency, however, was to put ridicule on the devil's side, to associate it with pride, derision, and contempt. Thus John Brown distinguishes between 'Pure *Wit*' and '*undesigning Laughter*' on the one hand, and 'Ridicule or Raillery' on the other. 'Pure *Wit*', he says, 'amuses and delights the Imagination by those sudden Assemblages and pleasing Pictures of Things which it creates . . . But *Ridicule* or *Raillery* . . . solely regards the Opinions, Passions, Actions, and Characters of Men: and may properly be denominated "that Species of Writing

---

[29] Corbyn Morris, pp. 36–7, 50.
[30] Charlotte Lennox, *The Female Quixote; or the Adventures of Arabella* (1752), ii. 144.

which excites Contempt with Laughter".[31] Similarly, Kames distinguishes between objects 'either *risible* or *ridiculous*' and contrasts the emotions they arouse:

A risible object is mirthful only; a ridiculous object is both mirthful and contemptible. The first raises an emotion of laughter that is altogether pleasant: the emotion of laughter raised by the other, is qualified with that of contempt; and the mixed emotion, partly pleasant partly painful, is termed *the emotion of ridicule*. I avenge myself of the pain a ridiculous object gives me by a laugh of derision. A risible object, on the other hand, gives me no pain: it is altogether pleasant by a certain sort of titillation, which is expressed externally by mirthful laughter.[32]

'Ridicule' was thus likened to 'satire' in being more mordant than 'raillery', yet its meaning tended to be vaguer and more general than that of 'satire'. Besides it was not normally considered to have the same reformative purpose as 'satire', but rather, like 'raillery', to concern itself with those insignificant failings which provoke amusement instead of dislike or detestation.

In those contexts where 'ridicule' referred to the '*act* or *practice* of making something or someone the object of laughter', and 'satire' to the finished product, to the work which performed the 'ridicule', 'ridicule' could be appropriately described as one of the means employed by 'satire'. Thus Charles Abbott spoke of 'satire' having 'invective' and 'ridicule' at its disposal and of 'ridicule' being the more effective instrument because its powers are more extensive and various than those of 'invective', which 'may deter or punish, but will seldom correct or improve'.[33] Most often, however, in eighteenth-century as in modern usage, 'ridicule' was the more inclusive term, as, for example, when Joseph Warton spoke of comedy, satire, and burlesque, as 'the three chief branches of ridicule'.[34]

(d) 'Libel', 'slander', 'lampoon', and 'satire'

No one appears to have been much troubled by the confusion of 'comedy' with 'satire' in the late seventeenth and early

---

[31] Brown (1751), pp. 41–3. See also Whitehead, *Essay on Ridicule*, p. 4.

[32] Henry Home (Lord Kames), *Elements of Criticism* (Edinburgh, 1762), i. 341.

[33] 'On the Use and Abuse of Satire' (1786), *Oxford English Prize Essays* (Oxford, 1836), i. 182.

[34] *The Adventurer*, No. 133.

eighteenth centuries: it suited the critics to take for granted the
close relationship of these terms rather than to discriminate
carefully between them. In this way the moral function of
'satire' could be attributed to 'comedy' and some of the good
nature of 'comedy' to 'satire'. The confusion of 'satire' with
'libel', 'slander', and 'lampoon', however, was of a different
order, if only because wherever it occurred it harmed the reputation of 'satire'. Often indeed the confusion was deliberately
created for this purpose by those critics who had a low regard
for satire generally or who were alarmed by the contemporary
trend of satirical writing. The defenders of satire naturally took
a different view: while they were disdainful of much contemporary satire, they deplored rather the current debasement of
the term and took pains to discriminate between 'true satire'
and the low forms of defamation and personal abuse with which
it had come to be associated. So T. Swift complained that 'the
world has of late years embraced a notion, that Personal Satire
and Lampoon are convertible terms';[35] and Pope condemned
the man

> Who reads but with a Lust to mis-apply,
> Make Satire a Lampoon, and Fiction, Lye.[36]

The standing complaint of the defenders was that the term
'satire' was being used as a cloak for slander and libel—

> When scandal has new minted an old lie,
> Or tax'd invention for a fresh supply,
> 'Tis called satyr, and the world appears
> Gath'ring around it with erected ears;[37]

—that in fact all the riff-raff of the literary underworld were
calling themselves 'satirists' in order to present a respectable
front to the world. Mr. Hyde, so it seemed, was posing as
Dr. Jekyll.

Does anyone asperse his neighbour's reputation? He instantly
vindicates his conduct by calling himself a Satirist. Does any
ungrateful bard repay the kindness of his friend, with the most gross
abuse? He is a Satirist. In short, the word, in its present corrupted
signification, implies, an undoubted right of censuring, scandalizing,
and venting the foulest reproaches on all mankind.[38]

[35] *The Temple of Folly* (1787), p. xiii.
[36] *An Epistle to Dr. Arbuthnot*, lines 301–2, Pope's *Poems*, iv. 117.
[37] William Cowper, 'Charity', *Poems* (1782–5), pp. 205–6.
[38] [William Combe], Preface to *The Refutation* (1778), p. 6.

In the dialogue between Candour and Satire in Charles Churchill's *An Epistle to William Hogarth* (1763), Candour upbraids Satire for 'libelling' the human race:

> Dost Thou pretend, and there a sanction find,
> Unpunish'd, thus to Libel human kind?[39]

Libel is used here in the sense of 'misrepresent' or 'cast a slur on', and in this vague sense both noun and verb were often used interchangeably with 'satire' and 'satirize'. 'Libel' and 'slander' referred to damaging statements concerning the honour or reputation of another person or persons, 'libel' being used particularly to describe a *written* statement of a defamatory nature. B. N. Defoe's *A Compleat English Dictionary* (1735) defined it as ' a little Book, also a scandalous and invective Pamphlet', and E[phraim] Chambers's *Cyclopaedia* (1728) as 'a Writing containing Injuries, Reproaches, or Accusations against the Honour and Reputation of any Person, particularly of a Superior, or Governour'. The 1738 edition instructed the reader also to 'see SATYR'. Clearly a 'satire' could also be a 'libel' or 'slander' in the popular sense of these terms. Just as clearly the apologists for particular satires, and for satire in general, would wish to establish a radical difference between 'satire' on the one hand and 'libel' and 'slander' on the other. The two were continually being confused, Steele said, because of 'the strange Delight Men take in reading Lampoons and Scandal'. They revel in it because it brings the virtuous down to their level and, accordingly, they overvalue it and give libellers all the encouragement they can:

> It is from this that Libel and Satyr are promiscuously joined together in the Notions of the Vulgar, though the Satyrist and Libeller differ as much as the Magistrate and the Murderer. In the Consideration of human Life, the Satyrist never falls upon Persons who are not glaringly faulty, and the Libeller on none but who are conspicuously commendable. Were I to expose any Vice in a good or great Man, it should certainly be by correcting it in some one where that Crime was the most distinguishing Part of the Character; as Pages are chastized for the Admonition of Princes. When it is performed otherwise, the Vicious are kept in Credit, by placing Men of Merit in the same Accusation.[40]

---

[39] *The Poetical Works of Charles Churchill*, ed. Douglas Grant (Oxford, 1956), p. 215.
[40] *The Tatler*, No. 92, 10 November 1709.

'Lampoon' acquired an increasingly harsh meaning during the eighteenth century. Early in the century it could refer to 'a Drolling Poem or Pamphlet in which some Person or Persons are treated with Reproach or abusive Language'.[41] Even here, however, it is noted that its ridicule is personal. Increasingly 'lampoon' came to mean ridicule of a particular person, and ridicule, moreover, of an exceptionally scurrilous kind. 'To lampoon' came to mean 'to abuse or satirize virulently in writing', and 'lampoon' 'a virulent or scurrilous satire upon an individual'. Throughout the period, one of the easiest ways to express disapproval of a satirist was to brand him 'a lampooner'. It will surprise no one familiar with Dennis's customary attitude to Pope that he called him by that name, adding 'infamous Libeller' for good measure:

> He has been so far from making that Distinction which he ought to have done, that his Malice has been levell'd most at those who have most Merit; which is a certain Proof, that this little envious Creature knows nothing of the Nature of Satire, which can never exist where the Censures are not just. In that case the Versifyer, instead of a Satirist, is a Lampooner, an Infamous Libeller.[42]

The need to mark the dividing line between 'lampoon' and 'satire' was recognized by both critics and satirists. Dr. Johnson considered the distinction important enough to include it in his definition of 'satire' in the *Dictionary*: 'Proper *satire* is distinguished, by the generality of the reflections, from a *lampoon* which is aimed against a particular person; but they are too frequently confounded.' In a most painstaking passage analysing the nature of satire in *An Essay Upon Publick Spirit* (1711), Dennis put 'lampoon' not only well below the best satire, which he maintained is general, but also below particular or personal satire:

> Yet are particular Satires, if they are just Satires, preferable by much to Lampoons or Libels: That only can be call'd a just Satire, whose Censures are always true; but that which endeavours to decry true Merit, out of Malice, or Passion, or Interest, is in spite of popular Applause a Lampoon, and an infamous Libel.[43]

[41] N. Bailey, *An Universal Etymological English Dictionary* (1721).
[42] *Remarks on Mr. Pope's Rape of the Lock* (1728), in *Critical Works*, ed. E. N. Hooker (2 vols., Baltimore, 1939), ii. 325.
[43] Ibid. 396–7.

Gildon complained in *The Laws of Poetry* (1721) that 'satire' had been debased, that it no longer signified the same kind of writing as it had among the Romans, and that, as a result of 'this misunderstanding of the very name of the poem', '*lampoons*, or copies of verses stuft with scurrillity and scandal', and full of personal abuse, had come to be referred to as 'satires'. Moreover, any scribbler, though he be utterly lacking in sense, learning, and knowledge of human nature, provided he had 'A great deal of malice, and a little wit', could set himself up as 'a great performer in this kind'. Returning to the theme later, he observed that the term had been so debased 'that we generally, at least, call a personal invective, and even a downright lampoon, by the name of *Satire*'.[44] The distinction continued to be emphasized throughout the century, which is evidence enough that Dennis and Gildon were right and that 'satire' and 'lampoon' tended to be confused in everyday usage. In *The Difference between Words Esteemed Synonymous in the English Language* (2 vols., 1766), J. Trusler summed up the main points of distinction as follows:

Satire, is general; being a poem, in which, the folly and wickedness of the times, are severely, censured; written with an intent to reform. *Lampoon*, is a poem also, but, personal; containing invective reflections against one person in particular; with a design, only to vex.

A *satire*, then, is commendable; a *lampoon*, scurrilous. The lash of *satire*, has been, often, found more beneficial to a state, than the scourge of power. The writer of a *lampoon*, may be well compared to a bee, whose sting, wounds but slightly, and, whose malicious act, is sure to be punished by the whole swarm.[45]

It is clear from these examples and the preceding brief account of the meanings of 'satire' and some related terms that anyone studying the theory of satire in the late seventeenth and eighteenth centuries must take into account not only what was said on 'satire', but also what was said on 'comedy', 'raillery', 'ridicule', 'libel', 'slander', and 'lampoon'. That is to say, he needs

[44] pp. 127, 136.
[45] ii. 25.

to acquaint himself with a whole family of terms and, in addition, to watch out for unobtrusive changes in the relationships of its members. In addition, he needs to inquire into current views of the derivation and historical usage of the word 'satire', for these views are also part of the meaning of 'satire' in the period.

3. Satire's Origin and History

ONE might reasonably wonder why Dryden gave such detailed consideration in his *Discourse* to the controversy, which had been a preoccupation of classical scholars for more than a hundred years, concerning the etymology of 'satire'. It was not simply because he was borrowing heavily from Dacier, and Dacier happened to have a clear and succinct account of it in his 'Préface sur les satires d'Horace'. Dryden was in command of his material, whether it was taken from Dacier or one of the other authorities he consulted, and he rejected what did not suit his purposes. The point was that this particular controversy was of much more than academic interest in the late seventeenth century, for it was not just a quarrel over the derivation of a critical term : it was also an attempt to determine the nature of the literary work to which that term referred.[1] For this reason all those critics, who wrote at any length on the history of satire, also reviewed the controversy and gave their opinions on it. Trapp and Gildon treated it as fully as had Dacier and Dryden; and Chambers summarized the main arguments systematically and impartially in his *Cyclopædia* (1728). These writers were not indulging in aimless pedantry. They clearly found the question of considerable critical importance; and this was because it helped them to determine their attitude to satire itself. The ideal of satire to which the Augustans were turning took root readily in the newly current view of 'satire' as deriving from *satura* instead of *satyrus*.

To appreciate the importance which the Augustans attached to the new derivation, it is necessary to look briefly at the notion of the origin and nature of satire, which was widely accepted during the sixteenth and the greater part of the seventeenth centuries, and to contrast it with the theory—first elaborated by

---

[1] 'This Controversy, then, about the *Name* of *Satire* . . . is the more material, because it in a great Measure defines its *Nature* . . .' (Trapp, p. 225).

Isaac Casaubon in 1605[2] and transmitted to England later in the century, mainly by Dacier and his translators—which the Augustans found more convincing as well as much more to their liking. In 1566 Thomas Drant described satire as

> . . . a tarte and carpyng kynd of verse,
> An instrument to pynche the prankes of men,[3]

and suggested that it might be derived from the Arabic for 'butcher's cleaver' or from 'Satyrus, the mossye rude, Vnciuile god'; but he did not mention the Roman *satura lanx*. John Florio defined satire as 'a kind of poeme rebuking evils and abuses, an invective, that regardeth no person',[4] and Randle Cotgrave defined it as 'an Invective, or vice-rebuking Poeme'.[5] Puttenham referred to it as 'the first and most bitter invective against vice and vicious men'.[6]

There is a notable absence of any mention of humour, wit, or fun, in these sixteenth- and early seventeenth-century definitions. For Englishmen of Tudor and Jacobean times, satire was harsh and punitive, full of stern reproof. Their model, Juvenal, they revered more as reformer than artist, especially as they had an exaggerated idea of the roughness of his verse and diction. Now Hall, Marston, Donne, and their contemporaries are usually said to have written harsh satire because they mistakenly associated the term with *satyrus*, and consequently believed that, to be true to itself, it had to be harsh and rough. So John Peter writes in his *Complaint and Satire in Early English Literature*: 'Undoubtedly it was the satire-satyr muddle that did most to persuade Elizabethan satirists that their poems could be satires proper only if they were barbarously phrased. . . .'[7] But this is to attribute a literary happening to a simple literary cause, when it it should be apparent that more complex social and psychological causes were at work. Elizabethan and Jacobean Englishmen demanded strong meat for their entertainment—comedies full of beatings and tragedies with plenty of bloody deaths —and strong medicine for their ills—satire that was harsh and

---

[2] *De Satyrica Graecorum Poesi et Romanorum Satira* (Paris, 1605).
[3] *Medicinable Morall*, sig. A4v.
[4] *A Worlde of Words* (1598).
[5] *A Dictionarie of the French and English Tongues* (1632).
[6] *The Arte of English Poesie* (1589), sig. Eivv.
[7] Oxford, 1956, p. 303.

purgative, and a satirist who would be surgeon, torturer, or executioner, as circumstances required.[8] Undoubtedly they found the current *satyrus* derivation much to their liking and convenience; but they would most likely have written harsh rough satire, even if it had not been to hand. In a similar way the Augustans, since they were developing a taste for social criticism and public censure of a more subtle and refined sort than that which had appealed to their predecessors, found the alternative derivation from *satura*, especially as it was associated with Roman satire and not with the Old Comedy (as *satyrus* was) much to *their* liking and convenience, and would almost certainly have preferred 'smiling' to 'savage' satire, even if the *satura* derivation had not been available to them. This may help to explain, too, why the *satura* derivation did not win general acceptance until the end of the seventeenth century, although it was expounded authoritatively at the beginning of the century by Casaubon. The spelling 'satyr' for literary mode, as well as legendary figure, persisted until well on in the eighteenth century. Some seventeenth- and early eighteenth-century dictionaries gave '*satura*' as the root-word; others simply noted the alternative meanings of 'demon-god' and 'invective poem' under the one word, spelt 'satyre' or 'satyr':

Satyre (from Satyrus) a certain deity of the wood . . . being all over hairy (from *Satyra*) a kind of sharp and invective Poem full of taunting expressions against any person or thing.[9]

Satyre, an hairy Monster, like a horned man with Goats feet; also an invective poem.[10]

With the publication of Dacier's 'Préface' in 1687, however, the *satyrus* derivation was pushed to one side, though by no means out of the picture altogether. It had after all been entrenched in scholarly commentary on Roman satire, and it continued to have (as it still does today) a superficial imaginative appeal. But the English neo-classical critics appear to have eagerly welcomed Dacier's lucid and exact statement of the view that satire is purely Roman both in its origin and history; and, in view of the considerable number of translations and

---

[8] See M. C. Randolph, 'The Medical Concept in English Renaissance Satiric Theory', *SP* xxxviii (1941), 125-57.

[9] P[hillips], *The New World of English Words* (1658).

[10] Coles, *An English Dictionary* (1676).

adaptations of the 'Préface' made in the late seventeenth and
early eighteenth century, and of the wide acclaim of Dacier by
English critics, it seems likely that most Augustan readers, from
the last decade of the seventeenth century onwards, got their
ideas on the derivation and history of satire from that source.[11]
Those writers, however, who had occasion to make a special
study of the history of satire, consulted also Casaubon, Heinsius,
Scaliger, and Rigault. Dryden mentions, too, 'the Dauphin's
Juvenal', that is Prateus's edition of Persius and Juvenal (1684);
Trapp deals at some length with Vossius, principally in order to
dismiss him; and Chambers's *Cyclopædia*, in the section on
SATYR, SATYRA, or SATIRA, refers to Spanheim in addition to
Casaubon, Heinsius, Scaliger, Vossius, and Dacier. As Dacier
was the most popular of these authorities on the 'original' of
satire, it will be best to examine his account first, then to note
the additions and alterations made to it by the English critics,
in particular by Dryden in his *Discourse on Satire* and by Joseph
Trapp in his *Oxford Lectures on Poetry (Praelectiones Poeticae,*
Oxford, 1711), in the light of their reading of the older authorities and of their own knowledge of Greek and Roman literature.

   After paying a tribute to Casaubon and the earlier classical
scholars generally—'ces Hommes extraordinaires, qui ne nous
ont precedez que pour nous guider'—Dacier makes it clear that
he intends to depart from them in certain particulars. He then
begins the main part of his essay by asserting forthrightly that
satire is purely Roman, that it has nothing in common with
the satirical poetry of the Greeks.[12] Dacier accepts Casaubon's
argument that 'satire' derives from *satur*, the Latin word for
'full', as used, for example, in the expression *satur color*. *Satur*
became *satura*, and was sometimes spelt *satira*, just as *maxumus*
and *optumus* were sometimes spelt *maximus* and *optimus*.
Although it was commonly used by itself, it was an adjective,
not a noun, the noun *lanx*, meaning 'a large dish' or 'platter',
being understood. *Satura*, however, was not used only in the
phrase *satur lanx*: its application was extended to cover a mixed
dish of meats; those laws (*leges saturas*), which had many heads

[11] For summary comments on Dacier's influence in England, see A. F. B.
Clark, *Boileau and the French Classical Critics in England (1660–1830)* (Paris,
1925), pp. 286–8.
[12] Dacier, sig. a iv.

or titles and were also called *Miscellas*; and history books such as those of Pescennius Festus. To take it another step, and apply it to Horace's satires, should not have presented any difficulty. In Dacier's opinion, however, the term had been previously applied to certain rustic entertainments (which he proceeds to describe) nearer in kind than laws or histories to satires, and from thence came to be applied to some of Horace's writings.

Dryden was content to repeat Dacier's account of the *satura* theory. He did not dispute any of its details, and added nothing except a graphic description of the *satyrus* and some ridicule of Scaliger's derivation of *satyrus* from σάθυ *salacitas*, with its (in Dryden's opinion) misleading association of 'wantonness and lubricity'.[13] Trapp, however, had doubts about the newer theory, and regretted that Horace, Juvenal, and Persius, in some of their satires, had only too clearly imitated the behaviour and customs of the satyrs:

Notwithstanding the learned Arguments which *Casaubon, Dacier,* and others have urg'd, for the Etymology of the Word Satire, I can't but think their Opinion has more Probability in it than Truth; nor can any sufficient Reason be assign'd, why it may not be as well deriv'd from *Satyrus,* a Satyr, as from *Satur,* full. There's certainly too much Reason to think that some Things in *Horace, Juvenal,* and *Persius,* were borrow'd from the supposed Manners and Customs of Satyrs; and I cannot but lament, that Writers so deserving in all other Respects, should reprove some Vices in such a Manner, as to teach them; and that while they are recommending Virtue, they should throw in some Expressions so injurious to it.[14]

One minor consequence of the adoption of the *satura* theory was that it prompted a change in spelling. Clearly, if *satura* were the root-word, then 'satire' was to be preferred to 'satyr'. Dryden repeated Dacier's argument in favour of the new spelling, though he did not adopt it himself, giving as his reason for this inconsistency that he had not thought to make the change soon enough,[15] which (if it be true) tells us a great deal about his methods of revision. By contrast, Trapp uses the 'satire' spelling, while remaining determinedly neutral on the *satyrus–satura* question.[16]

---

[13] Dryden's *Essays*, ii. 53.
[14] Trapp, pp. 224–5.
[15] Dryden's *Essays*, ii. 67.
[16] Trapp, p. 225.

To accept the *satura* in preference to the *satyrus* derivation was to accept the idea of satire as pre-eminently Roman, even while perhaps admitting that some Greek literature was in a satirical vein. And it is evident that the neo-classicists were pre-disposed to do this, because they thought of the Roman satirists, especially Horace, as much more civilized than, say, the writers of the Old Comedy. In their eyes the Romans were to the Greeks rather as they themselves were to the Elizabethans, that is to say they believed the Greeks had splendid imaginations, but that they were rude and undisciplined. They accepted Horace's account of Thespis bringing his actors in a rough cart before an audience of drunks, and of the Greek playwrights generally catering for the tastes of a coarse multitude.[17] Although they were inclined to favour the Romans, however, they did not regard the question as to whether satire was of Roman origin or had been invented by the Greeks and imitated by the Romans, as having been finally settled, at any rate not until the latter part of the eighteenth century. Newbery, who provides a reliable guide to contemporary opinion, certainly assumes that the question has been settled in favour of the Romans.[18] Dryden began his account proper of satire (having completed his com-ments on the epic) by listing the chief disputants: Scaliger and Heinsius in favour of a Greek origin, and Casaubon, Rigault, Dacier, and Prateus in favour of the Roman. Dryden takes up his own stand on a rise overlooking the combat: satire in its general sense of 'invective', he states at the outset, is universal— Did it not begin with Adam and Eve when they turned and railed at one another after the Fall? 'Scoffs and revilings are of the growth of all nations.'[19] For the same reason it is most probable, he argues, that satire as 'a species of poetry' grew up independently among both the Greeks and Romans. It is not necessary to posit a single origin. Dryden describes the early religious festivals of the Greeks and Romans and points out the similarities between them. Just as the Greeks brought in satyrs to lighten the more solemn and worshipful part of their festivals, so for the same purpose the Romans in their feasts of Saturn introduced rustic clowns who railed at one another in rough

---

[17] See, for example, *Ars Poetica*, lines 275–7; and Joseph Warton, *The Adventurer*, No. 133.
[18] *The Art of Poetry on a New Plan* (1762), ii. 99.
[19] Dryden's *Essays*, ii. 45.

SATIRE'S ORIGIN AND HISTORY

verse.[20] In Dryden's view, then, 'the Old Comedy of the Greeks',
and 'the Satire of the Romans' were 'of the same nature'.
Furthermore, their fortunes were the same: 'the Old Comedy
of the Grecians was forbidden, for its too much licence in exposing of particular persons; and the rude Satire of the Romans was
also punished by a law of the Decemviri . . .'[21] Although Dryden
points out these similarities between early Greek and early
Roman satire (using the term broadly), and although he stresses
that the need for satire is common to all peoples, 'as Nature is
the same in all places',[22] it is quite clear that he leans towards
Dacier's opinion that 'satire' in its modern sense, and particularly as a literary mode, was Roman in origin. Indeed, after
his summary account of the satyric dramas of the Greeks he
remarks how little resemblance there is between 'this satyric
tragedy, and the Roman Satire': 'The very kinds are different;
for what has a pastoral tragedy to do with a paper of verses
satirically written?' All they can be said to have in common is the
'character and raillery of the Satyrs'. Moreover, 'the first farces
of the Romans . . . were written before they had any communication with the Greeks, or indeed any knowledge of that
people'.[23] So Dryden concludes emphatically that Roman satire
was not borrowed from the Greeks but was 'of their own manu-
facture'; and, like Casaubon and Dacier, he cites Quintilian and
Horace as his authorities:

Quintilian says, in plain words, *Satira quidem tota nostra est*; and
Horace had said the same thing before him, speaking of his pre-
decessor in that sort of poetry, *et Græcis intacti carminis auctor*.
Nothing can be clearer than the opinion of the poet, and the orator,
both the best critics of the two best ages of the Roman Empire, that
Satire was wholly of Latin growth, and not transplanted to Rome
from Athens.[24]

While Dryden accepted these statements as conclusive testimony, Trapp once again was more cautious—'there is Reason,
indeed . . . to understand those Expressions of *Quintilian* and
Horace with some Abatement'.[25] He was not prepared to accept

[20] Dryden's *Essays*, ii. 47.   [21] Ibid. 49.   [22] Ibid. 46.
[23] Ibid. 51.   [24] Ibid. 53.
[25] Trapp, p. 219. For recent comments on the question, see G. L. Hendrick-
son, 'Satura tota nostra est', *CP* xxii (1927), 46–60; also C. A. Van Rooy,
Studies in Classical Satire and Related Literary Theory (Leiden, 1965),
pp. 124–43, 144–85.

Dacier's confident assertion that satire is purely Roman in origin, nor his contention that Roman satire has nothing in common with the satirical poetry of the Greeks. Trapp was willing to concede that Greek and Roman satire had appeared in different forms; but he argued forcefully that they possess the same properties of ridicule, banter, and censure, and therefore can be said to be related:

> Now will any one say, the *Grecian* and *Roman* Satire had nothing of this in common between them? Are Lasciviousness, Ridicule, and Banter, the exposing Vice, and the exciting Laughter, Properties in which the *Roman* Satire had no Share? We readily grant, indeed, that as it appear'd in a *different Form*, it was not the very *same Kind* of Poem with the *Grecian*: But surely there was some, nay, a great deal of Affinity between them; and the one, particularly, owes its Rise to the other.[26]

When they put aside their differences concerning the etymology of 'satire' and the relationship of Greek to Roman satire, and turn simply to the development of Roman satire, Dacier, Dryden, Trapp, Gildon, and the few others such as Harte, John Brown, and Newbery, who touch on the subject, are in fairly close agreement. They draw the greater part of their information from Horace, tracing Roman satire from its source in the impromptu verses, with their 'gross and rustic kind of raillery', delivered at ancient festivals of Saturn, through Andronicus, Ennius, Pacuvius, and Lucilius, to its high-water mark in the *saturae* of Horace, Persius, and Juvenal. With Horace and Juvenal, so all the critics agreed, satire came truly into its own. Any debate there was about these two great Roman writers turned on their relative merits: their superiority to their predecessors, and to Persius and all later satirists, except Boileau, was not disputed.

Accordingly, when the Augustans thought of 'satire' in its strict classical sense, they thought of the satires of Horace and Juvenal; and to enter fully into the Augustan viewpoint one must bear in mind the distinctive features of those satires. They were written in verse and in one metre, and they varied considerably in length; they were usually semi-dramatic and arranged in groups, which might or might not be introduced by a prologue; they took as their subject 'whatever men do', but

[26] Trapp, p. 226.

especially follies and vices, which they treated with ridicule and scorn; they also sometimes recommended virtue and included sermons and precepts on good conduct. In short, although it is true that 'satire' was a vague term in the late seventeenth and eighteenth centuries, denoting the spirit of a work rather than its form, the satires of Horace and Juvenal provided a centre of reference, a home-base to which critics could beat a quick retreat whenever they found themselves in difficulties. For the most part, in both the practice and theory of satire, the Augustans ranged much further abroad; but, having Horace and Juvenal there firmly behind them, they were able to do so with confidence.

Juvenal, however, presented them with something of a critical problem. By and large his satire was too serious and too scathing to comply with their neo-classical principles of moderation and decorum; yet they wholeheartedly approved of his moral indignation. As Dryden commented, 'he treats tyranny, and all the vices attending it, as they deserve, with the utmost rigour'.[27] Nor, presumably, was Dryden alone in finding Juvenal 'more nourishing' than Horace. After all, much of the satire of the age was more Juvenalian than Horatian—for example, *The Medall*; *Gulliver's Travels*, book iv; *The Dunciad*; *London* and *The Vanity of Human Wishes*; and *The Rosciad*. Consequently, Augustan critics were disposed to excuse or justify the harshness of Juvenal's satire by declaring it the natural and appropriate response to his times—'What honest heart could bear Domitian's age?' asked Walter Harte.[28] Dryden went so far as to say that Juvenal wrote the greater satire because his times were more suited to the satirist than Horace's.[29] Steele in *The Tatler*, No. 242, divided the honours evenly:

But in the Perusal of these Writers it may not be unnecessary to consider, that they lived in very different Times. *Horace* was intimate with a Prince of the greatest Goodness and Humanity imaginable, and his Court was formed after his Example: Therefore the Faults that Poet falls upon were little Inconsistencies in Behaviour, false Pretences to Politeness, or impertinent Affectations of what Men were not fit for. Vices of a coarser Sort could not come under his Consideration, or enter the Palace of *Augustus*. *Juvenal* on the

[27] Dryden's *Essays*, ii. 86–7.
[28] Harte, p. 17.
[29] Dryden's *Essay*, ii. 87.

other Hand lived under *Domitian*, in whose Reign every Thing that was great and noble was banished the Habitations of the Men in Power. Therefore he attacks Vice as it passes by in Triumph, not as it breaks into Conversation. The Fall of Empire, Contempt of Glory, and a general Degeneracy of Manners, are before his Eyes in all his Writings. In the Days of *Augustus*, to have talked like *Juvenal* had been Madness, or in those of *Domitian* like *Horace*. Morality and Virtue are every where recommended in *Horace*, as became a Man in a polite Court, from the Beauty, the Propriety, the convenience, of pursuing them. Vice and Corruption are attacked by *Juvenal* in a Style which denotes, he fears he shall not be heard without he calls to them in their own Language, with a bare-faced Mention of the Villanies and Obscenities of his Contemporaries.

This concept of the historical relativity of satire—the idea of different ages requiring different sorts of satire, and of certain ages being more suitable for satire than others—assumed considerable importance in the Augustan defence of satire. If the defenders (in most cases the satirists themselves) did not actually seize on it, at least they found it extremely useful not only to justify the harshness of Juvenal, but also—as we shall observe later with regard to personal satire—to excuse certain of their own more dubious satirical practices. But they had a more laudable motive also for taking the historical view. It appealed to them strongly as an approach to satire because it assumed that the satirist was primarily a practical reformer: he was out to reform his age—not just any age, but the one in which he lived. He wrote the kind of satire which would please the people of his own age, for he could not hope to influence and instruct them unless he first won their attention by pleasing them—so Aristophanes had written coarsely, and Plautus indulged in the 'basest buffoonery' in order to please the licentious multitude;[30] and, indeed, comedy, farce, and satire had come into being when the first dramatists discovered that tragedies were too solemn for their uncultivated audiences.[31]

Dryden's exposition of a historical approach to satire occurs at the point in his extended comparison of Horace and Juvenal where he is arguing that Juvenal is the finer satirist:

His thoughts are sharper; his indignation against vice is more vehement; his spirit has more of the commonwealth genius; he

---

[30] Joseph Warton, *The Adventurer*, No. 133.
[31] *Ars Poetica*, lines 220–4; and Rapin, p. 136.

treats tyranny, and all the vices attending it, as they deserve, with the utmost rigour: and consequently, a noble soul is better pleased with a zealous vindicator of Roman liberty, than with a temporising poet, a well-mannered court-slave, and a man who is often afraid of laughing in the right place; who is ever decent, because he is naturally servile. After all, Horace had the disadvantage of the times in which he lived; they were better for the man, but worse for the satirist. 'Tis generally said, that those enormous vices which were practised under the reign of Domitian were unknown in the time of Augustus Cæsar; that therefore Juvenal had a larger field than Horace. Little follies were out of doors when oppression was to be scourged instead of avarice: it was no longer time to turn into ridicule the false opinions of philosophers when the Roman liberty was to be asserted. There was more need of a Brutus in Domitian's days, to redeem or mend, than of a Horace, if he had then been living, to laugh at a fly-catcher. This reflection at the same time excuses Horace, but exalts Juvenal.[32]

Dryden goes on to explain that Horace wrote under restriction, for Augustus, with good reason wary of his own reputation, had proclaimed an edict against lampoons and satires, and Horace had no choice other than to obey this edict:

Horace, as he was a courtier, complied with the interest of his master; and, avoiding the lashing of greater crimes, confined himself to the ridiculing of petty vices and common follies; excepting only some reserved cases, in his Odes and Epodes, of his own particular quarrels, which either with permission of the magistrate, or without it, every man will revenge, though I say not that he should. . . . [33]

Dryden concludes that, as a result, Horace's subjects were 'of a lower nature' than Juvenal's, which is consonant with his theme throughout the comparison of the two poets: Juvenal is the better all round, having more power, more substance, a nobler soul, 'more of the commonwealth genius'. Dryden, embittered by the change in his fortunes after 1689, in particular by his loss of court favour, no doubt found consolation in the idea that a vicious and tyrannical reign had produced 'the greater poet . . . in satire'.[34]

One other kind of satire was mentioned by writers on the history of satire, usually quite briefly, namely Varronian or Menip-

[32] Dryden's Essays, ii. 87.
[33] Ibid. 90.
[34] Ibid. 86.

pean satire, so called after the Greek philosopher, Menippus, whose doctrines were popularized by Varro. The emphasis in all the descriptions of this kind of satire is on its variety; it was believed to have been varied not only in its subject-matter, but also in its mingling of several sorts of verse, of verse and prose, and even of Greek and Latin, in the one composition.[35]

Varronian satire thus also highlights the all-important idea implicit in *satura*, that of variety, or miscellaneity. This idea is brought out unfailingly by critics from Dacier onwards, with reference not only to the etymology of satire, but also to its diverse beginnings, its varied uses and subject-matter, and the many forms it has taken in its complicated history. Gildon, going one step further than Dacier, Dryden, and Trapp, says that any-one properly appreciating the meaning of *satura* is bound to accept the Romans' claim to have invented satire themselves, and not to have copied it from the Greeks; for, 'if either *Quintilian* or *Horace* had taken *Satire* in the sense that we do now, that is, of being a biting and personally invective poem only', they could not conceivably have claimed that it was purely Roman, 'since it is very well known that the *Iambic* poems of the *Greeks* were entirely invectives, and *Archilochus* is mentioned by *Horace* himself, in his *art of poetry*, as the inventer of that sort of verse . . .'. Moreover, when Horace wrote personal invectives, he wrote them in iambics and called them '*Iambics*, and not *Satires*, as is plain from the sixteenth *Ode* of the first book, which he directs to a young lady whom he had abused in *Iambics*'. Gildon concludes: 'It being thus evident that the *Romans* could not claim the invention of *Satire* to themselves, by its being a biting and invective poem, it is equally evident that the *Romans* deriv'd their right to it from that variety or medley of subjects which they contain'd, as is express'd by the very word it self, *Satura, Satira*; the biting quality being but one part of the whole. . . .'[36] Gildon's aim in bringing forward this argument is perfectly clear: he is attacking contemporary personal satire, and putting forward the stock eighteenth-century plea for 'smiling' as opposed to 'savage' satire. Dacier, Dryden, and Trapp also stress that 'satire' has come to have a much harsher and more restricted meaning in their times than *satura* used to have

[35] Dacier, sig. e ivv.
[36] *The Laws of Poetry*, pp. 136–7.

in the times of Horace and Juvenal. Dacier's comments on this point may appropriately be the ones quoted, as they are simply repeated by Dryden and Trapp:

Cependant le Lecteur doit se souvenir, que le nom de Satire en Latin ne convient pas moins à des Discours qui sont faits pour recommander la Vertu, qu'à ceux où l'on s'est proposé de décrier le Vice. Il n'en est pas de mesme dans nostre Langue, où le seul nom de Satire fait trembler ceux qui voudroient bien paroistre ce qu'ils ne sont pas. Car en François qui dit *satire*, dit *médisance*. Le mot ne laisse pourtant pas d'estré toûjours le mesme; Mais les Latins dans les titres de leurs Livres, n'ont souvent eu égard qu'au mot & à l'étendü de sa signification fondée sur l'étymologie, au lieu que les François n'ont regardé qu'au premier & au plus grand usage que l'on en a fait dans ses commencemens, de railler, & de médire.[37]

Trapp makes less than Gildon did of the *satura* derivation; nevertheless, after his recapitulation of Dacier's account of it, he comments that '*Satire* . . . when applied by a Metaphor to Writing, is a Miscellaneous Poem, full of Variety of Matter', and then quotes Juvenal's well-known lines:

> Quicquid agunt homines, votum, timor, ira, voluptas,
> Gaudia, discursus, nostri est farrago libelli.[38]

Trapp's choice of quotation is significant, for these lines from Juvenal's first satire crystallize the *satura* idea. They were a favourite eighteenth-century quotation, being used, for example, as the motto of the first forty numbers of *The Tatler* (though the list from *votum* to *discursus* was omitted), and also by Arthur Murphy for the *Gray's-Inn Journal*[39]—that is to say, they were considered most suitable for describing the intention and subject-matter of the satirical commentator at large in society.

By virtue of its diverse history, too, as well as its etymology, satire was regarded as miscellaneous in character. *Satyrica*, Old Comedies, *silli*, Fescennine verses, Andronicus' plays, Ennius' poems, and the satires of Menippus, all were thought to have been involved in some measure in its development. Dacier, it is true, maintained that satire was purely Roman in origin, but the Roman elements themselves, which he describes in the 'Preface', were heterogenous, and in the eyes of most of the

---

[37] Dacier, sig. i iv.
[38] Trapp, p. 220.
[39] 29 September 1753–21 September 1754.

authorities consulted by the Augustans, satire contained Greek elements also. Moreover, educated men of Dryden's, Pope's, and Johnson's times would have been well aware that much of the ethos of Roman satire was from Greek philosophy, from Stoicism and Cynicism especially.[40]

To add further to its motley character, satire had not been confined to one particular form, though it is true that Dacier had argued that it should be restricted to formal verse satire on the pattern set by Lucilius and perfected by Horace. In the majority of historical accounts it was associated with entertainments as diverse as rustic vaudeville, *exodia* of comedies, *silli*, the plays of Andronicus, and Horace's *sermones*. And in this connection it is worth noting again that it was not thought of as necessarily limited to any one metre, nor to verse rather than prose—even within the one satirical work.

Although, as we have just seen, the accepted view of the origin and history of satire emphasized its miscellaneity, there were two potent counterbalancing factors: first, the Horatian conception of literary (and social) history as a process of refinement towards a civilized ideal of order and harmony; and secondly, the classical models themselves, the actual satires of Horace and Juvenal. In the *Ars Poetica* Horace presents poetry both as an agent in the refining of human society and as itself something which had gradually become more refined. Similarly, Dryden remarks towards the end of his *Discourse* on the long refining process of literary history: 'And thus I have given the history of Satire, and derived it as far as from Ennius to your Lordship; that is, from its first rudiments of barbarity, to its last polishing and perfection. . . .'[41] Dryden may be dizzy from the altitude he has reached; but the same idea, though differently applied, is found in many critics. Abbott, for example, observes with regard to the progress of satire that, as society becomes more refined, 'the variety and caprice of artificial manners . . . multiply the objects of ridicule, and thus by perpetual exercise, improve and perfect the satiric muse'.[42]

As to the satires of Horace and Juvenal themselves, only a very superficial reader could think them artless and rambling.

---

[40] See Dryden's comments on the Stoicism of Persius, *Essays*, ii. 77–9.
[41] Dryden's *Essays*, ii. 99.
[42] In *Oxford English Prize Essays*, i. 181.

Horace's Satire, II i, for instance, through its colloquial manner and language and its semi-dramatic form creates the illusion of casual conversation; but actually it is a most carefully constructed rationale of the satirist's vocation. 'Why write satire?' is its theme; and, from Horace's self-deprecatory but challenging opening to Trebatius' shrug of acceptance and dismissal at the end, every line fits naturally into the dialogue and bears directly on the theme. Similarly, Juvenal's Satire III is far from being an incoherent outburst of rage. There is rage in it certainly; none the less it is constructed on well-established principles of rhetoric.[43] Moreover, Juvenal cleverly intensifies its impact on the reader's imagination by placing it in a dramatic frame—the subdued and sorrowful scene of farewell in Egeria's Glen. It would be equally mistaken to assume that the typical Augustan verse satire is artless. D. J. Greene comes very close to making this mistake when he accuses Dryden of 'anti-logical impressionism', and when he states that Pope 'rambles' in his epistles and satires and that Johnson in *London* and *The Vanity of Human Wishes* 'is entitled to little greater praise for logical structure than is Chaucer's Monk'.[44] But Greene is of course looking for *logical* order—needless to say, quite fruitlessly. He overworks the *satura* idea, implying that Dryden, Pope, and Johnson took it as referring to the form as well as the subject-matter of satire. Pope's *Epistles* may indeed appear loose and rambling at first glance; and his method of composition—in particular, that of working on a couplet or a paragraph as it came to him and fitting it into a poem at a later date, might not encourage us to expect a unified result. Actually, however, Pope's placement of the disparate parts often reveals not merely workmanlike care but a fine sense of timing and dramatic fitness as well, as, for example, with the attack on Sporus in the *Epistle to Dr. Arbuthnot*. Only on reflection do we appreciate how skilfully he has conducted us from the easy colloquial opening to this piece of brilliant invective—a fitting climax to the *Epistle*, for it presents in the evil person of Sporus a living proof of the necessity for satire.

Dryden's attempts to reconcile the demands of art and the implication of the *satura* idea occur in that part of the *Discourse*

---

[43] See Gilbert Highet, *Juvenal* (Oxford, 1954), pp. 65–75, 163–5.
[44] ' "Logical structure" in Eighteenth-Century Poetry', *PQ* xxxi (1952), 326–36.

where he sets down his 'thoughts, how a modern satire should be made'. He lets his readers into the 'important secret, in the designing of a perfect satire; that it ought only to treat of one subject; to be confined to one particular theme; or at least, to one principally. If other vices occur in the management of the chief, they should only be transiently lashed, and not be insisted on, so as to make the design double.' He regrets that though Horace must have recognized this principle 'for he gives this very precept *sit quodvis simplex duntaxat et unum*; yet he seems not much to mind it in his *Satires*, many of them consisting of more arguments than one; and the second without dependence on the first'. Dryden then deals directly with the opinion, which may be put forward in defence of Horace, that unity is not necessary in a satire, because the term by derivation means mixture, or variety. He points out that Persius, Juvenal, and Boileau all observed the principle of 'Unity of Design'; and that variety can be gained in a number of ways without breaking this principle.

I know it may be urged in defence of Horace, that this unity is not necessary; because the very word *satura* signifies a dish plentifully stored with all variety of fruits and grains. Yet Juvenal, who calls his poems a *farrago*, which is a word of the same signification with *satura*, has chosen to follow the same method of Persius, and not of Horace; and Boileau, whose example alone is a sufficient authority, has wholly confined himself, in all his *Satires*, to this unity of design. That variety, which is not to be found in any one satire, is, at least, in many, written on several occasions. And if variety be of absolute necessity in every one of them, according to the etymology of the word, yet it may arise naturally from one subject, as it is diversely treated, in the several subordinate branches of it, all relating to the chief. It may be illustrated accordingly with variety of examples in the subdivisions of it, and with as many precepts as there are members of it; which, altogether, may complete that *olla*, or hotchpotch, which is properly a satire.[45]

It is evident that the Augustans got a number of important ideas on satire from those scholarly sources of information on its origin and history which were available to them—ideas that partly determined and partly expressed their approach to satire. But, perhaps most important of all, they gained a sense of its

45 Dryden's *Essays*, ii. 102–4.

complexity. As Dacier commented, the greatest diffidence and
caution was necessary in approaching a subject so ancient and
obscure as satire. No critic who looked into the scholarly investi-
gations of its origin could be other than awed by the diversity
and complexity of the subject; no one who ventured into this
underground maze came out at the end with a simple and clear
idea of where he had been. Dryden, at the end of his explora-
tion, quotes Heinsius's definition:

Heinsius, in his dissertations on Horace, makes it for me, in these
words: 'Satire is a kind of poetry, without a series of action, invented
for the purging of our minds; in which human vices, ignorance,
and errors, and all things besides, which are produced from them in
every man, are severely reprehended; partly dramatically, partly
simply, and sometimes in both kinds of speaking; but, for the most
part, figuratively, and occultly; consisting in a low familiar way,
chiefly in a sharp and pungent manner of speech; but partly, also,
in a facetious and civil way of jesting; by which either hatred, or
laughter, or indignation is moved.'[46]

Dryden rightly describes this definition as obscure and perplexed, and he attempts to improve it; but, so obscure and
perplexed is satire itself, that he merely adds to the confusion
instead of diminishing it. As the definition stood, Dryden noted
that it failed to cover Juvenal's and Persius' satires, so he thereupon makes his illuminating plea for the 'Majestique way', for
epic satire, which Heinsius and many of the Augustans failed
to allow for in their critical pronouncements on satire.

Perhaps the most striking feature of Augustan historical criticism of satire is its neglect of earlier English satirists. It looks
wholly to the ancients, and to Rome rather than Greece. This
does not mean that the Augustans were ignorant of their English predecessors: rather that they felt them outside the tradition to which they themselves wished to belong—Donne, Hall,
Marston, and Cleveland were on the far side of the moon. Consequently, though they did comment on them and though Pope
imitated Donne's Fourth Satire, and also professed an interest
in Hall, their comments are sparse, perfunctory, and stereo-
typed.[47] On Donne, for example, the stock comment is that he

---

[46] Dryden's *Essays*, ii. 100.

[47] See Joseph Spence, *Observations, Anecdotes, and Characters of Books and
Men*, ed. James M. Osborn (Oxford, 1966), i. 185–8; and also, in this connection, Harold Williams, *Dean Swift's Library* (Cambridge, 1932).

took too little care of his numbers. The same is true of their comments on earlier Italian and French satirists, as is well illustrated by Harte in his *Essay on Satire*: '*Tassone* shone fantastic, but sublime', '*Rabelais* made the World his Jest', '*Marot* had Nature', and '*Regnier* Force and Flame'. When they come to Boileau, however, the response is different:

> Extensive Soul! who rang'd all learning o'er,
> Present and past—and yet found room for more.
> Full of new Sense, exact in every Page,
> Unbounded, and yet sober in thy Rage.[48]

Dryden referred to 'the admirable Boileau' as 'a living Horace and a Juvenal',[49] and William Shenstone commended him for 'uniting the style of Juvenal and Persius with that of Horace'.[50] 'William Cleland' (i.e. Pope) called him 'the greatest Poet and most Judicious Critic of his age and country' in his 'Letter to the Publisher' (1729), and implied that the author of *The Dunciad* was his counterpart in England.[51] In Boileau, then, satire had a modern champion (at least until something of a reaction set in against him in the latter part of the eighteenth century)[52] who was worthy to stand beside Horace and Juvenal. With the example of these three satirists behind them, the defenders of satire could face with confidence the formidable body of hostile criticism which was levelled against them.

[48] Harte, pp. 18–19.
[49] Dryden's *Essays*, ii. 26.
[50] 'Essays on Men, Manners, and Things', *Works* (1764), ii. 14.
[51] Pope's *Poems*, v. 17–18.
[52] See Clark, *Boileau and the French Classical Critics in England*, pp. 41–54.

4. Main Lines of the Attack

CERTAINLY satire had to face a formidable body of hostile criticism in the Augustan age. The charges made against it were many and varied. It was accused of great capacity for harm: as poetry could influence men for their good, so also through satire it could do them immeasurable injury. Historical examples of this abuse were not lacking—in the stories of Archilochus and Hipponax, for instance, and above all in the treatment of Socrates by Aristophanes. But there was no need to look to history for examples: the misuse of satire by contemporary writers was a scandal of the age; and Temple, Wolseley, Blackmore, Dennis, Addison, Steele, and scores of others inveighed against it. Obviously satire was a dangerous weapon, dangerous not only to society generally, but also to the satirist. It could injure worthy and innocent people, even when it was well intended. It was tainted at its source; its roots were in corruption. 'The vice and folly which overspread human nature first created the satirist.'[1] After all, had it not been for the Fall, it would not have become necessary. By virtue of its nature and function it had to soil its hands, to treat unpleasant, often sordid and repugnant subjects. It was accused of pandering to the worst in men's natures. Furthermore, satirists' motives were considered ignoble—envious, cowardly, cruel, sometimes even murderous—their dispositions malignant and cantankerous, and their personal conduct inconsistent with their presumption to judge others, with the high-minded attitudes they struck in their satirical writings. All in all, in the view of its opponents, satire was 'the least attractive of the Nine', 'that thorny, that unpleasing way'.[2]

The charges sound formidable when they are lumped together in this way. But of course in actual practice they never were; and, indeed, it is vitally important, when attempting to come

[1] Stevens, *A Lecture on Heads*, p. 100.
[2] George, Lord Lyttleton, *Epistle to Mr. Pope, from Rome*, 1730, *Works* (1774), p. 607.

to grips with this hostile criticism, to acknowledge its diversity. So far from being a single massive assault, it was rather a number of different sallies coming from different directions at different times. Sometimes only a certain kind of satirical writing was under attack, though general terms were used (as, for example, in Addison's celebrated attack on 'Arrows that fly in the dark' in *The Spectator*, No. 23, or in Pierre Bayle's chapter on 'Defamatory Libels' in his *Dictionary*); sometimes only the misuse of satire by contemporaries (as in Wolseley's Preface to *Valentinian* and Blackmore's *A Satyr Against Wit*); sometimes only a particular satirist, or group of satirists (as in Richardson's aspersions on 'Some of the Pieces of Pope, of Swift, and other eminent Authors, of the Poetical Tribe especially'); and sometimes merely the spirit of satire as it vaguely presented itself to men and women of goodwill (preachers like Glanvill and Tillotson, essayists like Addison and Steele, and authors of books on conduct and manners, like Eliza Haywood and Charlotte Lennox). It is always important, then, to determine the real object of any critical attack on satire, and to take into account the time and context in which it was written. In the late seventeenth and early eighteenth centuries, when critics were concentrating their fire on 'wit', they tended to think of satire as malicious and heartless, a mere display of cleverness; but when they were censuring the stage, they associated it rather with loose morals, obscene language, and a cynical addiction to ridicule; and when they had in mind 'the publick Scavengers of Scandal'[3] of the coffee-houses and Grub Street, they associated it with mischief-making, muck-raking, and back-stabbing, with libels, lampoons, and slander. During the twenties and thirties of the eighteenth century, however, the critical attack (especially when Pope and Swift were its objects) was aimed principally at personal satire and at the apparent preoccupation of these satirists with revolting subject-matter. After the death of Pope, and in the latter part of the eighteenth century, the attack tended to be both more general and more fundamental. An increasing number of critics, such as Joseph Warton, took it more or less for granted that satire had only a limited usefulness, and that it was one of the lesser and meaner kinds of writing.

[3] Dennis, 'An Essay Upon Publick Spirit', *Critical Works*, ed. Hooker, ii. 396.

The object of the present chapter is not (as the preceding comments might suggest) to trace the historical outlines of Augustan criticism of satire, but to sum up the main arguments which were brought against satire by its opponents. It is, however, necessary to keep the historical background in mind in order to guard against oversimplification and misinterpretation.

It was alleged by those hostile to satire that its principal capacity was for doing harm. This charge, which could be regarded as the most serious of all that were made, was in a way very flattering to the satirists for it credited them with extraordinary power—in fact, if the traditional tales of Archilochus and Hipponax were to be believed, with no less than the power of life and death. The story of Archilochus certainly illustrated the havoc that can be caused by satire. Because Lycambus had broken a promise he made to give his daughter to Archilochus in marriage, and broken it moreover in an insulting way, Archilochus attacked him in furious iambics. These were so powerful that Lycambus hanged himself; and, according to some accounts, the daughter who had been promised in marriage to Archilochus followed her father's example, whereupon her three sisters died of grief and despair. Another current story was that of Hipponax, the deformed sculptor, who sought revenge through satire on the two rival sculptors who had cruelly caricatured his misshapen body. To quote from Bayle's popular *Dictionary*: 'He discharged upon them a thundering legion of Iambic verses which so vexed them, that it has been reported they hanged themselves.'[4] Bayle concludes sombrely that Hipponax 'was neither the first, nor the only person who have forced people to make away with themselves by their invectives'; and in a footnote on this sentence he cites a score of minor historical figures (Archilochus first) who killed either themselves or their satirists. 'We need not wonder', he says, 'that a satire should cast men into despair, since a meer censure has sometimes had that fatal effect.' And he mentions the instance of the disciple of Pythagoras, who is said to have strangled himself, because Pythagoras had severely reprimanded him before many people. From that time on, Bayle comments, 'that Great Philosopher took care to censure only in private'.

Not too much importance should be attached to the stories of

---

[4] See Bayle's *Dictionary*, under 'Hipponax'.

Archilochus and Hipponax. These were, after all, legendary tales, and the Augustans had their minds 'too buckled and bowed unto the nature of things' to take them literally. Anyone repeating them, however, could not but allow them to colour his view of satire. Much the same can be said of traditional accounts of the fate of Isaac Casaubon and Joseph Scaliger—they were both said to have died from vexation and bitterness caused by the satires of Scioppius[5]—and also regarding Temple's comment that *Don Quixote* was responsible for the ruin of the Spanish monarchy.[6] Temple no doubt did not really believe this; but it suited his argument against what he believed to be the corrupting influence of ridicule in modern poetry to pretend that he did. By the same token Steele probably did not believe the story either when he repeated it in his attack on false raillery in *The Tatler*, No. 219 (2 September 1710). But those critics, who objected to Aristophanes' satire of Socrates, assuredly did believe what they said and wished it to be taken as written, for they were dealing with history not legend. Besides, Socrates might have been designed to be an eighteenth-century tragic hero, for he was a prime exemplar of the rational inquiring mind, who had been driven to his death chiefly on account of his unremitting pursuit of reason. It was no wonder, then, that Aristophanes' Νεφέλαι became by far the favourite instance in the eighteenth century of the misapplication of satire and its dire effects. The accepted Augustan view was that Aristophanes turned the Athenians against Socrates. 'Thus the enemies of *Socrates*,' wrote Richard Allestree, 'when they could no other waies suppress his reputation, hired *Aristophanes* a Comic Poet to personate him on the stage . . . ',[7] and by this means brought him first into contempt, then hatred. Addison, in *The Spectator*, No. 23, where he made his most sustained attack on ill-natured satire, portrayed Socrates as a tragic figure by having him, almost at the moment of his death, talk to Aristophanes more in grief than in anger.

The opponents of satire pointed out that it was dangerous not only to people generally, but also to the satirists themselves. Examples were not lacking of satirists who had been severely punished for their writings. Some kings and emperors had dealt

---

[5] See Bayle's *Dictionary*.
[6] 'An Essay upon the Ancient and Modern Learning', *Miscellanea*, ii. 70–1.
[7] [Richard Allestree], *The Government of the Tongue* (1674), p. 131.

savagely with those who had the temerity to ridicule them. Sextus Quintus, for example, when the author of a pasquinade confessed in order to claim the reward the Emperor had offered, gave him the reward as promised, but also removed his tongue and cut off both his hands. The dangerous and unrewarding nature of satire was an established theme of the satirist's apologia. Thus Boileau in Satire VII points out that cold panegyric is safer and more profitable than satire, for the latter arouses fear and hostility in all readers, not just in those who are personally ridiculed. No one much likes it, nor the person who perpetuates it.[8] Moreover, in so far as the satirist, through his satirical writing, became an active participant in political events—as he most often did in the late seventeenth century—he imperilled his livelihood, perhaps even his life. So Matthew Prior remarked that he 'did not launch much out into Satyr', because of the dangers involved: 'considering the uncertainty of Fortune, and the various change of Ministry, where every Man as he resents may punish in his turn of Greatness; and that in England a Man is less safe as to Politics, than he is in a Bark upon the Coast in regard to the Change of the Wind, and the Danger of Shipwreck'.[9]

Satire, it was widely agreed, was dangerous to everyone. It was a double-edged weapon. In the hands of a foolish, irresponsible, or simply unthinking person, it could smear virtue and degrade worth, drag the names of good men and their families in the dirt, and cause irremediable harm to innocent people; it could undermine the most sacred institutions of society and threaten the stability of government. Its indiscriminate use and its side-effects were a constant danger. Even 'fine raillery', the most delicate and subtle satire, as Dryden did not deny in his famous passage on the subject, could be expected to hurt. What one hoped (ideally) was that the victim would have the good sense and the good humour to see the point of the satire, and so not resent it too much.

In his *Letter Concerning Enthusiasm* Shaftesbury argued that truth and virtue could not be harmed by ridicule, for they occupy an impregnable citadel well out of its reach. During the

---

[8] Boileau's *Satires*, p. 90, lines 1–12.
[9] 'Heads for a Treatise upon Learning', *Literary Works*, ed. Wright and Spears, i. 583–4.

course of his argument Shaftesbury used the favourite
eighteenth-century example of Socrates, but in a novel way. He
cited Socrates as an example of truth triumphing in the end.[10]
Many of Shaftesbury's contemporaries, however, were not prepared to take so long a view. They were too well aware of the
harm injudicious and misplaced ridicule can do. John Brown,
for instance, though a champion of satire, gave the following
warning regarding ridicule:

> On truth, on falsehood let her colours fall,
> She throws a dazzling glare alike on all:
> Beware the mad advent'rer: Bold and blind
> She hoists her sail, and drives with ev'ry wind,
> Deaf as the storm to sinking virtue's groan,
> Nor heeds a friend's destruction, or her own.[11]

Shaftesbury's view that 'nothing can be made to appear ridiculous but what is *really* deformed' may be very well, Brown
considers, in a Platonic world; not so, however, in 'our *Gothic*
Systems', where 'it is the easiest of all Things to make that *appear*
ridiculous, which is not *really* deformed'. For the mere making
it appear false or deformed thereby renders it '*actually* contemptible and ridiculous'.[12] Brown gives historical examples to
support his contention, arguing at length that Aristophanes did
actually succeed in bringing Socrates into hatred and contempt.
So far from believing, like Shaftesbury, that just and sensible
men will not entertain false ridicule, he believes that the world
at large will swallow any falsehood, no matter how improbable.
'And where', he asks, 'was the Wonder or Improbability, that
the Wit of ARISTOPHANES should incite a *lewd Multitude* to
destroy the *divine Philosopher*?'[13] William Whitehead, who
was nothing if not wary of satire, feared that it may make most
men hypocrites: to avoid public ridicule they will conceal those
follies they are reluctant to abandon. He was afraid also that in
trying 'to laugh the Vice away', we may hurt some virtue, so
closely are virtues and vices intermingled in human beings.[14]
In an essay entitled 'On the Ill Effects of Ridicule, when

---

[10] pp. 17, 48.
[11] Brown (1745), pp. 17–18.
[12] Brown (1751), pp. 55–6.
[13] Ibid., pp. 57–63, 66.
[14] *Essay on Ridicule*, p. 16.

Employed as a Test of Truth in Private and Common Life',[15] Vicesimus Knox insists that

All the useful and amiable qualities, which sweeten private and domestic life, have occasionally been put out of countenance by the prevalence of the doctrine, that ridicule is the test of truth in common life. Conjugal attachment and fidelity, filial regard, regular industry, prudent œconomy, sincerity in friendship, delicate scruples, benevolence and beneficence have been destroyed by the pretender to wit, who from the malignant feelings of envy, has been prompted to bestow on them some ridiculous appellation.

He considers it a great mistake to think that great laughers are good-natured: 'I believe they are often particularly proud and malicious; for there is no method of gratifying pride and malice more effectually than by ridicule.'[16]

A more sophisticated and insidious criticism was that satire, even when it is well intended and well directed, may have bad results. A Tale of a Tub, for instance, was in John Brown's estimation 'an exquisite Piece of Raillery', and also a vindication of the English Church, which was decidedly in its favour; but for all that Brown thought it was bound to cause trouble and ill feeling—'its natural Effect is to create Prejudice, and inspire the contending Parties with mutual Distaste, Contempt, and Hatred . . . '.[17] Similarly, in Whitehead's view, ridicule of the sciences, though just, may have ill effects:

> We oft, 'tis true, mistake the Sat'rist's Aim,
> Not Arts themselves, but their Abuse they blame.
> Yet, if, *Crusaders* like, their Zeal be Rage,
> They hurt the Cause in which their Arms engage: [18]

Addison, in his comments on raillery, states 'that an indiscreet Man is more hurtful than an ill-natured one; for as the one will only attack his Enemies, and those he wishes ill to, the other injures indifferently both Friends and Foes'.[19] The harmfulness of raillery was indeed a favourite topic in the eighteenth century, treated at length in books on conduct, periodical essays, plays, novels, and autobiographies. For example, Arabella in Charlotte

---

[51] *Essays Moral and Literary* (3rd edn., 1782), i. 189. (The essay quoted did not appear in previous editions.)

[16] Ibid. 193, 195.

[17] Brown (1751), p. 102.

[18] *Essay on Ridicule*, p. 11.

[19] *The Spectator*, No. 23.

Lennox's *The Female Quixote*, representing the polite and sentimental attitude proper in a young lady of her period, warns that
it is 'almost impossible to use [raillery] without being hated or
feared; and whoever gets a Habit of it, is in Danger of wrong-
ing all the Laws of Friendship and Humanity'; and, under
Mr. Glanville's questioning, she reveals that there are really no
occasions on which she would permit raillery, though theoretic-
ally she approves of it when it is handled with sufficient
delicacy.[20]

The whole point is that satire was regarded as fundamentally
suspect—dangerous because untrustworthy. Even if it was not
necessarily evil in itself, it was at least dependent for its existence
on the workings of evil. It was a concomitant of man's failings, a
product of Original Sin and the Fall of Man.

> Yet the fair plant from virtue ne'er had sprung;
> And man was guilty e'er the Poet sung.[21]

After stating that satire, in its general sense of 'invective', may
be traced back to the railings of Adam and Eve after the Fall
and Job's curses against his Maker, Dryden confesses that 'This
original . . . is not much to the honour of satire . . .'.[22] Whitehead notes that laughter in the earliest ages of man was innocent,
merely the expression of benevolence, of 'th'o'erflowing Heart':

> A Brother's Frailties but proclaim'd him Man.
> Nought perfect here they found, nor ought required,
> Excus'd the Weakness, and the Worth admir'd.

In succeeding ages, however, as man became increasingly proud,
he resorted more and more to ridicule:

> Proud, and more proud, succeeding Ages grew;
> They mark'd our Foibles, and would mend them too.[23]

The outcome is a continuum of dissension and hostility:

> Keen Envy height'ning what weak Pride begun,
> The Sneer grows gen'ral, and Mankind's undone.

---

[20] i. 143–4. See also Colley Cibber, *Apology* (1740); James Forrester, *Polite
Philosopher* (Edinburgh, 1734); *The Rambler*, No. 174, 15 November 1751;
and, for further references, S. Tave, *The Amiable Humorist* (Chicago, 1960),
p. 251 n. 4.

[21] Brown (1745), p. 24.

[22] Dryden's *Essays*, ii. 44.

[23] *Essay on Ridicule*, p. 4.

Our mirthful Age, to all Extremes a Prey,
Ev'n courts the Lash, and laughs her Pains away.

... ...

No Truth so sacred, Banter cannot hit,
No Fool so stupid, but he aims at Wit.

... ...

Thrice happy we! how virtuous are we grown!
We hate all other Failings but our own.[24]

The emotions of satire, both those prompting people to write it and those aroused by it, were also regarded with suspicion. Richard Allestree, advising his readers from the standpoint of a Christian divine on 'the government of the tongue', condemns the emotions of satire as contrary to the humility and brotherly love which a true Christian should feel. He associates scorn and disdain with pride, and concludes that those who are at fault themselves are 'therefore very incompetent Correctors' of the faults of others. He mentions that it was once said of Diogenes that 'he trampled on *Plato*'s Pride with greater of his own'.[25] Walter Charleton describes 'MALIGNANT Wit' in similar terms:

that which is indeed quick of Apprension, but *void of Humanity*: being prone to exercise it self chiefly in re-searching into the Defects, Errors, and even the Infortunes of Others, such especially who by their Virtues have rendred themselves Conspicuous; and to delight in both aggravating and publishing them to their dishonour.[26]

Charleton states that men who possess this malignant kind of wit usually become critics, and he warns that '*Satyrists* and *Comical Poets*, those especially of the more licentious and railing sort', will not find it easy 'to exempt themselves from the same Tribe'. In *The Spectator*, No. 355 (17 April 1712), Addison says that he has often been strongly tempted to reply sharply to petty invectives and slights on his reputation, but he has not done so, because he does not approve of the feelings which prompted them, and which they arouse in himself. And, in the opinion of Vicesimus Knox,

The good reception which that species of poetry, called Satire, has commonly met with in the world, is perhaps owing to some dispositions in the human nature not the most amiable. It derives not its

---

[24] *Essay on Ridicule*, pp. 5–6.
[25] *The Government of the Tongue*, pp. 113–14.
[26] *A Brief Discourse Concerning the Different Wits of Men: Written . . . in the Year 1664* (1669), p. 112.

power of pleasing, like other poetry, from its effects on the imagination. It raises no enchanting prospects; it is not necessarily employed in fiction. A spirit of indignation is its essential principle, and by causing a similar spirit in the reader, it gently gratifies the irascible passions.[27]

If satire is essentially harmful and malicious, it follows that those who perpetrate it must be of bad character. 'A little wit, and a great deal of ill nature will furnish a man for Satyr. . . .'[28] 'Those who have a talent for ridicule, which is seldom united with a taste for delicate and refined beauties, are quick-sighted in improprieties; and these they eagerly lay hold of, in order to gratify their favourite propensity.'[29] In the opinion of many worthy men, satirists are cruel, untrustworthy, and treacherous. Young people should have nothing to do with them:

Have no Conversation with People delighting in Satyr and Raillery; Neither expect any Kindnesses from them after many Years Friendship, whatever Occasions you may have for their Assistance. If you make any false Steps, they'll be sure to laugh at you the first, and turn you into Ridicule. These people resemble some sort of wild Beasts, whom there's no Possibility of taming; but they'll still return to their savage Natures, and claw their Keepers.[30]

An even more unflattering picture of the person who delights in satire and raillery was drawn by the anonymous author of *Raillerie a la Mode Consider'd: or the Supercilious Detractor* (1763):

A *Detractor* is a kind of *Camelion*, that lives upon the worst sort of Air; at first bred up and suckled with sour Sustenance from the lank and flaggy Dugs of his lean and meager Mother *Envy*, he afterwards feeds on Fame; his words are worse than *Poyson* of *Asps*, and are a kind of *Witchcraft*, so that the *Sufferer* may justly be said to be *under an Evil Tongue*.

He is a sort of *turbulent* spirited *Furiozo*, continually *foaming* out his *frothy* Passion on all sides . . . he can find none to vouchsafe

---

[27] *Essays Moral and Literary* (1782), ii. 227.
[28] John Tillotson, 'The Folly of Scoffing at Religion', *Works* (1696), p. 41. See also Sir Thomas Pope Blount, *De Re Poetica* (1694), pp. 40–1; *The Ladies Library* (1714), i. 431; Giles Jacob, *The Poetical Register* (1723), p. xxiii; Elijah Fenton, 'Observations on Some of Mr. Waller's Poems', *The Works of Edmund Waller* (1729), p. iii.
[29] Kames, *The Elements of Criticism*, ii. 54–5.
[30] *An Essay on Polite Behaviour: wherein the Nature of Complaisance and True Gentility is Consider'd and Recommended* (1740), p. 46.

to vex him, till out of pure *spight* he is fain, at length, to be himself
both *Satyr*, *Answer*, and Reply.[31]

Even Boileau implies, though not altogether intentionally, that
there is something unpleasant about a satirist's character, when
he frankly admits that his Muse gets pleasure from administer-
ing lashes and grows bolder with each successive hit.[32] Bayle
thinks the typical satirist a man of 'peevish and splenetic' disposition, a 'morose bigot', or 'peevish fanatic'. He compares
satirists to mad dogs, whom people put down either lest they be
the next ones bitten or for much the same reason as they would
help put out a fire next door.[33] Samuel Richardson, although he
does not attack satirists generally, or satire itself, expresses in
a number of places his sense of outrage at the satires of Swift and
Pope. 'I am scandaliz'd for human Nature, and such Talents,
sunk so low': this is his comment on *The Dunciad* in a letter to
Aaron Hill.[34] It is in keeping with his usual comments on Swift's
yahoos and Pope's dunces. He recommends burning by 'the
Hands of the Common Hangman' of 'Some of the Pieces of Pope,
of Swift, & other eminent Authors, of the Poetical Tribe especially . . .'.[35] Richardson is especially disapproving of Swift, and
his criticism of him, unlike that of Pope, is *ad hominem*. He
wrote as follows to Lady Dorothy Bradshaigh: 'Swift, your Lady-
ship will easily see by his writings, had bitterness, satire, morose-
ness, that must make him insufferable both to equals and
inferiors, and unsafe for his superiors to countenance.'[36]

It is worth while to turn aside a moment to clarify Richardson's
attitude on this subject and towards satire generally. Obviously
he cannot be aligned with sentimental critics who were too
tender-minded to approve of the onslaughts of satirists and who
wanted to draw a veil over the nasty side of human nature.
Richardson, like the great majority of his contemporaries, was
a moral pragmatist. He could not, with any consistency, have
rejected satire as a moral weapon—and in fact he did not. In a
letter to Aaron Hill he refers to 'the good Effects' that could

---

[31] pp. 51–3.
[32] Satire vii, lines 47–54; Boileau's *Satires*, p. 94.
[33] *Dictionary*, i. xiii.
[34] 19 January 1743/4, John Carroll (ed.), *Selected Letters of Samuel Richardson* (1964), p. 60.
[35] Richardson to Dr. Cheyne, 21 January 1742/3, ibid., p. 57.
[36] 22 April 1752, *Letters*, ed. Carroll, p. 214.

have attended Pope's 'fine Satirical vein', had he not chosen 'to irritate rather than amend'.[37] Indeed, Richardson himself employed satire extensively, for example in the satirical 'characters' of Brand and Walden in *Clarissa* and *Sir Charles Grandison*, in Harriet Byron's sharp comments on London high life, and in the letters of Lovelace. But, although he no doubt saw some value in satire and on occasions wrote in satirical vein himself, he shows in his strictures on Swift and Pope that he held the strongest reservations about its nature and believed that it might very easily be put to bad uses. As John Carroll has shrewdly observed: 'It is not by chance that the most corrupt of Richardson's major characters has the clearest insight into the weakness and viciousness of human nature and the wit to exploit these frailties in his plot as well as in his style.'[38]

Richardson's comments on Swift and Pope indicate the need for caution in a survey of this kind. Most critics of satire in the period, like Richardson, have in mind particular satirists, or a particular sort of satire, when they are making their comments. They are seldom thinking of satire in general, though, as has already been observed, their use of general terms may sometimes lead one to suppose that they are doing so. This is true, for example, of Addison's essay in *The Spectator*, No. 23. Addison is thinking of slanderous satire only, yet he seems to call into question the nature and value of satire generally, and the character, motives, and conduct of satirists as a species of writers.

The attack is made under a pointed quotation from Virgil:

> Sævit atrox Volscens, nec teli conspicit usquam
> Auctorem, nec quo se ardens immittere possit.[39]

And the opening paragraph mixes in the one brew a number of the common charges made against satire and satirists in Addison's times:

> There is nothing that more betrays a base, ungenerous Spirit, than the giving of secret Stabs to a Man's Reputation. Lampoons and Satyrs, that are written with Wit and Spirit, are like poison'd Darts, which not only inflict a Wound, but make it incurable. For this Reason I am very much troubled when I see the Talents of

---

[37] 2 April 1743, ibid., p. 59.
[38] 'Richardson on Pope and Swift', *University of Toronto Quarterly*, xxiii (1963–4), 28.
[39] *Aeneid*, ix. 420–1.

Humour and Ridicule in the Possession of an ill-natured Man. There cannot be a greater Gratification to a barbarous and inhuman Wit, than to stir up Sorrow in the Heart of a private Person, to raise Uneasiness among near Relations, and to expose whole Families to Derision, at the same time that he remains unseen and undiscovered. If, besides the Accomplishments of being Witty and Ill-natured, a Man is vicious into the bargain, he is one of the most mischievous Creatures that can enter into a Civil Society. His Satyr will then chiefly fall upon those who ought to be the most exempt from it. Virtue, Merit, and every thing that is Praise-worthy, will be made the Subject of Ridicule and Buffoonry. It is impossible to enumerate the Evils which arise from these Arrows that fly in the dark, and I know no other Excuse that is or can be made for them, than that the Wounds they give are only Imaginary, and produce nothing more than a secret Shame or Sorrow in the Mind of the suffering Person. It must indeed be confess'd, that a Lampoon or a Satyr do not carry in them Robbery or Murder; but at the same time, how many are there that would not rather lose a considerable Sum of Mony, or even Life it self, than be set up as a Mark of Infamy and Derision? And in this Case a Man should consider, that an Injury is not to be measured by the Notions of him that gives, but of him that receives it.

For all its calm and lofty tone, this is a loaded passage. Addison may be discussing only ill-natured satire; but the fact that there may be another kind, basically noble in its motives and beneficial to society as a whole in its effects, as it is not mentioned, might easily be forgotten. The picture Addison draws is lurid and melodramatic. His satirist lurks in the shadows. He is ignoble, mean, secretive, cruel, and deadly. The wounds which he inflicts are incurable. Not only does he cause anguish to 'whole Families' and 'Uneasiness among near Relations', but he enjoys doing it. He is an enemy of society, for he harms chiefly its most upright members, and he makes a laughing-stock of everything that is worth while. Indeed, he is worse than a thief or a murderer for, in taking away the reputation of his victims, he robs them of something more precious than money or life itself.

Addison is shocked by the secretiveness of slanderous satire. He talks of 'secret Stabs' and 'Arrows that fly in the dark', and complains that the author of the mischief remains 'unseen and undiscovered'. Later in the same essay he remarks that he 'would never trust a Man that [he] thought was capable of giving these secret Wounds, adding that he 'cannot but think that [such a slanderer] would hurt the Person, whose Reputation he thus assaults, in his Body or in his Fortune, could he do it with the same Security'. This drastic charge, that satire may be a coward's substitute for violence and murder, is made much more strongly by Bayle:

we ought to believe that the same baseness which induces some people to fire a Musquet upon their Enemy, would induce them to defame him by a Satyr, if they had no other Arms but their Pen. 'Tis just as amongst Beasts; some don't gore with their Horns, but bite; 'tis because they have no Horns, and know how to use their Teeth. It may be said also, that a Satyrist who assaults the Honour of his Enemies with Libels, would attempt upon their Life with Sword and Poyson, if he had the same opportunity.[40]

Addison considers that another strong motive for satire is envy. Famous men, in his opinion, encourage detractors in proportion to their fame. Moreover, some people actually derive an inner satisfaction from ridiculing the great: 'A Satyr or a Libel on one of the common Stamp, never meets with that Reception and Approbation among its Readers, as what is aimed at a Person whose Merit places him upon an Eminence, and gives him a more conspicuous Figure among Men.'[41] For much the same reason, according to Joseph Glanvill, drolls (his term for those who use ridicule as a weapon in controversy) ridicule knowledge which is beyond their understanding.[42] Tillotson regretted that

The Wit of Man doth more naturally vent it self in *Satire* and Censure, than in Praise and *Panegyrick*. When Men set themselves to commend, it comes hardly from them, and not without great force and straining; and if any thing be fitly said in that kind, it doth hardly relish with most men: But in the way of *Invective*, the Invention of men is a plentiful and never-failing Spring. . . .[43]

Richard Owen Cambridge, with Aristophanes' parodies of characters and verses from Euripides particularly in mind, attributes a love of parody to envy: 'This love of Parody is accounted

---

[40] *Dictionary*, I. xxvii.

[41] *The Spectator*, No. 256, 24 December 1711.

[42] [Joseph Glanvill], 'Reflections on Drollery and Atheism', in *A Blow at Modern Sadducism* (1668), p. 151.

[43] *Works* (1728), i. 397.

for . . . from a certain malignity in mankind, which prompts them to laugh at what they most esteem, thinking they, in some measure, repay themselves for that involuntary tribute which is exacted from them by merit.'[44] Whitehead's questioning of satirists' motives is milder, but more profound. He wonders if they deceive themselves. It is possible that they write to relieve their own feelings instead of to check other people's? Does virtue really 'ev'ry Shaft supply'?[45] Some other critics, both before and after Whitehead, were more forthright in their questioning of the real motives behind the satirists' stated intention to reform society. Ambrose Philips, for instance, wrote in *A Reflection on Our Modern Poesy* (1695):

> *Satyr*, which was a wholsome Remedy,
> Prescrib'd to cure a People's Malady,
> When prudently apply'd doth Good produce;
> But as all *Goods* are subject to abuse,
> So this of Late no Publick Cure intends,
> But only serves to black Malicious ends.
> We dip our Pens in *Gall* when e'er we Write,
> And all our *Inspiration* is but *Spite*.[46]

Richard Bentley said that from his soul he abhorred

> The Name of Satirist, who to his Share
> Needs but an Ear to rhime, and Front to dare,
> To hide his splendid Bile in moral Mask.[47]

And William Shenstone, writing on Pope, stated that 'SATYR gratifies self-love', and that this was one of the reasons for Pope's popularity.[48]

The argument against the subject-matter of satire, that it tends to be trivial or nasty, or both, was put forward mainly with reference to individual satirists, for example Rochester, Swift, and Pope. Mulgrave censured Rochester for smuttiness, declaring 'Bawdry barefac'd, that poor pretence to Wit . . .'.[49] Richardson expressed wonder that Pope could find no better use for his abilities than to make satirical verses on dunces. 'Has he no Invention, Sir, to be better employ'd about? No Talents for worthier

---

[44] Preface to *The Scribleriad* (1752), p. iv.
[45] *Essay on Ridicule*, p. 13.
[46] p. 7.
[47] *Patriotism* (1763), pp. 64–5.
[48] *Works* (1764), ii. 14.
[49] *An Essay upon Poetry* (1682), p. 6.

Subjects?'[50] And with a memorable phrase for describing insignificant subjects, he dismisses Pope: 'Methinks, Sir, Mr. Pope might employ his Time, and his admirable Genius better than in exposing Insects of a Day. . . .'[51] As to the yahoos, Richardson was scandalized—even Lovelace was disgusted by them. So too for that matter were Dr. Johnson and Edward Young. Johnson wondered what abnormal or depraved streak in Swift's nature prompted him to take 'delight in revolving ideas, from which almost every other mind shrinks in disgust'.[52] And Young exclaimed:

If so, O *Gulliver*! dost thou not shudder at thy brother *Lucian*'s Vulturs hovering o'er thee? Shudder on! they cannot shock thee more, than Decency has been shock'd by thee. How have thy *Houyhnhunms* thrown thy judgment from its seat, and laid thy imagination in the mire? In what ordure hast thou dipt thy pencil? What a monster hast thou made of the
—*Human face Divine?* MILT.[53]

The opinion was not uncommon. The obscene antics of Pope's dunces and Swift's yahoos were too much for those Augustans who cherished standards of refinement and propriety, and who were advocating satire which would be both gentler and more genteel. The women of Juvenal's sixth satire were clearly too much for them also, though because of their high regard for Juvenal they were reluctant to admit it. At least they were able to excuse Juvenal on the ground that he lived in an exceptionally violent age. It is significant, however, that Boileau's Satire x and Pope's *Epistle to a Lady*, not to mention Edward Burnaby Greene's bowdlerized version of Juvenal's Satire vi,[54] are exceedingly mild by comparison.

The point has been made that most critics who attacked satire in the late seventeenth and eighteenth centuries had particular satires or satirists in mind, or were objecting to particular sorts of satire, such as that which contains libel or slander. But a much more important qualification is that they were for the most part attacking contemporary satire—that they were more concerned

---

[50] Richardson to Hill, 19 January 1743/4, *Letters*, ed. Carroll, p. 60.
[51] Richardson to Dr. Cheyne, 21 January 1742/3, ibid., p. 56.
[52] *Lives* (1779–81), ii. 428.
[53] [Edward Young], *Conjectures on Original Composition* (1759), p. 62.
[54] In *The Satires of Juvenal Paraphrastically Imitated and Adapted to the Times* (1763).

with contemporary practice than general principles. It was rather the defenders who turned attention to (in some instances, 'fell back on' would be the more appropriate phrase) general principles.

Much of the adverse criticism of satire arose from the moral reaction, which took place near the end of the seventeenth century, against the Court Wits and the contemporary theatre. Wit and all its by-products, such as scoffing, ridicule, mockery, satire, lampoon, burlesque, and parody were associated with the cuckoldry and obscenity of Restoration plays, with the scurrilous lampoons circulated in the coffee-houses, and with the notorious licentiousness of the Restoration rakes. Wit came to be regarded as inherently evil. Sir Richard Blackmore indeed noted in his Preface to *Prince Arthur* that wit is one of the attributes of Satan. A 'satyrical wit' was regarded as pre-eminently a 'debauchee',[55] and was associated with dissipation in the popular phrase 'a man of wit and pleasure'. Steele quoted with approval Blackmore's summary comment: 'The Wits of this Island . . . instead of correcting the Vices of the Age have done all they could to inflame them.'[56] Much earlier Allestree observed that wit had become an idol of the age: 'Indeed Wit is so much the *Diana* of this age, that he who goes about to set any bounds to it must expect an *uproar* . . . or at least to be judged to have imposed an envious inhibition on it, because himself has not stock enough to maintain the trade.'[57] It was not, he contended, that he wished everyone to be solemn all the time, but he objected to wit as a preoccupation. His own words show that he was not without wit himself: 'Tis sure we shall die in Earnest, and it will not become us, to live altogether in Jest.' The trouble is, he argues, that if jesting becomes a preoccupation, solid and worthwhile considerations go by the board: 'By this means it is, that the gift of Raillery has in this Age, like the lean Kine, devoured all the more solid worthy qualifications, and is counted the most reputable accomplishment. A strange inverted estimate, thus to prefer the little ebullitions of Wit, before solid reason and judgment.' Implicit in Allestree's comment on 'the

[55] Anthony à Wood, *Athenae Oxonienses*, ed. Philip Bliss (1813–20), vol. iv, col. 731.

[56] *The Tatler*, No. 159, 15 April 1710.

[57] *The Government of the Tongue*, p. 115.

gift of raillery' in the preceding quotation, is the popular notion that wit represents a corruption of parts, and is therefore doubly deplorable. Allestree himself argues that ingenuity and quickness of wit are blessings and so should be put to the good uses for which God surely intended them. They should not be used to ridicule natural defects but to help other people. There are many people who crave laughter so much that they would pull away a lame man's crutch in order to laugh when he stumbles.[58] If those who 'rally out the day' were to take stock at its end, they would find, so he believes, that their laughter adds up to no more than the crackling of thorns under a pot mentioned in Ecclesiastes.[59] Glanvill objects to such people chiefly because they scoff at the beliefs of others, in particular at his own belief in apparitions and witchcraft. Wit is best, in his opinion, as the spearhead of intellectual inquiry; and for this noble work the droll is totally unsuited.[60] In remarking on the difficulty of coming to grips with Shaftesbury in the *Characteristics* because of his bantering tone and his shifting and mingling of terms, John Brown depicts wit as a slippery customer who has logic and reason at a permanent disadvantage:

It must be confessed, that in the Conduct of the literary Warfare, they who depend on the Regularity and Force of *Arguments*, have but a sorry Chance against these nimble Adventurers in the *Sallies* of Wit and Ridicule; these *Hussars* in Disputation, who confide more in their Agility, than Strength or Discipline; and by sudden *Evolutions* and timely *Skulking*, can do great Mischiefs, without receiving any. Ill qualified, indeed, is the *saturnine* Complexion of the dry *Reasoner*, to cope with this *mercureal* Spirit of modern *Wit*: The Formalist is under a double Difficulty; not only to *conquer* his Enemy, but to *find* him.[61]

One should perhaps add that Brown's colourful comments are only faintly pejorative, being an exercise in the same sort of bantering tone he noticed in Shaftesbury.

Wit and ridicule, and by extension satire also, were frequently represented as a corrupting influence. As they are superficially attractive, the argument went, they encourage people to swallow untruths they would otherwise disregard. In Allestree's phrase,

---

[58] Ibid., pp. 119, 126-7.
[59] Ibid., pp. 123-4.
[60] *A Blow at Modern Sadducism*, pp. 142-4.
[61] Brown (1751), p. 9.

they give 'wings to a reproch'. Many a poor man's infirmities have been broadcast, he says, through being made the subject of witty mockery.[62] Temple believed that poetry had been corrupted by ridicule. Some fine works of satire and burlesque had been produced in modern times, he conceded, *Don Quixote* and *Hudibras* being his favourites. None the less, no matter how well it is done, satire's effect is to undermine and destroy both poetry and virtue.[63] Addison claims to have heard of men who have sacrificed friends' reputations just to be thought wits—'As if it were not infinitely more honourable to be a Good-natured Man, than a Wit.'[64] That was one of the commonplaces of the eighteenth century, repeated again and again in discussions of humour, comedy, wit, and satire. One finds it, for instance, almost at the end of the century in William Boscawen's *The Progress of Satire* (1798): 'Could we bring all the satirists who ever wrote to an ingenuous confession, how few (if any) would declare that they invariably had forborne from a witty remark, or humourous description, when it appeared to violate the laws of candour and good-nature.'[65]

Not only the severe moralists, the Blackmores and Colliers, reacted strongly against wit and its by-products in the late seventeenth century. Tom Brown, who was far from being puritanical in life or letters, Shaftesbury, who became the champion of ridicule, and Wolseley, who was a great admirer of Rochester, also censured the trend of contemporary wit and satire. The immorality of the court, Tom Brown remarks in his 'Short Essay on English Satyr', was learned from France during the Prince's 'unhappy Exile', and this immorality 'and the Luxurious Idleness which succeeded the long fatiegues of our Civil Wars, frequently gave Births to Lampoons and Satyrs . . .', of which the former were 'perfectly Malicious' and the latter pointed too much to Great Men, lashing the Persons more than the Vices . . .'. Fortunately most of these writings are now forgotten, buried in 'Tombs of Forgetfulness'.[66] Shaftesbury, for all his advocacy of the moral and intellectual utility of ridicule found much that was regrettable in its practice. The satire of the day he

---

[62] *The Government of the Tongue*, p. 115.
[63] *Miscellanea*, ii. 49–51.
[64] *The Spectator*, No. 23.
[65] p. 4.
[66] *Works* (1707), i. 34.

considered 'scurrilous, buffooning and without Morals or Instruction'.[67] In Wolseley's opinion, satire was being employed
irresponsibly and indiscriminately, with the result that it was
doing all sorts of harm everywhere, but in particular to women's
reputations.

> For Satyre, that most needful part of our Poetry, it has of late
> been more abus'd, and is grown more degenerate than any other;
> most commonly like a Sword in the hands of a Mad-man, it runs a
> Tilt at all manner of Persons without any sort of distinction or
> reason, and so ill-guided is this furious Career, that the Thrusts are
> most aim'd, where the Enemy is best arm'd. Womens Reputations
> [of what Quality or Conduct soever,] have been reckon'd as lawful
> Game as Watchmen's Heads, and 'tis thought as glorious a piece of
> Gallantry by some of our modern Sparks, to libel a Woman of
> Honour, as to kill a Constable who is doing his duty;[68]

Wolseley declared that such satirists were unjust, superficial, and
ignorant, and that their readers—those at least who were prepared to credit such empty slanders—were equally foolish. Moreover, he confirmed, often they did not even have the excuse of
vengeance, for they hurt people who had done them no harm.
Nor could they be dismissed as mere buffoons: they were doing
too much mischief for that. Indeed, 'falling in with the baseness
of a corrupt Age' they were bidding 'defiance to the unalterable
Essence of things, by calling *Good Evil, and Evil Good*':

> Heroes have been hung up *in Effigie* who deserv'd Statues, while
> the worst of men have been *cens'd* with the Praises of demi-Gods;
> Betrayers of their Trust, and little servers of Turns have been
> idoliz'd, while Patriots of an unstain'd Honour, and unreproachable
> Conduct, who were in truth the *Dii Tutelares* of their distracted
> Countrey, have been openly blasphem'd with an impudent and wit-
> lesse Scurrility; in a word, those chiefly have been the Authors of
> Satyres, who ought to be the Subject, and 'tis become much more
> scandalous to be thought to write the best, than to be put into the
> most abusive.[69]

Contemporary satire, in the opinion of these writers, of Addison,
Blackmore, Collier, Dennis, Shaftesbury, Steele, Whitehead,
Wolseley, and countless others throughout the Augustan period,
needed to be purged of malice and pettiness.

---

[67] *Advice to an Author* (1710), p. 109.
[68] Preface to *Valentinian* (1685), sig. a2v.
[69] Ibid., sigs. a2v–a3r.

> Most sat'rists are indeed a public scourge,
> Their mildest physic is a farrier's purge,
> Their acrid temper turns as soon as stirr'd
> The milk of their good purpose all to curd,
> Their zeal begotten as their works rehearse,
> By lean despair upon an empty purse;[70]

Humour was needed instead of wit, and humour moreover that was imbued with good nature and fellow feeling.

With the development of this new kind of humour, and the growth of sentimentalism generally, we move from the area of stated objections to satire, which is properly the subject of this survey, to that of the underlying causes of its decline, which forms merely a part of the background. It need not be examined in any detail here, especially as it has been thoroughly traversed already by a number of critics.[71]

The principal impulse towards satire in the Augustan age was said in Chapter I to be, on the one hand, a yearning for moderation and order in every aspect of life, and on the other, the guiding belief that men could achieve this goal by the exercise of free will in the light of reason. One would expect, therefore, that satire's decline occurred when people became tolerant again of extremes and idiosyncrasies, of diversity, and when they began to lose their faith in man's ability to govern his conduct, and order society, by rational principles. And this is roughly what happened. As society and government became more settled and secure, and the tensions of the Civil War and post-Civil War period were relaxed, the need grew for a kindlier, more tolerant kind of humour. People no longer wanted comic characters who were so vicious as to demand the lash of satire, but those they could laugh at and enjoy. They wanted comic characters whom they might conceivably welcome into their homes, not those (like, let us say, Volpone and Mosca) whom they wished to see reduced to penury or sent to the galleys. In short, they preferred the amiably idiosyncratic *Spectator* characters to Shadwell's 'humorists'; and the inimitable Falstaff to Morose or Abel Drugger. Corbyn Morris said that 'it is impossible to *hate* honest

---

[70] William Cowper, 'Charity', *Poems* (1782–5), i. 205.

[71] e.g. Andrew M. Wilkinson, 'The Decline of English Verse Satire in the Middle Years of the Eighteenth Century', *RES* n.s. iii (1952), 222–33; E. N. Hooker, 'Humour in the Age of Pope', *HLQ* xi (1948), 361–85; and S. Tave, *The Amiable Humorist*.

Jack Falstaff, indeed 'it is impossible to avoid *loving* him' for he is 'the most delightful *Swaggerer* in all Nature'. He admits that there is humour in Ben Jonson's characters, and that they are drawn with masterly skill; but they are 'of a *satirical*, and *deceitful*, or of a *peevish*, or *despicable* Species: as *Volpone*, *Subtle, Morose,* and *Abel Drugger* . . .'. While admitting, however, that Jonson, like Shakespeare, wrote well in his way, Corbyn Morris leaves the reader in no doubt where his own preference lies:

> *Johnson* in his COMIC Scenes has expos'd and ridicul'd *Folly* and *Vice*; *Shakespear* has usher'd in *Joy, Frolic* and *Happiness.*—The *Alchymist, Volpone* and *Silent Woman* of *Johnson*, are most exquisite *Satires*. The *comic* Entertainments of *Shakespear* are the highest Compositions of *Raillery, Wit* and *Humour. Johnson* conveys some Lesson in every Character. *Shakespear* some new Species of Foible and Oddity. The one pointed his Satire with masterly Skill; the other was inimitable in touching the Strings of Delight. With *Johnson* you are confin'd and instructed, with *Shakespear* unbent and dissolv'd in Joy.[72]

What Corbyn Morris and critics like him were in fact asking for was comedy without satire. Similarly they wanted laughter free of any tincture of contempt. In Hobbes's view, which went largely unchallenged in the late seventeenth century, laughter was essentially derisive, set off by a sudden revelation of one's superiority. But this view was repeatedly challenged in the eighteenth century, and intimations of a kindlier approach to laughter, which had been voiced previously, were taken up and expanded. Descartes had said that laughter is permissible provided that we feel no hatred towards its victims,[73] and in the Preface to *Absalom and Achitophel*, as well as in the *Discourse*, Dryden propounded the ideal of a kind of satire which would amuse its victims as well as everyone else, and which if it wounded would at least do so painlessly. The contrast between the older and newer attitudes is interestingly illustrated by two of Addison's essays. In *The Spectator*, No. 47, he goes along happily enough with the Hobbesian view. He quotes the famous 'sudden glory' passage from Hobbes's *Discourse on Human Nature*, then observes: 'According to this Author therefore, when

---

[72] Corbyn Morris, pp. 29–30, 33.
[73] *Passiones Animae* (Amsterdam, 1650), Pt. III, art. clxxx, p. 34.

we hear a Man laugh excessively, instead of saying he is very Merry, we ought to tell him he is very Proud.' And, in the behaviour of those around him he finds many instances to confirm this view. But in *The Spectator*, No. 249, where he is intent on developing a benign notion of laughter, he leaves Hobbes far behind. Laughter in itself he finds both 'amiable and beautiful', the companion of love and beauty (Venus is 'the Laughter-loving Dame'), and though it 'slackens and unbraces the Mind' we should 'take care not to grow too Wise for so great a Pleasure of Life'. Francis Hutcheson in his *Reflections Upon Laughter* (Glasgow, 1750), points out that, if Hobbes is right, there can be no laughter except when we compare ourselves to others, or our present state to one that is worse. But of course this is not so, for parody (to take one example) may arouse laughter in those 'who have the highest veneration for the writing alluded to'. Moreover, the sudden appearance of superiority may excite the opposite of laughter. If we see someone in pain we are more inclined to weep than laugh, 'and yet here is occasion for Hobbes's sudden joy'. What a merry state a fine well-dressed gentleman must be in, Hutcheson reflects, when he passes through a street full of 'ragged beggars, and porters and chairmen sweating at their labour'! And what a pity it is not to have 'an infirmary or lazar-house to retire to in cloudy weather, to get an afternoon of Laughter'! [74]

Addison and Hutcheson and certain other critics, such as Anthony Collins,[75] succeeded in establishing a distinction between two sorts of laughter, the comic and the satiric, between 'innocent' laughter, on the one hand, and 'judicial' or 'derisive' laughter, on the other; and the opponents of satire used this distinction to express their distaste for ridicule in all its manifestations. In his essay on laughter in *The Spectator*, No. 249, Addison ruled that 'The Talent of turning men into Ridicule, and exposing to Laughter those one converses with, is the Qualification of little ungenerous Tempers.'

A young Man with this cast of Mind cuts himself off from all manner of Improvement. Every one has his Flaws and Weaknesses; nay, the greatest Blemishes are often found in the most shining Characters; but what an absurd thing is it to pass over all the

---

[74] pp. 8, 11–12.
[75] *A Discourse Concerning Ridicule and Irony in Writing* (1729), *passim*.

valuable Parts of a Man, and fix our Attention on his Infirmities; to observe his Imperfections more than his Virtues; and to make use of him for the Sport of others, rather than for our own Improvement. Very often those who are 'the most accomplished in Ridicule' never produce anything worth while themselves; without ever perhaps writing a single good line they achieve a reputation as eminent critics. Addison would not mind so much if ridicule were applied where it is deserved: 'If the Talent of Ridicule were employed to laugh Men out of Vice and Folly, it might be of some use to the World; but instead of this, we find that it is generally made use of to laugh Men out of Virtue and good Sense, by attacking every thing that is Solemn and Serious, Decent and Praise-worthy in Human Life.' Again and again it is the contemporary misuse of ridicule—and of its various modes, raillery, banter, burlesque, and satire—that is the target of hostile criticism. Thus Knox observed: 'Ridicule, indeed, seems to become a weapon in the hands of the wicked, destructive of taste, feeling, morality, and religion.'[76]

No doubt it was the growing distaste for ridicule which caused Shaftesbury's contention that it could be used effectively against propositions which reason found untenable, that it could function as a test of truth, to arouse such a hostile reaction. It should be noted at the same time, however, that Shaftesbury found himself with at least as many supporters as opponents. Ridicule evidently was an effective catalyst of eighteenth-century opinion. Those, whose outlook one may broadly describe as satirical, saw it as a most valuable means of exposing departures from the norms of reasonable thinking and conduct. Through ridicule they felt that follies and vices could be laughed away. For those who believed in satire (like John Brown for instance), Shaftesbury's main assertion, even though it could not be accepted without qualification, provided satire with a philosophical justification, a rationale—as Brown's *Essay on Satire* and *Essays on the Characteristics* amply demonstrate.[77] On the other hand, Shaftesbury's contention angered those who were aware of the considerable harm that could be and was being done by misplaced ridicule. One of the chief arguments against ridicule, both before

[76] *Essays Moral and Literary* (1782), ii. 165.
[77] See R. L. Brett, *The Third Earl of Shaftesbury: A Study in Eighteenth Century Literary Theory* (1951), pp. 174–7.

and after Shaftesbury, was that so far from fostering truth and
virtue it frequently traduced and injured them. 'What means
all this *Railing* and Libelling? Can any man of Common Sense
think, this is the Method to *Promote Truth?*' asked John
Sergeant. 'Invectives cast such a Shadow upon the clearest
Truths' that 'the best Efforts of *Exact Reason* will be turn'd into
Buffoonery.'[78] In a poem entitled *Candour, or an Occasional
Essay on the Abuse of Wit and Eloquence* (1739), the anonymous author protests against satire's continual railing against
the age and its vices, seeing that satire herself respects neither
religion nor government. He advises her in effect either to prove
her charges, or be quiet:

> Enough has Satire vicious Times bewail'd
> Error expos'd, and at Corruption rail'd;
> Satire herself, a public Grievance grown,
> Nor spares the Altar, nor reveres the Throne.
>
> .   .   .
>
> Whence all this Clamour of Decay in Parts,
> In martial Prowess, and in civil Arts?
> Prove, SATIRE, prove, where *Britain's* Genius fails;
> Where sacred Justice boasts more equal Scales,
> Where Learning, Worth, or Glory more prevails.[79]

And in the debate between Candour and Satire in Churchill's
Epistle to William Hogarth (1763), one of Candour's main
charges is that Satire, overcome by discontent and ill nature,
wilfully misrepresents the truth and gives a false view of human
nature:

> Cease then thy guilty rage, thou wayward son,
> With the foul gall of discontent o'er run,
> List to my voice—be honest, if you can,
> Nor slander Nature in her fav'rite man.
> But if thy spirit, resolute in ill,
> Once having err'd, persists in error still,
> Go on at large, no longer worth my care,
> And freely vent those blasphemies in air,
> Which I would stamp as false, tho' on the tongue
> Of Angels, the injurious slander hung.
>
> .   .   .

---

[78] J. S., *Raillery Defeated by Calm Reason: or, the New Cartesian Method
of Arguing and Answering Expos'd* (1699), sig. A2r, and p. 2.
[79] pp. 5, 10.

Hast Thou, maintaining that which must disgrace
And bring into contempt the human race,
Hast Thou, or can'st Thou, in Truth's sacred court,
To save thy credit, and thy cause support,
Produce one proof, make out one real ground
On which so great, so gross a charge to found?[80]

In the latter part of the eighteenth century the feeling was abroad that the time for satire was over. It spread even to satirists —'Satyr has long since done his best', wrote William Cowper in 'Table Talk'.[81] Satirists were still plentiful enough—Churchill, Combe, Cowper, Gifford, Mathias, 'Pasquin', 'Peter Pindar'—but confidence in satire's function was diminishing, as also in its standing among the kinds of poetry. Thomas Blackwell referred to its province as 'the most unpoetical of Parnassus'.[82] James Beattie put it among 'the lower kinds' along with pastoral and song.[83] John Aikin noted that 'satire . . . is still sufficiently vigorous and prolific; but its offspring is little suited to please a mind sensible to the charms of genuine poetry'. He classed it with the other 'enfeebled' kinds.[84] And Joseph Warton, in comments which have long been famous, denied that a satirist could ever be regarded as a true poet:

a clear head, and acute understanding are not sufficient, alone, to make a POET . . . the most solid observations on human life, expressed with the utmost elegance and brevity, are MORALITY, and not POETRY . . . the EPISTLES of Boileau in RHYME, are not more poetical, than the CHARACTERS of Bruyere in PROSE . . . it is a creative and glowing IMAGINATION 'acer spiritus ac vis', and that alone, that can stamp a writer with this exalted and very uncommon character, which so few possess, and of which so few can properly judge.[85]

Warton believed that the works of 'wit and satire' were in a separate (and inferior) category from those of 'nature and passion'—'WIT AND SATIRE are transitory and perishable, but NATURE and PASSION are eternal'[86]—and, by putting *The Rape of the Lock* above Pope's later satires, Warton showed clearly that he preferred light and comparatively harmless to profound and

[80] *Epistle to Hogarth*, pp. 14–15.
[81] *Poems* (1782), i. 38.
[82] *Letters Concerning Mythology* (1748), p. 14.
[83] *Essays* (1776), p. 297.
[84] *Essay on the Application of Natural History to Poetry* (1777), pp. 3–4.
[85] Warton (1756), pp. iv–v.
[86] Ibid., p. 334.

devastating satire—satire in fact, which was perhaps not properly satire at all, but nearer in spirit to comedy. Of all the attitudes which were adopted towards satire in the eighteenth century, this was the most damaging, for it implied that satire did not have to be taken very seriously, that it was of only minor importance. Throughout this chapter it has been emphasized that the main attack was directed against contemporary satire. Doubting Thomases there were certainly, who had no time for satire at all; but most of satire's opponents objected only or mainly to its abuses. Satire fell into decline in the latter part of the eighteenth century, not because it was crushed by critical arguments, nor because the defence put up by its advocates was feeble, irrational, inappropriate, or otherwise faulty, but because both friends and enemies no longer took for granted that there was something there that really needed or was worth defending. Less than a hundred years after Pope had proclaimed himself 'arm'd for Virtue' and held satire high above his head like a flaming sword, Byron wrote to his friend Murray: 'You are too earnest and eager about a work [Don Juan] never intended to be serious. Do you suppose that I could have any intention but to giggle and make giggle?'[87] Admittedly elsewhere[88] Byron described *Don Juan* as 'the most moral of poems'; nevertheless, the facetiousness of his comment to Murray is more typical both of his satirical pose and of his age's taste in satire.

[87] *The Works of Lord Byron: Letters and Journals*, ed. R. E. Prothero (1898–1901), iv. 343.
[88] Ibid. iv. 279.

5. Core of the Defence: the Moral Function of Satire

'THE Greatest Satire is Non-Moral.' This pronouncement (actually the title of an essay by Wyndham Lewis)[1] is startling, as it was no doubt intended to be. It is as though Lewis has pulled satire up by its roots and is waving it in the air to gain our attention. If we are at first startled, however, this might well be less because we disagree with the pronouncement than because we have not previously turned our minds to the traditional assumption which it so forthrightly contradicts. We are inclined to accept without question today the idea that a work of art, though its concerns may be moral, cannot put a case for a specific moral code without damaging itself as art. Indeed to discuss a work of art as though it were a moral tract appears a heinous sin to many modern critics. 'The moralistic view of art', writes John Crowe Ransom, 'is the immoral recourse of thinkers with moral axes to grind; or it is the decision of harried and unphilosophical thinkers who cannot think of anything else to think.'[2] Even those who would not be prepared to go as far as Professor Ransom, and who firmly believe in the moral value of art, nevertheless insist that its moral effects must be indirect and unobtrusive, in short that however moral it may be in essence it fails as art the moment it becomes moralistic.

This is a far cry from the orthodox viewpoint of the Augustan critics. In the late seventeenth and eighteenth centuries, as for that matter throughout the Renaissance and in classical Roman and Greek times, poetry like all art was expected to profit as well as please. Its capacity to instruct was upheld as its *raison d'être*: it had to be manifestly useful to individuals and to society as a whole, to church and government, God and the commonweal: *utile* was its end, *dulci* merely the means. Possibly, too, as

---

[1] *Men Without Art* (1934), pp. 103–14.
[2] 'Ubiquitous Moralists', *The Kenyon Review*, iii (1941), 99.

F

J. W. Draper has observed, this traditional didactic approach became more pronounced in England as a result of the frequent attacks made by the Puritans on literature and the theatre:

> Ever since the rise of Puritanism in the reign of Elizabeth, the fundamental problem in England of every art has been to justify its existence in the face of a religious sect that dominated the bourgeoisie—a sect that required of every human activity a direct religious sanction . . .[3]

Certainly the idea that art need not be directly useful was scarcely even entertained, although one comes on intimations of it in the writings of exceptionally sensitive critics, such as Sidney[4] and Dryden,[5] when they are giving full expression to their delight in literature. The orthodox view, handed down to the Augustans and accepted by them as an article of faith, was that literature aims to instruct its readers at the same time as it delights them.

> For no other end is *Poetry* delightful then that it may be profitable. Pleasure is only the means by which the profit is convey'd . . .[6]

> As the Inventions of Sages and Law-givers themselves, do please as well as profit those who approve and follow them; so those of Poets, Instruct and Profit as well as Please . . . and the happy mixture of both these, makes the excellency in both those compositions . . .[7]

> To instruct delightfully is the general end of all poetry.[8]

For the most part late seventeenth- and eighteenth-century critics evidently considered there was no need to discuss these precepts or to put a case for them. They felt that it was enough to repeat them—which they did as the occasion demanded, either self-righteously in the course of an essay, as though making the gestures required of them by tradition and public opinion, or defensively on behalf of a literary work, which they liked and admired, but whose moral usefulness had been called into question. They agreed, admitted, or reluctantly conceded, according to their individual temperaments, that literature gives

---

[3] 'The Theory of the Comic in Eighteenth Century England', *JEGP* xxxvii (1938), 212.

[4] *An Apologie for Poetrie* (1595). See also G. Gregory Smith's comments in *Elizabethan Critical Essays* (Oxford, 1904), i. xxiv–xxvii.

[5] In his comments on Juvenal, for example, Dryden's *Essays*, ii. 84–5.

[6] Rapin, p. 13.

[7] Temple, 'Of Poetry', *Miscellanea*, ii. 3.

[8] Preface to *Troilus and Cressida* (1679), Dryden's *Essays*, i. 209.

and should give pleasure; at the same time they found it necessary to repeat time and time again, *ad nauseam,* that this
pleasure should be only a means to the profit.

Nothing could have been easier, then, since the established view
of the worth of literature was its capacity to instruct, than to defend satire on the grounds of its moral utility. It was the obvious
line to take, for after all, to the moralist, satire is the most patently
moral of all literary modes, provided of course that it is
responsibly employed. Indeed what happened, as has already
been pointed out,[9] was that other modes were sometimes justified
in terms of their satirical elements or, in extreme instances, made
out to be essentially satirical. Tragedy, for example, was praised
for showing that crime does not pay, and comedy and burlesque
for making fools appear ridiculous and contemptible.

And for the reformation of Fopps and Knaves, I think Comedy
most useful, because to render Vices and Fopperies very ridiculous,
is much a greater punishment than Tragedy can inflict upon 'em.
There we do but subject 'em to hatred, or at worst to death; here
we make them live to be despised and laugh'd at, which certainly
makes more impression upon men than even death can do.[10]

For the thorough-going moralist, all literature has only one
aim (albeit a two-fold aim): the destruction of vice and the
promotion of virtue. He reduces literature to two principal kinds,
satire and panegyric. Thus he views tragedy as savage satire, and
comedy as laughing satire. Both furnish negative examples
designed to deter men from vice. Heroic drama and the epic, on
the other hand, are types of panegyric, exalting virtue and providing examples for imitation. In his Preface to *Prince Arthur*
(1695) Blackmore observes that in antiquity tragedies were part
of the divine service. As their object was to dissuade men from
vice and impiety they showed how the bad actions of great men
inevitably brought about their ruin. Comedy, he says, has the
same object, but it employs a different method, for it dissuades
men from vice by making vicious men appear ridiculous. Satire,
according to Blackmore's description, differs from comedy only
in using the harsher laughter of scorn and reproach.[11] As was
pointed out in the opening chapter, the same identification of

---

[9] Chapter 2, pp. 14–15.
[10] Thomas Shadwell, Preface to *The Humorists*, sig. a 1r.
[11] Preface to *Prince Arthur*, first unsigned gathering [2v].

tragedy with savage satire, and comedy with laughing satire, was made by Collier at the very beginning of his attack on the contemporary stage. The paradox is that the two late seventeenth-century critics who launched the heaviest assaults on contemporary satirical practice laid a wider basis at a theoretical level for the defence of satire than any of its avowed champions. But that is by the way. The important point to notice here is that in such a mileu as has been indicated, one in which literature generally was viewed as an instrument of reform, the justification of satire on the grounds of its moral and social function was a comparatively easy matter. It followed predictable lines.

There were, for example, the proclamations of its general moral purpose:

> The principal end of *Satyr*, is to instruct the People by discrediting Vice.[12]

> The true end of *Satyre*, is the amendment of Vices by correction.[13]

> The End of Satyr is Reformation . . .[14]

Any society benefits from satire, it was argued, but especially one which is ailing, for no remedy is more effective in curing social ills than satire.

> Speak, *Satyr*; for there's none can tell like thee,
> Whether 'tis Folly, Pride, or Knavery,
> That makes this discontented Land appear
> Less happy now in Times of Peace, than War:[15]

In similar terms Horace Walpole begs Mason to use to the full his talent for satire: 'for Heaven's and England's sake do not let it rust. You have a vein of irony and satire that the best of causes bleeds for having wanted.'[16] As satire is an ideal remedy for social ills, it is as ridiculous to regard the satirist as society's enemy, as it would be to regard the physician as the enemy of his patient. So Dryden added the following comment to his statement (quoted above) of the general moral purpose of satire: 'And he who writes Honestly, is no more an Enemy to the Offendour,

---

[12] Rapin, p. 137.
[13] 'To the Reader', *Absalom and Achitophel*, Dryden's *Poems*, i. 216.
[14] Daniel Defoe, Preface to *The True-Born Englishman* (1701), sig. Aivr.
[15] Ibid., sig. A2r.
[16] 27 March 1773, *Horace Walpole's Correspondence*, ed. W. S. Lewis, xxviii. 77.

than the Physician to the Patient, when he prescribes harsh Remedies to an inveterate Disease.'[17] As a sick society needs satire if it is to recover, so a healthy society welcomes it because it recognizes its uses. In his letter to Arbuthnot, 26 July 1734, Pope observed that 'much freer Satyrists' than himself 'enjoy'd the encouragement and protection of the Princes under whom they lived. Augustus and Mecœnas made Horace their companion, tho' he had been in arms on the side of Brutus. . . .' Then he adds that, although he would not presume to compare himself with Horace, nor with Virgil, who also found favour with Augustus and Maecenas, 'nor even with another Court-favourite, Boileau', he does wish to point out 'that it was under the greatest Princes and best Ministers, that moral Satyrists were most encouraged; and that then Poets exercised the same jurisdiction over the Follies, as Historians did over the Vices of men'.[18]

In addition to its broad social uses, satire is 'a shining *supplement* to publick *laws*'.[19] It can serve as an extra arm of government and the law, for it can reach out and expose those malefactors who in the normal run of events would probably escape unscathed and perhaps even unnoticed.

. . . Law can pronounce judgment only on open Facts, Morality alone can pass censure on Intentions of mischief; so that for secret calumny or the arrow flying in the dark, there is no publick punishment left, but what a good writer inflicts.[20]

But there are Crimes of a very high Nature, which are not cognisable in the ordinary Courts of Justice, such as Ingratitude, the denying a Deposit, the betraying a Friend's Secrets; and among these I may reckon such Frauds, as for want of legal Evidence escape with Impunity. These and all other Evils, which are not punishable by the Civil Magistrate are surely the proper Objects of Satire; nor is the Satirist obliged to stop short, because the Criminal may happen to die, while he is telling his Story.[21]

There are many grievous excesses which Law does not reach, and concerning which the menaces of Religion are ineffectual. Satire

---

[17] 'To the Reader', *Absalom and Achitophel*, Dryden's *Poems*, i. 216.
[18] Pope's *Correspondence*, iii. 420.
[19] [Edward Young], *Love of Fame, The Universal Passion*, Second Edition Corrected, and Altered (1728), p. 4.
[20] William Cleland, 'A Letter to the Publisher, Occasioned by the present Edition of the Dunciad', Pope's *Poems*, v. 14.
[21] [William King], The Translator's Preface to *The Toast, An Heroick Poem* (1736), p. xxxix.

takes, as it were, the middle way; supplies, in some measure, the defects of Law in creating a Tribunal of its own; and by erecting a sensibility to its own severities, prepares the mind to be affected by those of Religion.[22]

Steele had put this same argument in *The Tatler*, No. 61 (30 August 1709), where he told of a gentleman of his acquaintance maintaining that it is permissible in certain instances for satire to injure reputations:

It is a common Objection against Writings of a Satyrical Mixture, that they hurt Men in their Reputations, and consequently in their Fortunes and Possessions; but a Gentleman who frequents this Room declar'd, he was of Opinion it ought to be so, provided such Performances had their proper Restrictions. The greatest Evils in human Society are such as no Law can come at; as in the Case of Ingratitude. . . . And is it not lawful to set Marks upon Persons who live within the Law, and do base Things? Shall not we use the same Protection of those Laws to punish 'em, which they have to defend themselves? We shall therefore take it for a very moral Action to find good Appellation for Offenders, and to turn 'em into Ridicule under feign'd Names.

The fullest and most carefully reasoned statement of the argument, however, was made by Swift in *The Examiner*, No. 38 (26 April 1711):

But to return from this Digression; 'tis very plain, that considering the Defectiveness of our Laws; the variety of Cases, the weakness of the Prerogative, the Power or the Cunning of ill-designing Men, it is possible, that many great Abuses may be visibly committed, which cannot be legally Punish'd: Especially if we add to this, that some Enquiries might probably involve those, whom upon other Accounts, it is not thought convenient to disturb. Therefore, it is very false Reasoning, especially in the Management of Publick Affairs, to Argue that Men are Innocent, because the Law hath not pronounc'd them Guilty.

I am apt to think, it was to supply such Defects as these, that Satyr was first introduc'd into the World; whereby those whom neither Religion, nor natural Virtue, nor fear of Punishment, were able to keep within the Bounds of their Duty, might be withheld by the Shame of having their Crimes expos'd to open View in the strongest Colours, and themselves rendered odious to Mankind. Perhaps all this may be little regarded by such harden'd and abandoned Natures as I have to deal with; but, next to taming or binding a Savage—

[22] [William Combe], Preface to *The Justification* (1777), p. iii.

Animal, the best Service you can do the Neighbourhood, is to give them warning, either to Arm themselves, or not to come in its way.

Of all the social services which satire could perform, none was considered more urgently necessary than the extermination of the whole race of scribblers who (as in Pope's picture of them in *The Dunciad*) threatened to over-run the polite world of letters and learning. To leading Augustans like Addison and Pope, and Dennis too for that matter, scribbling appeared to have reached epidemic proportions. It was often described as a plague or infection and the scribblers themselves as insects, locusts, grasshoppers, bugs, or vermin.

> Fierce Insect-Wits draw out their noisy Swarms,
> And threaten Ruin more than Foreign Arms.
> O'er all the Land the hungry Locusts spread
> Gnaw every Plant, taint every flowry Bed,
> And crop each budding Virtue's tender Head.[23]

Pope compared the scribblers who attacked Dryden in the latter part of his life to 'Gnats in a Summer's evening, which are never very troublesome but in the finest and most glorious Season'.[24]

In campaigning against bad writing, the English neo-classicists were no doubt self-consciously following in a well-established tradition—'*Semper ego auditor tantum?* . . .'[25]—but it would be wrong to imply that they were doing no more than that, for they were genuinely alarmed by the rabble of inferior writers who were 'loading the presses' and 'choking the stage'[26] with their illiterate productions:

Never was there known so many Versifyers, and so few Poets; every Ass that's Romantick, believes he's inspir'd, and none have been so forward to teach others as those who cannot write themselves; every man is ready to be a Judge, but few will be at the trouble to understand, and none are more blind to the faults of their own Poetry, than those who are so sharp-sighted in other men's; Every Fop that falls in Love, thinks he has a Right to make Songs, and all kind of People that are gifted with the least knowledge of *Latin* and *Greek*, pretend to translate; the most reverenc'd Authors of Antiquity, have not been able to escape the Conceitedness of

---

[23] Blackmore, *A Satyr against Wit* (1700), A2r
[24] Pope to Wycherley, 26 December 1704, *Pope's Correspondence*, i. 2.
[25] Juvenal, *Satires*, i. i.
[26] Thomas Otway, 'To Mr. Creech upon his Translation of *Lucretius*', *The Works of Thomas Otway*, ed. J. C. Ghosh, ii. 439–40.

Essayers, nor *Hudibras* himself, that admirable Original, his little Apers, tho' so artless are their Imitations, so unlike and so liveless are their Copies, that 'twere impossible to guess after what Hands they drew, if their Vanity did not take care to inform us in the Title-Page.[27]

With regard to 'the occasion and cause' of *The Dunciad,* Martinus Scriblerus comments:

[The author] lived in those days, when (after providence had permitted the Invention of Printing as a scourge for the Sins of the learned) Paper also became so cheap, and printers so numerous, that a deluge of authors cover'd the land: Whereby not only the peace of the honest unwriting subject was daily molested, but unmerciful demands were made of his applause, yea of his money, by such as would neither earn the one, or deserve the other:[28]

In such an age the duty of the satirist was unmistakable:

> Exert your self, defend the Muse's Cause . . .
> For of all Natures Works we most should scorn
> The thing who thinks himself a Poet born . . .[29]

Pope, through Scriblerus, warned his readers against dismissing scribblers too lightly, reminding them 'what the *Dutch* stories somewhere relate, that a great part of their Provinces was once overflow'd, by a small opening made in one of their dykes by a single *Water-Rat*'.[30] In his *Life of Pope* Dr. Johnson, while admitting that 'there was petulance and malignity enough' in the design of *The Dunciad,* justified it and similar works on the ground that they serve to check bad writers and refine public taste.[31] And, according to Wolseley, Rochester in his lifetime had just this effect. Wolseley compares him to an eagle majestically circling above the lesser birds of the air and frightening them into subjection:

he who by his great Mastery in Satyre seem'd to be particularly trusted with the Justice of *Apollo,* did not use to let the Purloiners of Wit retail their stollen Goods to the People, without bringing 'em to open shame, nor *Quacks* and *Mountebanks* in Poetry, furnish'd with nothing but a few borrow'd *Recipes,* to put on the Face and

27 Wolseley, Preface to *Valentinian,* sig. A2r.
28 Pope's *Poems,* v. 49.
29 Otway, *Works,* ed. Ghosh, ii. 439.
30 Pope's *Poems,* v. 192 (note to line 337).
31 *The Lives of the English Poets* (1779–81), ii. 428.

Gravity, and appear in publick with the pride and positiveness of Doctors; the vainest Pretenders in his time, the most confident *Essayers*, cow'd and aw'd under the known force of a sence so superiour to their own, were glad at any rate to keep their empty Heads out of Observation, as the Fowl of a whole Countrey creep into the Bushes, when an Eagle hangs hovering above 'em.[32]

In keeping law and order, in maintaining moral and literary standards, and generally in the exercise of its moral function, satire was thought to have special advantages over rival media. It was considered much more effective than teaching, for example—as Francis Hutcheson put it, 'Men have been laughed out of faults which a sermon could not reform . . .'[33]—and more effective also than philosophical discourse or rational argument:

> And without doubt, though some it may offend,
> Nothing helps more than satire to amend
> Ill manners, or is trulier virtue's friend,
> Princes may laws ordain, priests gravely preach,
> But poets most successfully will teach.[34]

According to Rapin,[35] the Greeks had found tragedy too grim and frightening to exercise a generally reformative influence. Bolingbroke remarked in a letter to Swift, March 1731/2, on the powerlessness of philosophy, politics, and divinity to reform the age. Satire alone, he felt, could do any good, for those who are ashamed of nothing else are ashamed of being made to look ridiculous.[36] In Addison's opinion, satire (of the kind he and Steele advocated) is capable of redeeming apparently hopeless cases, malefactors beyond the reach of every other means of reform:

> It also awakens Reflection in those who are the most Indifferent in the Cause of Virtue or Knowledge, by setting before them the Absurdity of such Practices as are generally unobserved, by Reason of their being Common or Fashionable: Nay, it sometimes catches the Dissolute and Abandoned before they are aware of it; who are often betrayed to laugh at themselves, and upon Reflection find, that they are merry at their own Expence.[37]

---

[32] Preface to *Valentinian*, sigs. a1v–a2r.
[33] *Reflections upon Laughter*, p. 35.
[34] Sir Carr Scroope, 'In Defense of Satire', in *Poems on Affairs of State*, ed. Lord, i. 364.
[35] Rapin, p. 136. See also Horace, *Ars Poetica*, lines 220–4.
[36] Swift's *Correspondence*, iii. 276.
[37] *The Free-holder*, No. 45, 25 May 1716.

Pope wrote to Arbuthnot that nothing had comforted him more, nor afforded him greater encouragement to proceed with his satirical writing, than to observe 'that those who have no shame, and no fear, of any thing else, have appeared touch'd by my Satires'.[38] A special advantage of satire, when delicately handled, was held to be its ability to administer reproof and correction without arousing antagonism. 'I hope', says Fielding's Medley, 'to expose the reigning Follies, in such a Manner, that Men shall laugh themselves out of them before they feel that they are touched.'[39] Anthony Collins, after relating an anecdote of a satirical remark made by Waller to Charles II, at which the King laughed heartily, commented on the exceeding usefulness of irony 'that can convey an Instruction to a vicious, evil, and tyrannical Prince, highly reflecting on his Conduct, without drawing on his Resentment'.[40] But the famous instance of course is Dryden's claim regarding his portrait of Zimri—'he, for whom it was intended, was too witty to resent it as an injury'.[41] It may be doubted whether Buckingham took it as lightly as Dryden supposed. Certainly the lines[42] he wrote in response seem to show that he was hurt by the portrait. But the important point no doubt is that the satire was so skilful and entertaining that he could only have lost face by showing any resentment of it.

Broadly speaking, satire was held to instruct by the use of negative examples—examples of the kind of conduct which leads to misery, or misfortune, or public ridicule. It is the task of writers of comedy, Shadwell advised, 'to render their Figures of *Vice* and *Folly* so ugly and detestable, to make people hate and despise them, not onely in others, but (if it be possible) in their dear selves'.[43] By this means the foolish or evil person is shamed into reforming himself; while the virtuous person feels both confirmed in his virtue and mindful of the need to take extra precautions against any possible lapse. When a reaction set in against Restoration Comedy in the earlier part of the eighteenth century, the question was raised as to whether negative examples were as effective as positive ones. Steele believed that

---

[38] 26 July 1734, Pope's *Correspondence*, iii. 419.
[39] *The Historical Register For the Year 1736* (1736), p. 4.
[40] *A Discourse Concerning Ridicule and Irony in Writing* (1729), pp. 16–17.
[41] Dryden's *Essays*, ii. 93.
[42] 'To Dryden', *Poems on Affairs of State*, ed. Lord, i. liii.
[43] Preface to *The Humorists*, first unsigned gathering [4ᵛ].

young people should be shown models of virtue, which they might endeavour to emulate;[44] and Moore made fun of the view that instruction may be drawn from plays notable chiefly for their celebration of immorality. A brothel, he thought, could be recommended on the same grounds.[45] Satirists and defenders of satire, however, continued to argue the superiority of negative examples.

> The *Moral* must be clear and understood;
> But finer still, if negatively good:
> Blaspheming *Capeneus* obliquely shows
> T'adore those Gods *Aeneas* fears and knows.[46]

Fielding maintained on a number of occasions that satiric portraits of social abuse have greater impact than examples of good actions:

> Examples may perhaps have more Advantage over Precepts, in teaching us to avoid what is odious, than in impelling us to pursue what is amiable.[47]

> I shall venture . . . to assert that we are much better and easier taught by the examples of what we are to shun, than by those which would instruct us what to pursue.[48]

And Goldsmith alleged that sentimental comedy, through its avoidance of realistic depiction of current follies and vices, was failing to carry out comedy's function of moral reform.[49]

To instruct successfully, to achieve the maximum impact, critics from Dryden and Wycherley to Fielding and Goldsmith believed that satire (like comedy—in this context, no distinction was made between the two) must be realistic. Indeed they regarded its realism as the basis of its moral value. The function of the satirist was to show people as they were and the age what it was like. Bayle may have accused the satirist of being unable to resist the temptation to tamper with facts in order to make an entertaining story, and the wits may have acquired a bad name for telling lies or slanders about their fellows in order to raise a

---

[44] cf. *The Conscious Lovers* (1722), and John Hughes's attack in *The Tatler*, No. 76, 4 October 1709, on 'Reformation by Opposites'.
[45] *The World*, No. 9, 1 March 1753.
[46] Harte, p. 10.
[47] *The Covent Garden Journal*, No. 21, 14 March 1752.
[48] *The Champion*, 10 June 1740.
[49] *The Westminster Magazine*, 1 January 1773, *Goldsmith's Works*, ed. Friedman, iii. 209–13.

laugh; some satirists like Gay may have had recourse to fable, and some like Swift to allegory; nevertheless, the satirists and defenders of satire distinguished this mode of writing from others closely related to it by its superior realism, and justified it on the ground that it faithfully reflected the times. Pope, referring to his portrait of the Man of Ross, pleaded that he should be allowed some 'small exaggeration . . . as a poet', but none the less insisted that he 'was determined the ground work at least should be *Truth*' and to that end had been 'scupulous in [his] enquiries'.[50] Fielding stated in the Preface to *Joseph Andrews* that 'a Comic Writer should of all others be the least excused for deviating from Nature, since it may not always be easy for a serious Poet to meet with the Great and the Admirable; but Life every where furnishes an accurate Observer with the Ridiculous'.[51] And the anonymous author of *A Vindication of the Stage* (1698), claimed that

> . . . Plays are the Glasses of Human Actions, and reflect the true Images of the People; as you see the Errors of your Complexion by a view in a Glass, so in the Play-House you see the meanness and folly of your Vices, and by beholding the frightful Image, you grow asham'd, and perhaps may Reform, whereas had they never been expos'd, they had still been your Darling Companions, tho' all the Pulpits in Town had thunder'd never so loudly against them.[52]

The idea was repeated again and again in prologues and epilogues, and in dedications and prefaces, throughout the period. It was fundamental to the Augustan appreciation of satire. For example, it was the accuracy of Gay's picture in *The Beggar's Opera* that Swift regarded as its outstanding merit.[53] And it was the very realism, the truth to life, of contemporary comedy which, according to its apologists, most offended certain people (those who were exposed by it). 'But, now I mention Satyr,' wrote William Wycherley with regard to *The Plain Dealer*, 'some there are who say, 'Tis the Plain-dealing of the Play, not the obscenity; 'tis taking off the Ladies Masks, not offering at the

---

[50] Pope to Tonson, sen., 7 June 1732, Pope's *Correspondence*, iii. 290.
[51] (1752), I. vii.
[52] p. 15. cf. Sir John Vanbrugh, Prologue to *The Provok'd Wife* (1697):
   Since 'tis the Intent and Business of the Stage,
   To Copy out the Follies of the Age;
   To hold to every Man a Faithful Glass,
   And shew him of what Species he's an Ass.
[53] See quotation, Chapter 2, p. 14.

Pettycoats, which offends 'em . . .'.[54] Allegorical satires and satirical fables were written, certainly, but in such works the allegory
and fable tended to be merely cypher, less a means of transporting
the reader to another world than of making the writer safe in
this one. By recounting fantastic tales of pigeons, buzzards, and
swallows, wolves, and pigs, he could avoid open political and
personal reference. Most Augustan satirists, especially in the
late seventeenth century, dealt directly with the men and affairs
of the day, and they usually felt no inclination or need to depart
much from the facts. Dryden's satirical portrait of Zimri is
remarkably accurate historically; so also is Marvell's satirical
account of England's defeat by the Dutch in 1667 and of the
political intrigues which surrounded it.[55]

It was only to be expected that the Augustans would demand
of the literary modes which they used most that they be realistic,
as well as practical and instructive. In an age in which reason was
put before imagination, and judgement before fancy, in which
things were to be preferred to words, plain statements of fact to
figurative expressions—*ignes fatui*, as Hobbes called them[56]—
empirical procedures to intuitive speculations, and sober observation and reasoning to 'the Quaintest plays and sportings of
wit',[57] satire was expected to deal with everyday life, with current
fads and fancies, real dunces and real villains, and to deal with
them, moreover, in a practical, straightforward fashion, without
recourse to allegory, or deliberate mystification of any kind. Epic
and tragedy could treat noble heroes and their exploits, admirable and marvellous happenings, and scenes drawn from pagan
antiquity and the Garden of Eden. Satire, however, was to be a
mirror of the times. It was in fact often referred to as a glass or
mirror;[58] and the accuracy of its reflection was put forward as
the principal source of its reformative power.[59]

One might well ask whether, amid so much high-minded

[54] Dedication of *The Plain Dealer*, 1677, sig. +2r.

[55] See Lord's comments, *Poems on Affairs of State*, i. xlvii.

[56] Thomas Hobbes, *Leviathan* (1651), p. 22.

[57] Samuel Parker, *A Free and Impartial Censure of the Platonick Philosophie* (Oxford, 1666), p. 73.

[58] See Swift, Preface to *The Battle of the Books* (1704), Swift's *Prose Works*,
i. 140; and Pope, *The First Satire of the Second Book of Horace, Imitated*,
line 57, Pope's *Poems*, iv. 11.

[59] See Edwin E. Williams, 'Dr. James Drake and Restoration Theory of
Comedy', *RES* xv (1939), 184.

justification, any doubts at all were expressed by the defenders of satire as to its capacity to reform the world. That those critics who were hostile to satire would question it on this score was to be expected; and, as has previously been noted,[60] Blackmore and Bayle flatly denied that the world was one whit better for all the satires that had ever been written. The more interesting question, however, is whether any of satire's protagonists were prepared to set aside this leading argument in its defence, and substitute for it a more modest claim, one which we should regard as sounder and more discerning. For the generally acceptable view today would surely be that a satire has done its work when it has effectively demonstrated the failings of its subject, and that it cannot be expected to remove them as well; or to put the matter another way, that a satire is valuable for the insights it gives into moral problems, not for providing solutions to them. It can indeed be argued, from first principles as well as from ample historical evidence, that the worth of a satire is in inverse proportion to its capacity to bring about reforms—the better the satire, the less likely it is to change anything. Topical satires may occasion improvements in—let us say—political policies or social institutions, but these improvements will necessarily be of a superficial and adventitious nature. For those satirical works— the classics of the genre—which deal with basic features of human nature and society can never bring about any improvement, simply because neither human nature nor society is capable of fundamental change. Meanness does not disappear with a Molière, nor hypocrisy with a Fielding; nor have totalitarianism and utopianism vanished for ever with George Orwell.

Few Augustans were willing to contemplate so complete a reversal of the orthodox view of their times on the moral function of satire. Reservations were expressed, it is true, by a number of critics, and such reservations tended to become more sweeping as the period wore on. William Cowper probably expressed the feelings of many people in the latter part of the eighteenth century when he despaired of satire's ability to correct any but insignificant failings—

> Yet what can satire, whether grave or gay?
> It may correct a foible, may chastise
> The freaks of fashion, regulate the dress,

[60] Chapter 4, pp. 46, 47, 60.

Retrench a sword-blade, or displace a patch;
But where are its sublimer trophies found?
What vice has it subdued? Whose heart reclaim'd
By rigour, or whom laugh'd into reform?
Alas! Leviathan is not so tamed.[61]

Dryden and Pope regretted that fools, who are obviously proper targets for satire, usually prove insensitive to it. 'A witty man is tickled while he is hurt in this manner, and a fool feels it not', said Dryden of fine raillery.[62] And Pope repeated the same idea in a famous couplet:

You think this cruel? take it for a rule,
No creature smarts so little as a Fool.[63]

It was not only fools, however, who might fail to recognize themselves in a satire, and so be unaffected by it. According to Swift's much-quoted comment, everyone tends to treat satire as 'a sort of *Glass*, wherein Beholders do generally discover every body's Face but their Own; which is the chief Reason for that kind of Reception it meets in the World, and that so very few are offended with it'.[64] Moreover, the very subtlety of good satire may prevent it from striking home openly and unmistakably. As Dryden put it, a man may be 'secretly wounded' by fine raillery in a way that he could not be by coarse abuse, by 'slovenly butchering'.[65] Whitehead observed that although the use of fable may enable satire to rise above personal reference, it may also cause it to fly beyond its target. The satire may be disregarded by those who most need to take note of it—'They view the Face, but soon forget 'tis theirs'.[66]

Such minor reservations are to be found scattered in Augustan writings on satire; but they are after all merely minor, and probably they are more often used for effect or to express a passing mood than as considered statements of opinion. For example, in a letter written towards the end of his life, Pope remarks regretfully that he has lost his taste for all writing, even for satire, because 'no body has Shame enough left to be afraid of

---

[61] 'The Task', *Poems* (1782–5), ii. 61–2.
[62] Dryden's *Essays*, ii. 93.
[63] *An Epistle from Mr. Pope to Dr. Arbuthnot* (1734), lines 83–4, Pope's *Poems*, iv. 101.
[64] Preface to *The Battle of the Books*, Swift's *Prose Works*, i. 140.
[65] Dryden's *Essays*, ii. 93.
[66] *Essay on Ridicule*, p. 16.

Reproach, or punish'd by it'.[67] Similarly, in his Satire ix Boileau laments that frequently all the satirist succeeds in doing is to confer immortality on coxcombs; and in his Satire viii he cites, as a prime instance of man's neglect of his faculty of reason, the satirist's persistence in writing satire when his reason tells him that it is a totally unrewarding task.

Of the major writers only Swift entertained serious doubts about the reformative effects of satire. This is not to say that he did not subscribe to it on occasion—for example, in his vindication of *The Beggar's Opera* and in *Verses on the Death of Dr. Swift*[68]—but when his numerous comments on the question in letters, poems, and prefaces are taken into account, and when due weight is given to the satirical import of his major satires, it can be seen that basically he had no faith in it. In a letter to Charles Ford, 5 April 1733, after saying how he envied Pope the attacks being made on him, he expressed the opinion that 'all men of wit should employ it in Satyr, if it will onely serve to vex Rogues, though it will not amend them'.[69] In *A Letter of Advice to a Young Poet* (1721),[70] he ridiculed the extremes to which the belief that satire benefits mankind have been carried; and in his poem *On Censure* he declared that it cannot do harm either:

> For, let Mankind discharge their Tongues
> In Venom, till they burst their Lungs,
> Their utmost Malice cannot make
> Your Head, or Tooth, or Finger ake:
>
> . . .
>
> Nor can ten Hundred Thousand Lyes,
> Make you less virtuous, learn'd, or wise.[71]

Then, although it is claimed on the title-page of *A Tale of a Tub* that the book has been written for the universal improvement of mankind. Swift parodies pretensions of this kind throughout the book itself and, in the Preface, openly ridicules the common claim that the chief aim of satire is reform:

I have observ'd some Satyrists to use the Publick much at the Rate that Pedants do a naughty Boy ready Hors'd for Discipline: First expostulate the Case, then plead the Necessity of the Rod, from

---

[67] Pope to Earl of Orrery, 13 January 1742/3, Pope's *Correspondence*, iv. 437.
[68] Swift's *Poems*, ii. 571.
[69] Swift's *Correspondence*, iv. 138.
[70] p. 23.   [71] Swift's *Poems*, ii. 414.

great Provocations, and conclude every Period with a Lash. Now, if
I know any thing of Mankind, these Gentlemen might very well
spare their Reproof and Correction: For there is not, through all
Nature, another so callous and insensible a Member as *the World's
Posteriors*, whether you apply to it the *Toe* or the *Birch*.[72]

As to Gulliver's statement that his 'principal design' has been
'to inform, and not to amuse',[73] this is an obvious example of
irony, as is the claim that *Gulliver's Travels* would wonderfully
mend the world. Swift's doubts regarding the moral efficacy of
satire are indicated too in the last book of the *Travels*, though
by no means unequivocally. Swift is having so much fun at
Gulliver's expense, especially in the last chapter, that it is difficult
to determine how deep his ridicule goes and where it shades off
into assent. Gulliver is so consumed with self-disgust that he
behaves absurdly: forcing himself to look often at his body in
the mirror so that he may come in time to tolerate the sight of
human creatures; and stuffing his nostrils with rue, lavender,
and tobacco leaves when his wife comes near him because he
cannot bear her Yahoo smell. He is a figure of fun, a misan-
thropic clown; so we may not take his opinions too seriously.
Nevertheless, the acquaintanceship with reason that he has
formed in the country of the Houyhnhnms, although it has
unbalanced him personally, has enabled him to see his fellows
and English society in a clearer light than after his earlier
voyages. And, however absurd much of his behaviour may be,
he can now appreciate (Swift is surely assenting here) that, for
as long as human nature and society continue, there will be
fools and rascals, hypocrites and cheats: 'I am not in the least
provoked at the Sight of a Lawyer, a Pick-pocket, a Colonel, a
Fool, a Lord, a Gamester, a Politician, a Whoremunger, a
Physician, an Evidence, a Suborner, an Attorney, a Traytor, or
the like: This is all according to the due Course of Things.'[74] But
Swift goes on to imply through Gulliver (and the implication is
emphasized by being in the concluding paragraphs of the book)
that pride can be reduced or at least contained; for pride is
principally a failure to recognize our own limitations and weaknesses, a 'want of thoroughly understanding Human Nature, as
it sheweth it self in other Countries'. Satire then may not be

---

[72] Preface to *A Tale of a Tub*, Swift's *Prose Works*, i. 29.
[73] Swift's *Prose Works*, ii. 291.
[74] Ibid. 296.

able to counter 'the due Course of Things', but it provides rational perspectives and standards so that, however unsettling it may be, it enables us to *understand* ourselves and other people better: it may never enable us to attain the ideal of reason (which, at any rate, as personified by the Houyhnhnms, is slightly ludicrous); but it may perhaps enable most of us to appreciate the respects in which we fall short of that ideal.

Such would appear to be Swift's mature view of the function of satire, as expressed in his most deeply imagined writings. In this connection it is instructive to contrast *A Tale of a Tub* and *Gulliver's Travels* with an occasional piece like the vindication of *The Beggar's Opera*. One would hardly have expected Swift to subscribe to an oversimplified notion of satire's social utility that satisfied a Blackmore or a Collier; yet, as we have seen, it would be going too far to suggest that he rejected the moral view entirely. Rather, he gave such a view a colouring of scepticism, and found room in it for a number of important reservations and misgivings.

Swift was the only satirist of the age to look on his vocation with such honest discernment. Either from conviction, or for reasons of expediency, his fellow satirists preferred to present themselves to the public as practical reformers. Their claims were frequently grandiose. Satire, they declared, is on the side of the angels, of the king and the state. It is the public conscience, an arm of government and the law, the destroyer of vice and the champion of virtue. Did it not come into being for the express purpose of uplifting mankind?

> T'Exalt the Soul, or make the Heart sincere,
> To arm our Lives with honesty severe,
> To shake the wretch beyond the reach of Law,
> Deter the young, and touch the bold with awe,
> To raise the fal'n, to hear the sufferer's cries,
> And sanctify the virtues of the wise . . .[75]

Satire, according to John Brown, calms turbulent emotions, indicates the hard climb to glory, and teaches wise restraint to those who are reckless through ambition. She strikes sparks from stone, and

> Like the nice BEE, with art most subtly true
> From poys'nous vice extracts a healing dew.

[75] Harte, p. 5.

She humbles pride and rewards virtue, fearlessly attacks tyranny and, 'Pow'rful as death', defies the sycophants and slaves who cluster around a tyrant's throne. So powerful is she that the wicked hate and fear her, as well they might, for 'When love of virtue wakes her scorn of vice', she is remorseless and unbending:[76] But Satire's sternness and severity in the face of vice should not be held against her: it only makes her the greater friend to virtue. For it is by her ultimate purpose and effects that she should be judged, not by her acts of vengeance against the guilty. If she is judged fairly in this way, she will be seen to stand on a pinnacle of light, splendid and triumphant, the embodiment of divine virtue and truth.

> When fell Corruption dark and deep as fate,
> Saps the foundation of a tottering state:
> When Giant-Vice and Irreligion rise
> On mountain'd falsehoods to invade the skies: - - -
> When warmer numbers glow thro' SATIRE's page,
> And all her smiles are darken'd into rage:
> On eagle wing she gains Parnassus' height,
> Not lofty Epic soars a nobler flight;
> The conscious mountain trembles at her nod,
> And ev'ry awful gesture speaks the God:
> Then keener indignation fires her eye,
> Then flash her light'nings, and her thunders fly;
> Wide and more wide the flaming bolts are hurl'd,
> Till all her wrath involves the guilty world.[77]

The impressive range of Augustan achievement in satire, together with a background of traditional belief in the moral function of literature, evidently meant that such claims as Brown's could be announced with ringing confidence. If they sound somewhat absurd to a modern reader, this is probably largely because of the fulsomeness of Brown's diction. For, if we turn from the passages quoted above to Pope's apostrophe to satire in the *Epilogue to the Satires* (1738), we discover (particularly if we keep the finest of Pope's own satires in mind) that we are moved beyond questioning to assent and acclaim—

> O sacred Weapon! left for Truth's defence,
> Sole Dread of Folly, Vice, and Insolence!
> To all but Heav'n-directed hands deny'd,
> The Muse may give thee, but the Gods must guide.[78]

---

[76] Brown (1745), pp. 10–12.   [77] Ibid., p. 22.
[78] Lines 212–15, Pope's *Poems*, iv. 325.

6. Motives and Character of
the Satirist

AUGUSTAN satirists frequently accused one another, or were accused by their critics, of writing from bad motives. It is the perennial charge; but it was made with exceptional vigour and frequency in the Augustan period simply because that period furnished exceptionally ample grounds for it. A great deal of the satirical writing of Dryden's and Pope's times was in fact as scurrilous and libellous as it was said to be. As Pope acknowledged, there was a genuine need for an Addison to 'whiten the page'.[1] Anyone wishing to confirm this has only to glance at the printed attacks on Pope which he collected himself and had Tonson bind for him.[2] To acquire a balanced understanding of Augustan satire, it is necessary to poke about in the undergrowth as well as to admire 'the timber trees'.[3] The satirists and their supporters, however, were determined to keep their gaze turned upwards. They spoke of their intentions and aspirations and the outstanding achievements of the classical past. Besides, they were attempting to counter their opponents' unflattering picture of the satirist as a mean and petty-minded person full of spite and jealousy. They sought to present him instead as a man with an exceptionally keen sense of public duty, one who was so outraged by a foolish or wicked act that he felt he must speak out against it, but who for all that was full of sympathy for his fellows, even those who had erred and whom he felt it his duty to reprove. 'A Satyric Author', observed Des Maiseaux,

---

[1] *The First Epistle of the Second Book of Horace, Imitated*, line 216, Pope's *Poems*, iv. 213.

[2] These four volumes of pamphlets, given by their binder the general title 'Tracts on the works of Pope', press-mark B.M. C. 116 b. 1–4, possess such titles as, for example, *The Curliad* (vol. iv (1)), and many of them were published by Curll. The title of the first pamphlet in vol. i is *Reflections critical and satirical, upon a late rhapsody, call'd, An essay upon criticism. By Mr. Dennis* [i.e. John Dennis] (London, printed for Bernard Lintott [1711]).

[3] Dryden's term, *Essays*, ii. 52.

'is commonly represented as a Malicious, Envious, Sullen and Ill-natur'd Person: But there's nothing more unreasonable than this Prejudice.' And he proceeded to give the standard defence of the satirist's motives and character:

> It is not, either, Malice or Envy or a sour captious Humour that inclines him to write; but the sole Desire of making Men better. It is the Consideration of their Disorders that Angers him; his Sharpness proceeds only from his Vexation to see Vice, Error, or Folly, prevail. As he has a Natural Sense of Good-nature, Justice and Humanity, he Interests himself in every Thing that Concerns other Men; he Sympathizes with their Misadventures; and the Wrong they receive, either in their Person or Reputation, makes as quick an Impression upon him, as if himself had suffer'd those Indignities.[4]

'I hate no human Creature,' Pope wrote to the Earl of Marchmont, '& the moment any can repent or reform, I love them sincerely';[5] and on an earlier occasion he had assured Swift, 'as for Anger I know it not; or at least only that sort of which the Apostle speaks, "Be ye angry and sin not" '.[6] This is where the satirists took their stand: they insisted that they had been provoked into writing satire not by malice, pique, or anger, but by righteous indignation. Their model was Dorset, 'the best good Man, with the worst natur'd Muse'.[7] Critics might accuse them of mere irritability—'You seem . . . to have been angry at the rain for wetting you, why then would you go into it?' Colley Cibber remarked with reference to The Dunciad[8]—but neither Pope nor any of the other satirists admitted that irrisio rather than indignatio might have sometimes been the inspiration of their writings. 'Quid verum atque decens, curare, & rogare, nostrum sit'—'We spend our Time in the Search and Enquiry after Truth and Decency'.[9] Gay and Pope quoted the line from Horace with approval in a letter to Swift. A satirist, Rapin maintained, is one who speaks out with 'true zeal' against the evils of his times.[10] One of Goldsmith's reasons for regarding Butler as a better

---

[4] 'The Life of Monsieur Boileau Despreaux', prefixed to The Works of Monsieur Boileau. Made English . . . by several hands (1711–12), i. clvii.

[5] 10 October 1741, Pope's Correspondence, iv. 364.

[6] 28 May 1733, ibid. iii. 372.

[7] John Wilmot, Earl of Rochester, 'An Allusion to Horace The 10th Satyr of the 1st Book', line 60, Poems, ed. V. de Sola Pinto (1953), p. 97.

[8] A Letter from Mr. Cibber to Mr. Pope (1742), p. 13.

[9] 1 December 1731, Swift's Correspondence, iii. 510.

[10] Rapin, p. 138.

satirist than Swift was that Butler had a more thorough detestation of vice.[11] In addition to presenting the satirist as a champion
of virtue, his supporters had to defend him against the charge,
which was made repeatedly in the eighteenth century, that he
was lacking in candour and good nature. They had to show that
his stern mien was adopted only in order to awe the vicious,
and that fundamentally he was benevolent and magnanimous:
'Kind, even in vengeance kind to virtue's foes'.[12] 'I've often
thought', Pope wrote to Fortescue, 'Good nature, properly felt,
would make a rigorous Judge, & give a sort of Joy in passing
the Sentence, both as it is *Justice*, and as it is *Example*.'[13]
Candour and good nature were not to be identified with weakness, irresponsibility, and soft-hearted tolerance. John Brown
forcefully dismissed this sentimental approach to satire:

> O sordid maxim, form'd to screen the vile,
> That true good-nature still must wear a smile!
> In frowns involv'd her beauties stronger rise,
> When love of virtue wakes her scorn of vice:
> Where justice calls, 'tis cruelty to save;
> And 'tis the law's good-nature hangs the knave.[14]

Probably no satirist protested his honourable intentions more
often than Pope. In the storm that followed the publication of
the *Epistle to Burlington* in December 1731, he wrote a long letter
of defence to Gay, in which, among other things, he bewailed the
public's misunderstanding of satire, and pictured the author—
Pope was writing under the pseudonym of 'William Cleland'—
as one who would grieve should he give the least hurt to another
person, unless that person deserved it:

Could there be a more melancholy Instance how much the Taste
of the Publick is vitiated, and turns the most salutary and seasonable
Physick into Poyson than if amidst the Blaze of a thousand bright
Qualities in a Great Man, they should only remark there is a
Shadow about him, as what Eminence is without one? I am confident the Author is incapable of imputing any such to a Person,
whose whole Life (to use his own Expression in Print of him) *is a
continued Series* of good and generous Actions. I say I am confident,
for I have known this Author long and well; and I know no good

[11] Goldsmith's *Works*, ed. Friedman, iv. 269–77.
[12] Brown (1745), p. 13.
[13] 16 August 1736, Pope's *Correspondence*, iv. 27.
[14] Brown (1745), p. 12.

Man who would be more concerned, if he gave the least Pain or
Offence to another; and none who would be less concerned, if the
Satire were challenged by any one at whom he would really aim it.
If ever that happens, I dare engage he will own it, with all the Free-
dom of a Man whose Censures are just, and who sets his Name to
them.[15]

In July 1734, when Dr. Arbuthnot was ill with the disease from
which he died, and was therefore in the frame of mind to give
Pope solemn advice about his future conduct as a satirist, he
wrote to Pope entreating him as a 'Last Request' to 'continue
that noble *Disdain* and *Abhorrence* of Vice, which you seem
naturally endu'd with',[16] and Pope replied that 'What you
recommend to me with the solemnity of a Last Request, shall
have its due weight with me. That disdain and indignation
against Vice, is (I thank God) the only disdain and indignation
I have: It is sincere, and it will be a lasting one.'[17] Promises made
over death-beds or in response to 'last requests' are seldom
notable for their realism. Moreover in this letter Pope was
writing not to Arbuthnot but to a wider public. The letter may
not in fact have been sent to Arbuthnot.[18] Pope was not writing
familiarly to a close friend, but polishing his public image for
the benefit of posterity. His statement consequently reflects his
ideal of himself as satirist: it presents him as he would like to
have been thought, and no doubt as he would really like to have
been. It would be too facile altogether to accuse him of dis-
honesty, for he undoubtedly took his role as satirist very seriously
and was proud of his impact on contemporary society:

That I am an Author whose characters are thought of some
weight, appears from the great noise and bustle that the Court and
Town make about any I give: and I will not render them less important or interesting, by sparing Vice and Folly, or by betraying the
cause of Truth and Virtue. I will take care they shall be such as no
man can be angry at but the persons I would have angry. You are
sensible with what decency and justice I paid homage to the Royal
Family, at the same time that I satirized false Courtiers, and Spies,
&c. about 'em. I have not the courage however to be such a Satyrist
as you, but I would be as much, or more, a Philosopher. You call

---

[15] 16 December 1731, Pope's *Correspondence*, iii. 256–7.
[16] 17 July 1734, ibid. iii. 417.
[17] 26 July 1734, ibid. 419.
[18] See Pope's *Poems*, iv. xxi, n. 1.

your satires, Libels: I would rather call my satires, Epistles: They will consist more of morality than wit, and grow graver, which you will call duller. I shall leave it to my Antagonists to be witty (if they can) and content myself to be useful, and in the right.[19]

For a more realistic appraisal of the satirist's motives, one must turn to Swift, and to Rochester before him. In reply to Burnet's charge that revenge and falsehood are characteristic faults of satire, Rochester (so Burnet recounts) declared:

A man . . . could not write with life, unless he were heated with Revenge, for to make a Satire without Resentments, upon the cold Notions of Philosophy, was as if a man would in cold blood cut men's throats, who had never offended him. And he said, the lyes in these Libels came often as in ornaments that could not be spared without spoiling the beauty of the Poem.[20]

As for Swift, though he was capable of claiming a moral purpose when he found it expedient to do so, he none the less reveals in numerous comments his delight in the whips and knives of satire: 'when you think of the world give it one lash the more at my Request', he instructs Pope; he considers satire worth while if only 'to vex Rogues, even though it will not amend them'; and with regard to *Gulliver's Travels* he states that 'the chief end I propose to my self in all my labors is to vex the world rather than divert it', adding that if he 'could compass that designe' without injury to himself, he 'would be the most Indefatigable writer you have ever seen . . .'[21] At another time he speaks enthusiastically of cutting off Curll's ears, a commendable project and if anything unduly limited in scope, but admittedly not an edifying subject for discussion.[22] Pope believed in setting a higher moral tone. It is difficult, however, to represent Swift's views accurately because of his keen sense of irony and his enjoyment of ridicule: he was more likely to make light of his motives and achievements in order to avoid being pretentious than to give an accurate account of them. Furthermore, his letters, unlike many of Pope's, are not carefully calculated public statements. Where he does make a direct public statement on the intentions of the satirist, in his vindication of Gay

[19] Pope to Swift, 2[0] April 1733, Pope's *Correspondence*, iii. 365–6.
[20] Quoted in Poems by *John Wilmot, Earl of Rochester*, ed. V. de Sola Pinto (1953), p. lxvi.
[21] Swift to Pope, 29 September 1725, Swift's *Correspondence*, iii. 102–3.
[22] Swift to Pope, 30 August 1716, ibid. ii. 214.

in *The Intelligencer*, No. 3, he takes an orthodox didactic line. Even here, however, his realistic appraisal of human motives is still in evidence, for he admits that the satirist derives considerable personal satisfaction from seeing his satirical shafts strike home:

> *There* are two Ends that Men propose in writing Satyr, one of them less Noble than the other, as regarding nothing further than personal Satisfaction, and Pleasure of the Writer, but without any View towards *Personal Malice*; the other is a *Publick Spirit*, prompting Men of *Genius* and Virtue, to mend the World as far as they are able. And as both these Ends are innocent, so the latter is highly commendable. With Regard to the former, I demand whether I have not as good a Title to laugh, as Men have to be ridiculous, and to expose Vice, as another hath to be vicious. . . .
> But if my Design be to make Mankind better, then I think it is my Duty; at least I am sure it is the Interest of those very *Courts* and *Ministers*, whose Follies or Vices I ridicule, to reward me for my good Intentions: For if it be reckoned a high Point of Wisdom to get the Laughers on our Side, it is much more Easy, as well as Wise to get those on our Side, who can make Millions laugh when they please.

As to his notorious statement regarding 'the great foundation of Misanthropy' on which *Gulliver's Travels* is erected.

> I have ever hated all Nations professions and Communityes and all my love is towards individualls for instance I hate the tribe of Lawyers, but I love Councellor such a one, Judge such a one for so with Physicians (I will not Speak of my own Trade) Soldiers, English, Scotch, French; and the rest but principally I hate and detest that animal called man, although I hartily love John, Peter, Thomas and so forth. this is the system upon which I have governed my self many years (but do not tell) and so I shall go on till I have done with them I have got Materials Towards a Treatis proving the falsity of that Definition *animal rationale*; and to show it should be only *rationis capax*. Upon this great foundation of Misanthropy (though not Timons manner) The whole building of my Travells is erected: And I never will have peace of mind till all honest men are of my Opinion.[23]

This is not the simple admission that it is usually taken to be. Swift is declaring his disappointment in man as maker and member of institutions, professions, societies, and nations, and

---

[23] Swift to Pope, 29 September 1725, ibid. iii. 103.

in mankind because it is 'only *rationis capax*' not '*animal rationale*'. Yet at the same time he insists that he loves individuals: 'I hartily love John, Peter, Thomas, and so forth.' And Pope, on reading the letter, evidently took Swift's insistence on love of individuals as his main point. 'I really enter,' he wrote in reply, 'as fully as you can desire, into your Principle, of Love of Individuals: And I think the way to have a Publick Spirit, is first to have a Private one.'[24] On examination then, it can be seen that the point of view Swift is expressing transcends misanthropy: it is the outlook less of a misanthrope than a moralist, or moral philosopher, who has a profound sense of the limitations of human achievement and the shortcomings of human beings in the performance of their social duties and functions. If only Swift had denied himself the rhetorical flourish of 'the great foundation of Misanthropy' and had written instead that 'on this realistic basis' or 'on this commonsense truth my book about Gulliver has been erected', he would have saved himself much misinterpretation.

In their efforts to build up a picture of themselves as worthy citizens performing a public duty, the satirists stressed their lack of personal ambition and their lack of concern for their personal safety. Gay's constant complaint was that he had been denied preferment at court because of his satirical writing. In *The Intelligencer*, No. 3, Swift mentions Gay's having been unjustly refused promotion and states in *Verses on the Death of Dr. Swift* that he himself would have had a more successful career had he not been a satirist:

> Had he but spar'd his Tongue and Pen,
> He might have rose like other Men:[25]

In Pope's letter to Arbuthnot, 26 July 1734, he thanked Arbuthnot for worrying about his safety, but professed to have no fear of the persons he had exposed in his satires—'Such in particular as have the meanness to do mischiefs in the dark, have seldom the courage to justify them in the face of day; the talents that make a Cheat or a Whisperer, are not the same that qualify a man for an Insulter; and as to private villany, it is not so safe to join in an Assassination, as in a Libel.' From such cowardly

---

[24] Pope to Swift, 15 October 1725, Pope's *Correspondence*, ii. 333.
[25] Lines 355-6, Swift's *Poems*, ii. 567.

slanderers Pope was confident that he had nothing to fear, and
he declared roundly: 'I will consult my safety so far as I think
becomes a prudent man; but not so far as to omit any thing
which I think becomes an honest one. As to personal attacks
beyond the law, every man is liable to them: as for danger within
the law, I am not guilty enough to fear any.' He considers himself wise enough, moreover, to know that 'the good opinion of all
the world . . . is not to be had'; but he hopes that he will not
forfeit the esteem of worthy men. As to that of the great and
powerful, he says: 'I may wish I had it, but if thro' misrepresenta-
tions (too common about persons in that station) I have it not,
I shall be sorry, but not miserable in the want of it.'[26] The elegiac
note perceptible in this letter is much more pronounced in one
written seven years later to the Earl of Marchmont. It also deals
with Pope's general intentions as a satirist. He would have
Marchmont think of him as having passed beyond worldly
concerns. He no longer feels either ambition or resentment and
he bears ill will to no man, but sincerely loves those who turn
from their evil ways. He has reached an age (fifty years) when
he feels he must write for the good of others, not for amusement. For a number of reasons, however, he has resolved to
publish no more in his lifetime:

For I may tell you, that I am determined to publish no more in my
life time, for many reasons; but principally thro' the Zeal I have to
speak the *Whole Truth*, & neither to praise or dispraise by halves,
or with worldly managements. I think fifty an age at which to write
no longer for Amusement, but for some Use, and with design to do
some good. I never had any uneasy Desire of Fame, or keen Resentment of Injuries, & now both are asleep together: Other Ambition
I never had, than to be tolerably thought of by those I esteem'd,
and this has been gratify'd beyond my proudest Hopes. I hate no
human Creature, & the moment any can repent or reform, I love
them sincerely. Public Calamities touch me; but when I read of Past
Times, I am somewhat comforted as to the present, upon the Comparison: and at the worst I thank God, that I do not yet live under
a Tyranny, nor an Inquisition: that I have thus long enjoyed Inde-
pendency, Freedom of Body & Mind, have told the world of my
Opinions, even on the highest subjects, & of the Greatest Men, pretty
freely; that good men have not been ashamed of me; and that my
Works have not dy'd before me (which is the Case of most Authors)

---

[26] Pope's *Correspondence*, iii. 419–20.

and if they die soon after, I shall probably not know it, or certainly not be concern'd at it, in the next world.[27]

Another favourite plea of the satirists was that they were victims of misunderstanding. According to Oldmixon, the English as a race were unable to understand criticism and as a result habitually mistook it for 'an Effect of Envy, Jealousy and Spleen'.[28] Satire certainly was most often described as a result of these motives. Consequently, the satirists protested that they had been misunderstood and misinterpreted. That was the burden of Boileau's reply to those who adjudged *Le Lutrin* a mischievous satire on the ministers of the Church. In January 1732 Pope claimed that he was withholding his *Epistle to Bathurst* from publication because, if he were to allow it to be printed, he felt sure it would be misinterpreted by Malice—'& I find it is Malice I am to expect from the World, not Thanks, for my writings'.[29]

One other kind of misunderstanding which satirists pleaded they had to suffer was that of being taken too seriously. Although there first line of defence was that they were moralists and reformers, they also liked to repeat Horace's modest avowal that he wrote merely for his own pleasure and that of a few close friends. Their writings, they hinted, were not to be taken too seriously. Thus Boileau said that *Le Lutrin*, so far from having been written to discredit the Church, was merely the result of a wager. M. Lamoignon, a good friend of Boileau's, had jokingly challenged him to write a mock epic based on the incident of the lectern, and he had done so light-heartedly without any thought of offending anyone. He would not have dreamed of ridiculing the ministers of the Church, for he had the highest opinion of them, especially the Canons.[30] No doubt the satirists wanted to have it both ways, to be regarded at one and the same time as harmless jesters and serious reformers. So Swift added to his comment on having been only 'a Man of Rhimes' ('I have been only a Man of Rhimes, and that upon Trifles, never having written serious Couplets in my Life') the saving

---

[27] 10 October 1741, Pope's *Correspondence*, iv. 364.

[28] *An Essay on Criticism* (1728), p. 3.

[29] Pope to the Earl of Oxford, 22 January [1731/2], Pope's *Correspondence*, iii. 267.

[30] Author's Preface to *Boileau's Lutrin: A Mock-Heroic Poem* (1708), sig. A2v.

clause 'yet never any without a moral view'; and he remarked later in the same letter, 'You see *Pope, Gay*, and I, use all our Endeavours to make folks Merry and Wise, and profess to have no Enemies, except Knaves and Fools.'[31]

The high esteem in which Boileau was held by English writers and critics in the late seventeenth and eighteenth centuries has already been mentioned.[32] He was apparently revered as much for his moral character as for his literary achievements. Yet his French critics, Des Maiseaux states in his brief biography of Boileau, represented him as 'a Slanderer, an Envyer, a Detractor, and one who only study'd how to establish his own Reputation upon the Ruin of that of other Men'.[33] Des Maiseaux insists that this was the opposite of the truth: 'never was Man more exempt from all these Faults than [Boileau], or more strongly addicted to the contrary Virtues.' Otherwise he would not have won the esteem of so many worthy people. 'His Justice, his Rectitude, and his Sincerity, were so well establish'd, that he made no difficulty of publishing them himself in his *Epistle to his Book*, and to make it a Matter of Glory to himself. . . .' It was Boileau's 'Integrity and Innocence', says Des Maiseaux, 'which did, as it were, give him a Right to Compose *Satires*'; and Des Maiseaux thereupon commits himself to the exceedingly perilous argument that a satirist must be a good man if he is to have the right to ridicule his fellows:

An author that shou'd reprehend in others such Faults as he himself is guilty of, wou'd be expos'd to the public Laughter, and regarded by none. A Satiric Poet, shou'd, to a great share of Equity and Uprightness, joyn an ardent Love for Virtue and a perfect Exemption from the Vices which he Lashes in his Writings: By this he gains the Favour of good Men, and secures himself against the Malice of his Enemies.[34]

This is surely a glass house few satirists would dare to live in. One might well wonder if any satirist has been able to boast 'perfect Exemption from the Vices which he Lashes in his Writings'.

In the preceding observations from his 'Life of Boileau', Des

[31] Swift to Charles Wogan, July–2 August 1732, Swift's *Correspondence*, iv. 52–3.
[32] Chapter 3, p. 43.
[33] *Works of Boileau* (1711–12), I. clv–clvi.
[34] Ibid. clvi.

Maiseaux spoke up for one distinguished satirist; but in so doing he defended the motives and characters of satirists generally, as also did the other writers whose incidental comments have been quoted in this chapter. For the full-scale defence of the satirist in his public role, however, we must turn now to the apologias current in the Augustan age. In these by tradition the satirist donned a mask even when he used his own name or initial. His object was to justify his public role as a satirist, rather than his private conduct and circumstances. The apologias are therefore especially valuable to anyone studying the critical defence of satire in the Augustan period, for they are designed as statements of general principle: they present the satirist in his ideal character declaring his vocation to the world. In the following pages the chief classical apologias studied in the Augustan age will be examined in some detail, then the outstanding imitations of them by Boileau and Pope, and finally a few poems (Swift's *Verses on the Death of Dr. Swift*, Churchill's *An Epistle to William Hogarth*,[35] and William Combe's *The Justification*) which put forward some of the same arguments and have similar characteristics.

The classical apologias (Horace, *Satires*, i. iv and x, and ii. i; Persius, Satire i; and Juvenal, Satire i) all follow the same basic pattern. In all of them an interlocutor counsels the author to give up writing satire and try his hand at something more profitable and less hazardous, such as epic, or (better still) panegyric. He warns the author of the dangers of satire: he will lose friends and make enemies; he may be punished severely, perhaps even put to death. In response to these warnings the author states that he cannot keep himself from writing satire, either because it is part of his nature, or because the times are so corrupt that he feels he must speak out against them. Anyway, why not write satire? It has a noble tradition. The satirist was once both feared and respected: when Lucilius was alive the guilty trembled; yet he retained the friendship of the greatest men of his times. In all these apologias, the satirist of course has the better of the argument; but in all of them, too, either in the interests of dramatic plausibility or in order to demonstrate that he is

---

[35] Churchill's *The Apology* (1761), despite its name, resembles a classical apologia less than does the *Epistle to Hogarth*, and contains less discussion of the principles of satire.

a reasonable man, he makes some small concession to his counsellor. He promises, for example, to avoid mentioning living people or those at least who are politically powerful.

So far as eighteenth-century English poets and critics were concerned, it was Horace who established the pattern of the apologia, although it was accepted that Lucilius had invented it. Horace, by his own account, set out to be a kind of satirist quite different from Lucilius: an urbane commentator on his country-men's follies, rather than a prosecutor armed with a writ against wicked men.[36] Through both his arguments and practice he attempted to create a more refined kind of satire, and a more attractive public image for the satirist. In short, the neo-classicists saw him as having done what they themselves were trying to do, and his apologias gave them just the sort of justification they wanted.

In *Satires*, i. iv, Horace begins by remarking on the enviable freedom with which the writers of the Old Attic Comedy attacked vice. In Roman literature Lucilius had been equally bold and he had admirable qualities as a satirist; but he took too little trouble over his versification. Horace believes he knows why some people abhor his own satire: they realize that they deserve it. So they warn everyone to avoid him, implying that he is wild, perhaps a little crazy. Now Horace puts his defence. First, he does not claim to be a poet, for his verses are prosaic, colloquial. The title of poet should be reserved for those who are divinely inspired. Secondly, no one—not even a guilty man—need fear his verses, for they are not on the bookstalls, and only when pressed to do so will he recite them privately to friends. Thirdly, so far from being a person who delights in giving pain, he has no time for the man who makes damaging remarks about an absent friend, who fails to defend a friend's reputation when others are attacking it, who goes out of his way to gain the reputation of a wit, and who makes up tales and cannot keep secrets. Such a man is black at heart and a good Roman should shun him. Horace gives his word that such malice shall be far from his pages. He does admit, however, that he may have been a little too free in his writings (Horace is implying that he may have made a few too many personal allusions); but his excuse is that his father—the best of fathers—taught him to

---

[36] Horace, *Satires*, i. iv. 70.

avoid bad behaviour by pointing to actual examples of it. Thanks to this training he has been able to escape degrading vices, though no doubt he is subject to some lesser frailties which he hopes his friends will excuse.

In *Satires* I. x, Horace seeks to clarify his attitude to Lucilius, for he has been taken to task by some critics for his earlier derogatory remarks. Here he emphasizes that, though he admires the satiric power of Lucilius, he disapproves of his roughness and wordiness. Horace unequivocally advocates a restrained and polished style in satire, and recommends gentle ridicule in preference to severe invective:

> est brevitate opus, ut currat sententia, neu se
> impediat verbis lassas onerantibus auris;
>
> .   .   .
>
> ridiculum acri
> fortius et melius magnas plerumque secat res.
> (lines 9–10, 14–15)[37]

Horace is always careful to show that he does not take himself too seriously. He says that he is not really a poet, just a versifier. In the all-important first satire of Book II he passes off his satire as a mere hobby: some men like to drink, others to try their luck at the races, but he likes writing satires. Trebatius, his lawyer-friend, tells him that he should work off his worries, or his surplus energy, in some more innocuous way, say by swimming the Tiber three times before retiring. Alternatively he could try his hand at composing epics. Horace jokingly protests that, coming as he does from frontier stock, satire is all he can write. But he uses it only for defence, only when he is provoked. It is his natural weapon; as the wolf defends himself with his fangs, and the bull with his horns, so he with his satire. Then, says Trebatius, your life will be short. Why should it be? Horace retorts. Lucilius attacked both great and small, yet continued to enjoy the friendship of Scipio and Laelius. Trebatius concedes that this was so, but points out that laws have been passed since then against bad—that is, libellous—verses. And what if a man write good verses? asks Horace, playing on the two senses of *malum*, 'of bad quality' and 'libellous'. In that event, Trebatius

---

[37] 'You need terseness, that the thought may run on, and not become entangled in verbiage that weighs upon wearied ears . . . Jesting oft cuts hard knots more forcefully and effectively than gravity' (Loeb translation).

replies, the case will be dismissed with a laugh, you will get off scot-free. And the apologia ends on this light-hearted note, with a laugh and a shrug of the shoulders, the implication being that, all things considered, Horace really has not much to worry about.

Juvenal's and Persius' apologias bring forward the same essential arguments as the three satires by Horace which have just been discussed. As they differ greatly in tone from Horace's, however, as well as from each other, they create quite different impressions of the satirist's motives and character. Both Juvenal and Persius protest that they cannot help writing satire, but for different reasons. Persius gives as his chief reason his wayward sense of humour: when he looks about him at the gloomy way of life and the affected morality of his fellow Romans, he cannot help laughing. Besides he has a secret, and with this secret (that all men are fools) continually in his mind, he can hardly help but be a satirist. Juvenal's reasons are more serious and profound. Faced with the vice and corruption he sees everywhere, he cannot keep silent. Examples pour from him in a flood. When was there a greater profusion of vices? Would you not feel like filling up a whole notebook while standing at a street corner? he exclaims. Although his natural inclination is to say nothing, he cannot. His indignation compels him to speak out. Juvenal's attack is more general than Persius': it is directed at the declining morals and changing social order of Rome, whereas Persius' concentrates on the prevailing bad taste in literature. Both writers turn scornfully away from other kinds of writing. Juvenal dismisses the odes and epics of his day as trivial and irrelevant, mere literary exercises. Persius ridicules the bombast of contemporary heroic poetry. It is frothy, inflated stuff, he says, utterly lacking in honesty. Both Persius and Juvenal appeal to the example of Lucilius and both are warned by their interlocutors of the dangers of continuing to write satire. Your friends will shut their doors against you, Persius' counsellor says. The warning given to Juvenal is much grimmer: if he is not careful he will be burned at the stake and his dead body dragged through the arena. Finally, both satirists give undertakings regarding their future practice as satirists, Juvenal that he will name only the dead, and Persius that he will content himself with a limited though discriminating audience.

The uniformity of the arguments in these apologias is striking; but what is even more striking and surprising is that it extends to apologias written seventeen centuries later. Boileau's two principal exercises in the form, Satires VII and IX,[38] repeat the classical arguments with only minor additions and variations. Satire VII describes satire as an unrewarding and dangerous occupation by contrast with 'cold panegyric', which has no enemies other than moths and dust. Most readers Boileau considers hypocritical in their attitude to satire. They blame the satirist while they are reading him, yet go on reading and laughing. Boileau says he writes satire because it suits him. It is plain and prosaic, and he has never pretended to have the ability to write inspired poetry. Some will pity him, saying that he is bound to suffer for his satire. Why should he? Were Lucilius, Horace, and Juvenal made to suffer for exposing the vices of their times? Moreover, he writes anonymously, and only after persuasion will he read his satirical verses to entertain a friend. But above all he will continue to write satire because it is his natural mode of expression. The attempts he has made at other modes, such as elegy and epic, have been dull and pedestrian. Yet immediately he feels the satirical impulse take hold of him, he cannot restrain himself.

> Mais quand il faut railler, j'ay ce que je souhaite:
> Alors certes alors, je me connois Poëte.
> Phébus, dés que je parle, est prest à m'exaucer.
> Mes mots viennent sans peine, & courent se placer.
>
> .   .   .
>
> Je sens que mon esprit travaille de genie.
>
> .   .   .
>
> Mes vers, comme un torrent, coulent sur le papier.
>
> (lines 33–6, 41, 43)

He returns to the theme repeatedly in this satire, describing the exhilaration he experiences in satirical composition, warning that his satire spares no one when the frenzy seizes him, and declaring that no threats, not even of death, and no promises, not even the promise of a long and peaceful life, could wean him from satire.

---

[38] See Boileau's *Satires*, pp. 90–7, 119–40.

A Rome ou dans Paris, aux champs ou dans la ville,
Deust ma Muse par là choquer tout l'Univers,
Riche, gueux, triste ou gay, je veux faire des vers.

(lines 66-8)

In Satire IX, after commenting at some length on the inefficacy
and ephemerality of satire, he comes back again to the old theme
of its dangers. The satirist runs the risk of being beaten or
drowned, gets involved in endless quarrels and, though he may
make a few merry souls laugh, he incurs the hatred of hundreds.
Despite its dangers, however, satire is a genre rich in common
sense and pleasing instruction, as Lucilius, Horace, and others
knew very well. Boileau states that satire has been his guide to
proper conduct and his arbiter of literary taste since boyhood.
But to placate his Muse, the interlocutor of this apologia, he
pretends for a moment that he is willing to give up satire for
panegyric. He would do so, if he thought any good might come
of it. What is likely to happen, however, is that his incredulous
readers will mistake his flattery for raillery. Therefore he is
resolved to continue, whatever the dangers, expecting no reward
for his feeble writings, except that of being able to use the same
pen, which has previously been used to lash fools, to praise his
King.

It is the same old story all over again. Boileau has been content
merely to recapitulate the traditional arguments of the apologia.
His treatment of them, however, is not without originality. In
Satire VII, for instance, he gives new colouring and force to the
traditional argument that the satirist is powerless to restrain
his passion for satire. He does this first by making it his main
argument and secondly by giving it an intimately personal
quality. Both Satires VII and IX are more personal, more auto-
biographical, even than Horace's apologias. In Satire IX, for
example, Boileau tells us of his boyhood training and indicates
the fine relationship between himself and his father. As a result
the satirist comes through as a warmer and more sympathetic
character than he does in the classical satires, one who is able
more easily to win his way into the reader's confidence.

Pope also accentuated this personal, introspective quality in
his imitations of Horace. *An Epistle to Dr. Arbuthnot* seeks to
defend 'His Father, Mother, Body, Soul, and Muse' against the
attacks which have been made on them by 'the *Two Curls* of

Town and Court' (lines 380–1) and it includes a filial tribute to that 'good Man', Pope's father, and an expression of Pope's tender regard for his mother's welfare in her declining years. In *The First Satire of The Second Book of Horace Imitated*,[39] Pope comments pleasantly on his grotto, and on the friends who come to Twit'nam and assist him in the arrangement of his quincunxes, vines, and vistas. And he does not merely pass off his satire as a harmless hobby, as Horace does, but talks of it also in a sincere, direct way as the mirror of his soul:

> I love to pour out all myself, as plain
> As downright *Shippen*, or as old *Montagne*.
> In them, as certain to be lov'd as seen,
> The Soul stood forth, nor kept a Thought within;
> In me what Spots (for Spots I have) appear,
> Will prove at least the Medium must be clear.
>
> (lines 51–6)

This idea that the satirist himself comes within the scope of his satire is much in advance of that of the satirist as 'the best good man', for it brings him down from his pedestal or pulpit and allows him to mingle with mankind, with other friends and sinners. It is no doubt a pity that Pope did not develop it further for in addition to being sounder in principle it would have provided him with a much better *persona* than that of the Man of Virtue, which he tried so hard and constantly, and sometimes so deviously, to maintain.

An Epistle to Dr. Arbuthnot[40] opens with a winning appeal for sympathy, all the more winning through being comical as well as familiar. Again, the basic idea is not new. It creates a picture a satirist liked to have of himself, that of a man of achievement pestered by insignificant and envious scribblers. For example, in *The Spectator*, No. 355 (17 April 1712), Addison complains about the malicious witlings who are perpetually snapping at his heels. He takes as little notice of them as possible, and he certainly feels too disdainful of them to retaliate in kind. He quotes Jean-Louis Balzac[41] to the effect that attacks from envious persons should be regarded as tributes, like the stones which travellers in some eastern countries throw on the bodies of

---

[39] Pope's *Poems*, iv. 5–21.

[40] Ibid. 96–127.

[41] Jean-Louis Guez de Balzac (1597–1654), 'le grand épistolier de France'. See *The Spectator*, ed. Bond, iii. 324, n. 1.

dead men—the bigger the mound of stones the greater the tribute.
Later in the same essay he recounts a fable of Boccalini's about
a traveller 'who was so pestered with the Noise of Grasshoppers
in his Ears that he alighted from his Horse in great Wrath to
kill them all'. This, Addison says, was to take unnecessary
trouble. Had the traveller gone on his way without taking notice
of them, they would have died in a week or so and he would
have suffered nothing from them. Pope's, however, remains the
most telling image of the satirist beset by 'the common Fry of
scribblers'. He has filled in the details of the picture, making it
not only more graphic and cogent but also more appealing than
it had been previously. The situation is one which we may
instantly recognize, or at least readily imagine. Scribblers or
students, tourists, picnickers, salesmen, or collectors for chari-
ties, it does not matter which, for they are all familiar disturbers
of peace and privacy. We are predisposed to identify ourselves
with Pope and share his ironic self-pity. Poor man! we feel,
partly amused, partly sympathetic. No wonder he has taken to
satire, if only in self-defence! 'Out, with it, *Dunciad*!'

An Epistle to Dr. Arbuthnot follows the classical pattern of
the apologia, although it is called an 'epistle', and although it is
not printed as a dialogue (that is, with the interjections attributed
to Arbuthnot) in the approved text.[42] Pope, like Horace, Persius,
and Juvenal, is interrupted from time to time by a friend, who
advises him to watch his step, to leave 'Queens, Ministers, or
Kings' unnamed and keep to safe if trivial subjects, to take care
in naming dangerous persons, and to refrain from insulting the
poor or affronting the great. Pope replies with the full battery
of defensive arguments. He was born a writer, he could not
help it:

> What sin to me unknown
> Dipt me in Ink, my Parents', or my own?
> (lines 125–6)

In his youth he was content to paint pleasant country scenes;
but he has been turned into a satirist by the injuries he has
suffered. Yet he has been slow to rouse—

> Full ten years slander'd, did he once reply?
> Three thousand Suns went down on Welsted's Lye:
> (lines 374–5)

---

[42] Octavo edition, 1734. See Pope's *Poems*, iv. 93.

He has been tolerant of his critics, no matter how they have raged at him. He has not yearned for money, power, fame, or friendship. He has wanted merely to lead a quiet, decent life, as did his father. He is essentially 'soft by Nature', good rather than clever, sensitive not cruel. Anyone who thinks him cruel is forgetting that those he has attacked are too stupid to realize that they are being attacked, so they are not hurt. He has been much maligned and misunderstood. His satire has been misapplied. Other writers' scurrilous pieces have been attributed to him. Yet he would suffer anguish if a single line of his should cause an innocent person the slightest harm or sorrow. Virtue is his goddess, and her enemies are his, whether they be rich or poor, great or small. He desires no reward, but is happy in the knowledge that he leads a righteous life. Having begun the apologia with an amusing bid for his reader's sympathy, he ends it with a sentimental appeal, with a prayer for his friend, and a humble vow to care for his mother in her last years:

> Me, let the tender Office long engage
> To rock the Cradle of reposing Age,
> With lenient Arts extend a Mother's breath,
> Make Languor smile, and smooth the Bed of Death,
> Explore the Thought, explain the asking Eye,
> And keep a while one Parent from the Sky!
>
> (lines 407–13)

The appeal is undoubtedly sentimental. There is a coyness about the diction and an archness of manner—'And keep a while one Parent from the Sky!'—which makes one suspect the speaker's sincerity. He sounds a little too good to be true. So it is too with his curse on any writings that tend to give

> ... Innocence a fear
> Or from the soft-ey'd Virgin steal a Tear!

In short, in these parts of the apologia the satirist overstates his case. And in certain other parts he allows himself flashes of wit or malice which puncture his arguments. For example, he concludes the passage on his desire for a peaceful and righteous life with a keen thrust at Dennis (lines 261–70), which shows pretty clearly that other thoughts than prayers occasionally pass through his mind, and that he is concerned to maintain other things than 'a Poet's Dignity and Ease' (line 263). Perhaps the

point to make here is that Pope is indulging himself a little
because he knows that the basis of his case is entirely acceptable
to his readers. Orthodox ideas can be playfully elaborated and
exaggerated in a way that a new line of thought can never be.
It has to be presented, if it is to win any converts, seriously and
directly, and with evident sincerity.

There is a marked difference in depth and tone between *An
Epistle to Dr. Arbuthnot* and the two dialogues 'Something like
Horace', which were later jointly renamed *Epilogue to the
Satires*.[43] Pope was very likely moved by Arbuthnot's advice in
his letter of 26 July 1734, on avoiding ill will in future, to put
together into a single poem the miscellaneous pieces of attack
and defence which he had written at various earlier times. The
Epilogue, on the other hand, was written specifically in response
to criticism of the *Imitations of Horace*, and it was composed, so
Warton reports, with the most painstaking care.[44] Whether for
these reasons, or because it was written nearer the end of his
career, it strikes deeper than *An Epistle to Dr. Arbuthnot*; and
it replies directly and forcefully to the most serious charges
which had been levelled against Pope, namely that his satire was
malicious and mordant, and often repellent in its subject-matter
and allusions. Pope ridicules with devastating irony his friend's
advice that he should write mild innocuous satire, such as 'Boys
may read, and Girls may understand' (Dialogue I, line 76), and
that he should attack vices without naming persons—'How Sir!
not damn the Sharper, but the Dice?' (II. 13). Pope's defence of his
scatology succeeds because of its straightforwardness and vigour
and also partly as a result of Pope's clever placement of it in the
poem. First, he provides an example by comparing courtly wits
to hogs which feast on each other's excrement, and when his
friend exclaims in disgust,

> This filthy Simile, this beastly Line,
> Quite turns my Stomach,

he retorts:

> So does Flatt'ry mine;
> And all your Courtly Civet-Cats can vent,
> Perfume to you, to me is Excrement.
>
> (II. 182–4)

---

43 Pope's *Poems*, iv. 297–309, 313–27.
44 See ibid. xxxix.

Pope argued in *An Epistle to Dr. Arbuthnot* that he looked on knaves as knaves no matter where he found them. The greater part of the *Epilogue* is taken up with this same argument, and with commentary on the corruption of the age, particularly as it was manifesting itself among those in power. Vice is so general, Pope remarks at the opening of the second dialogue, that it is difficult for the satirist to keep up with it:

> Vice with such Giant-strides comes on amain,
> Invention strives to be before in vain;
>
> (II. 6–7)

And the first dialogue concludes with a passage reminiscent of the grand finale of *The Dunciad* in its picture of a society in which all values have been turned upside down:

> All, all look up, with reverential Awe,
> On Crimes that scape, or triumph o'er the Law:
> While Truth, Worth, Wisdom, daily they decry—
> 'Nothing is Sacred now but Villany.'
>
> (I. 167–70)

Around this worship of inverted values and celebration of vice and villainy, the satirist's is the lone small voice of protest:

> Yet may this Verse (if such a Verse remain)
> Show there was one who held it in disdain.
>
> (I. 171–2)

It is his mission to attack folly and vice wherever he sees them. He must not yield to cowardly fears nor allow himself to be diverted from his stern duty by . . .

> . . . Pity for the needy Cheat,
> The poor and friendless Villain . . .
>
> (II. 44–5)

Satire must attack both the high and low, or else leave rogues alone altogether. Moreover, he does give praise where it is deserved. It is random praise which he abjures. But why attack those who have done you no injury? his friend asks—'Hold Sir! for God's-sake, where's th'Affront to you?' (II. 157). Pope's reply is incontestable. May not a pastor, he inquires, blame a wife who has been unfaithful unless he is himself a cuckold? Must

> each Blasphemer quite escape the Rod,
> Because the insult's not on Man, but God?
>
> (II. 195–6)

He then states—once and for all, we may feel—his sufficient

reason for being a satirist. He has been provoked not by any-thing trivial or personal, but simply by his sense of truth and virtue:

> Ask you what Provocation I have had?
> The strong Antipathy of Good to Bad.
> When Truth or Virtue an Affront endures,
> Th'Affront is mine, my Friend, and should be yours.
> Mine, as a Foe profess'd to false Pretence,
> Who think a Coxcomb's Honour like his Sense;
> Mine, as a Friend to ev'ry worthy mind;
> And mine as Man, who feel for all mankind.
>
> (II. 197–204)

Certainly he is proud, proud to see

> Men not afraid of God, afraid of me.
>
> (II. 208–9)

For, after all, his mission is no less than divine—

> Truth guards the Poet, sanctifies the line,
> And makes Immortal, Verse as mean as mine.
>
> (II. 246–7)

The formal apology has risen no higher than this either in its aspirations or in the quality of its expression. The three other poems to be considered in this chapter are of a lower order. This is true even of *Verses on the Death of Dr. Swift*,[45] which is none the less a humorous and diverting poem, in some parts brilliant and, as a whole, moving. Like Pope's *Epistle to Dr. Arbuthnot*, it is Horatian in outlook and manner and employs the stock arguments of the apologia; but it lacks the underlying pattern of Pope's poem. In the *Epistle* it is as though each powerful set of feelings, each emotion, just at the moment its energy is spent, releases the spring of a consequent emotion. So Pope's pride in his refusal to curry favour with the *literati* is followed immediately by laughing contempt for Bufo and his cultural pretensions; or—to take the most striking example in the poem—so Pope's righteous hatred of the evil Sporus is followed immediately by righteous ('self-righteous' if you will) admiration of himself as poet and man—

> Not proud, nor servile, be one Poet's praise
> That, if he pleas'd, he pleas'd by manly ways...
>
> (lines 336–7)

---

[45] Swift's *Poems*, ii. 553–72.

Verses on the Death of Dr. Swift appears to proceed more casually from one idea, or one line of commentary, to the next. Thus the relaxed opening remarks on Rochefoucault's maxim that

> In all Distresses of our Friends
> We first consult our private Ends

lead to plausible, though humorously exaggerated, speculation on the comments which his acquaintances may be making on him as he approaches senility, thence to more keenly satirical speculation on the comments with which his death will be greeted by the Town—by the Queen and Bolingbroke, and by his female acquaintances—and thence to a supposed post-mortem discussion of his qualities by 'A Club assembled at the *Rose*'. It is in this part, the tavern discussion, that the form of the traditional apologia can be most easily discerned under the vagaries of Swift's invention, for the impartial critic—'One quite indiff'rent in the Cause' (line 305)—is equivalent to the satirist of the traditional apologia, and the other members of the Club to the interlocutor, who characteristically finds it hard to get a word in edgeways. Swift's apologist, the one 'impartial' critic, allows that the Dean may have had a defect—'too much Satyr in his Vein' (line 456)—but otherwise has nothing but praise for him. The grounds of his praise are perfectly conventional, either in the context of the classical apologia or that of the body of eighteenth-century opinion on satire generally. So he informs us that Swift wrote

> As with a moral View design'd
> To cure the Vices of Mankind:
> His Vein, ironically grave,
> Expos'd the Fool, and lash'd the Knave:
>
> (lines 313–16)

Swift was never ill received at Court, and he was popular with readers—at any rate they all bought his books. He was neither a snob nor a flatterer, but a humble and generous man who 'gave himself no haughty Airs' and 'Spent all his Credit for his Friends' (lines 330–2). He was always impartial in his revelations of evil, not sparing even fellow clergy. He distinguished between the fool whom he merely exposed and the knave whom he lashed. He chose friends of worth and took pains to aid 'Virtue in Distress' (line 335). With princes he observed due decorum but that was all. He loved virtue for its own sake and he was prepared to die for liberty. Had he not spoken and written his mind so freely, he would have risen higher in the world. But he gave no thought to power or money, aiming only to help his country through bad times. If he was too inclined to satire, perhaps this was a good thing, for 'no Age could more deserve it' (line 458). Furthermore, he never wrote from malice and never personally; he satirized only those defects which can be corrected, and to his dying day he was never sour or splenetic, but always cheerful.

All this is pretty shopworn stuff, and it is only partly redeemed by witty turns of phrase and telling details—some of the details unfortunately are merely topical and trivial. It would hardly be worth a second reading, if it were presented simply as statement, that is to say if it were not qualified by the unfavourable comments on Swift which are made before line 300, when the Club assembles at the Rose, and if it were not also modified by the tone of self-mockery of which one is aware throughout the poem and which comes plainly to the surface in the brilliant concluding lines on the bequest to the Irish nation. Swift may be joking in these verses on his own death, but that is not to say that he believed that the weaknesses mentioned in the earlier part of the poem were purely imaginary. It is interesting to note in this connection that he had already enumerated in his 'Resolutions When I Come to Be Old', which he wrote in 1699, certain of the failings which he supposes his 'special Friends' of the *Verses* attributing to him in his old age—notably that of repeating the same story to the same people again and again, and that of imposing himself on young people when they do not really desire his company. The comments of the 'impartial' critic, moreover, cannot blot out entirely the unfavourable comments made on Swift before the Club assembles. But that is not the crux of the matter either, which is to be found rather in the impression of the author emerging from the poem as a whole. Underneath the levity of the *Verses* there is self-irony, a half-mocking regret at the Dean's failure to rise above himself, to be better than he was or became. Was he too proud, too unyielding, to adapt himself to everyday realities? He is presented as one who retreated from the political scene in despair to spend the latter part of his life in exile in a barbarous country—'a Land of

Slaves and Fens'—doing a few good deeds and remaining out-
wardly cheerful. The implication is that inwardly he despaired,
hence his final ironically defiant gesture of leaving 'the little
Wealth he had' to build a lunatic asylum in Ireland. Swift does
not wear his heart on his sleeve in these verses on his own death,
as does Pope in the *Epistle to Dr. Arbuthnot*, yet his personal
involvement is in a way greater than Pope's, for Swift seems
anxious to convince not only the reader, but himself as well,
of his moral integrity. In parts of the *Verses* one senses a debate
taking place in the author's conscience: it is being conducted no
doubt in what has often been called in recent times the Oxford
manner, with wit and levity, but that is not to say that the
proposition under debate is necessarily being taken lightly.

The exact measure of Swift's seriousness and of his personal
involvement is as hard to gauge in the *Verses* as in many other
of his writings. That need not delay us here, however, for the
relevant point is that *Verses on the Death of Dr. Swift*, like *An
Epistle to Dr. Arbuthnot*, is a good eighteenth-century example
of the satirist's apologia, largely traditional in content and form,
but given a marked personal slant and informed by strong
personal feeling.

In both Churchill's *An Epistle to William Hogarth* (1763),
and William Combe's *The Justification* (1777), the framework is
a dialogue between the satirist and a representative of what we
may loosely call the eighteenth-century sentimental viewpoint.
In Churchill's poem the dialogue is between Candour and Satire
and the arguments are a medley of the stock arguments of the
apologists and those of the so-called sentimental critics. Candour,
who is characterized at the opening as a milksop, accuses Satire
of misrepresentation, of drawing an exaggerated picture of vices
for effect, and of doing it moreover from dubious motives.

> Doth not humanity condemn that zeal
> Which tends to aggravate and not to heal?
> *(Poetical Works*, ed. Grant, p. 215)

Does Satire claim some special licence to slander mankind?
Following the beaten track of the classical apologia, Candour
asks why Satire did not choose panegyric, which would have
been easier and more profitable:

> What but rank Folly, for thy curse decreed,
> Could into SATIRE's barren path mislead,

When, open to thy view, before thee lay
Soul-soothing PANEGYRIC's flow'ry way?
There might the Muse have saunter'd at her ease,
And, pleasing others, learn'd herself to please,
Lords should have listen'd to the sugar'd treat,
And *Ladies*, simp'ring own'd it vastly sweet;
Rogues, in thy prudent verse with virtue grac'd,
Fools, mark'd by thee as prodigies of Taste,
Must have forbid, pouring preferments down,
Such Wit, such Truth as thine to quit the gown.
Thy sacred Brethren too (for they, no less
Than Laymen, bring their off'rings to Success)
Had hail'd Thee good if great, and paid the vow
Sincere as that they pay to God, whilst Thou
In *Lawn* hadst whisper'd to a sleeping croud,
As dull as R[OCHESTER], and half as proud.

(pp. 215–16)

Satire in reply proudly proclaims his freedom from self-interest:

I cannot truckle to a Fool of State,
Nor take a favour from the man I hate.

(p. 216)

Had he, as many renowned satirists have done, publicly
exposed a friend through envy, or had he spared hypocrites,
offended modesty, or injured worth, then he would hate himself
and curse his Muse. But as he fights only for virtue, he will not
allow himself to be swayed by Candour's mawkish advice:

But shall my arm—forbid it manly Pride,
Forbid it Reason, warring on my side—
For vengeance lifted high, the stroke forbear,
And hang suspended in the desart air,
Or to my trembling side unnerv'd sink down,
Palsied, forsooth, by Candour's half-made frown?
When Justice bids me on, shall I delay
Because insipid CANDOUR's bars my way?

(p. 217)

Virtue must be strong and fearless, not an 'equal-blooded judge'
nor a 'lukewarm drone' like Candour. The times demand stern
correction. And Satire asks Juvenal's question: How can he lack
a subject when vice is so rampant? Again Candour accuses Satire
of exaggeration. Satire, she says, blights the hopes of mankind
with fear and gives an utterly dispiriting and desolate picture of

the world. Therefore Candour bids him cease railing unless he can produce one person as bad as he makes out all men to be. Satire eagerly rises to the occasion and names Hogarth.

Combe's *The Justification* follows the standard pattern of argument and counter-argument between the satirist and a friend who is eventually won over to the satirist's viewpoint. The friend begins by remarking that he has for a long time wanted the satirist to turn from 'the rugged way' of satire to the flowery paths of panegyric. Is it not possible, he asks, to help virtue by tender means? The satirist of course believes that the harsh remedy of satire is more effective, especially in an age when vice is so rampant. He points out that guilt is a powerful force in human nature; accordingly, if satire is able to arouse feelings of guilt in guilty men, then it is working directly for the good of mankind. The friend, however, doubts whether the claims made for satire as an instrument of reform can be substantiated. He cites instances of contemporaries who continue to flaunt their vices even though they have been severely satirized. Naturally, the satirist replies, men who are vicious by nature will take care not to betray any sign of 'the biting pangs' that satire has made them feel. They feel the pangs none the less: they smile in public, but they weep at home. Satire can therefore be regarded as part of 'the glorious design' of Providence, and as an aid to 'the Minister of God'. It has to be cruel to be kind, especially as some vices are too malignant for tender treatment—

> To such diseases Satire must apply
> The keenest probe of mental surgery.
>
> (p. 22)

The satirist has only too evidently been allowed the best of the argument. His friend, however, still has a pointed question to ask. Does the satirist himself lead a blameless life? Can he 'boast the Censor's spotless name'?

> Does no base passion urge you to declare
> With Vice and vicious men this open war?
>
> (p. 26)

But the satirist sidesteps the question. As we are all imperfect, he argues, we just have to do the best we can and help virtue whenever we see an opportunity to do so. If we were to wait 'till Angels held the pen', then 'base degenerate men' would far too long go unchecked and unpunished. He is resolved to attack vice whenever he sees it, in high places as well as low. Even the King will not be sacrosanct. His friend cries out for him to stop. Should he not be more cautious? Is it not possible for him to soften his satire a little? Is there no one he can find to praise? Whereupon the satirist, responsive to this cry from his friend's heart (and to show that he is not really hard-hearted), makes a concession: he lists those he will praise—Saville, Camden, Rockingham—and declares that he will single out for special mention Chatham from politics and Lowth from the Church. Concluding the dialogue, his friend exclaims joyfully that at last he sees that the satirist is as capable of praise as of censure, and thus well suited to brand vice with the crimson dye of shame, and to confer on the good their immortality.

No one it seems could be worthier, nor more commendable, than the satirist. He emerges from the apologias like a knight in shining armour from a dark cloud. About Churchill's and Combe's poems especially there is a ceremonial and celebratory air which removes them from reality. In a sense of course all the apologias are ritual performances and should be taken as statements of an ideal: they are not intended to be faithful documentaries. Yet the claims made for the satirist in the incidental comments discussed earlier in the chapter were not less extravagant. It seems that, in countering the image of the malignant satirist, which was painted by some critics of satire, apologists went to the opposite extreme, whether they were writing in prose or poetry, and whether they were writing apologias, essays, or biographies, or simply making genial comments in passing. In place of the malignant and envious scribbler, they drew the portrait of a paragon: no satirist could possibly live up to it. But, as was mentioned a moment ago, the apologists, in putting this portrait before the public, were not attempting to be realistic. Their pretences to realism, to be telling the simple prosaic truth, were largely rhetorical. What they were endeavouring to do was to counterbalance the exaggerations of their opponents. It is perhaps worth remarking that these opponents may not always have been contemporary critics: they may sometimes have been doubts and qualms in their own minds.

7. Personal Reference

MANY Augustans experienced troubling doubts concerning the ethics of personal satire. When satire was personal in the sense of being written out of revenge, or to bring down a rival, it was clearly difficult to justify on moral principles. At best it might be excused on the ground that the satirist had been 'notoriously abused'. There was a sense, however, in which all personal satire could be regarded as inexcusable: it is against charity, and so against Christianity. As Dryden observed, 'in Christian charity, all offences are to be forgiven'; and he confessed that he had often trembled while he was saying the Lord's Prayer because in that prayer we ask forgiveness of God on the 'plain condition' that we forgive others for injuries they have done to us.[1] Like the majority of his contemporaries, Dryden was inconsistent on the subject of personal satire. He disapproved of it in principle, except under the most stringent conditions; yet his own satire failed to observe these conditions, especially *Mac Flecknoe* which was written for revenge and which referred unmistakably to a personal rival.

Most satire of the late seventeenth and eighteenth centuries was personal: Dryden's occasional poems, the satires of Rochester and Pope, the operas of Gay, and Fielding's plays, pamphlets, and his *Jonathan Wild* fall into this category, to mention only some of the works of the more responsible writers. Even *The Spectator* and *The Tatler*, which we rightly regard as initiating a milder kind of satire, contained a considerable amount of personal reference. Steele's boasts in *The Tatler*[2] of threats of violence, which had been provoked by certain numbers, do not prove that the journal in fact contained intentional ridicule of particular individuals; but they do indicate how used readers were to a personal element in satire, and how much they were on the look-out for it. In the concluding number of *The Tatler*,

---

[1] Dryden's *Essays*, ii. 79–80.
[2] No. 84 (22 October 1709), and No. 164 (27 April 1710).

Steele thanked a major-general, a brigadier, and an admiral, for
having volunteered to defend him against attacks by angry
readers, who imagined they had been personally satirized in one
number or another of the journal. The motto of the first forty
numbers of *The Tatler* was part of the familiar quotation from
Juvenal's first satire (*Quicquid agunt homines* . . .) with 'votum,
timor, ira, voluptas, gaudia discursus' omitted. The omission
possibly reflects the determination of such writers as Steele and
Addison to be mild and restrained in their commentary; but
equally the use of the first half of the quotation shows that the
journal was intended to give a realistic commentary on everyday
life. And to comment realistically and pertinently on social
behaviour without being personal is an impossibility.

The political satire of the period was personal and topical. *The
Poems on Affairs of State* (1697 et seq.), for example, as the title
signifies, were concerned with contemporary men and affairs.
They were on the events of the day—plots, treaties, military and
naval actions, battles, acts of parliament—and on the men and
women directly involved in these happenings—the King, members of the Court, ministers, royal mistresses, heirs to the throne,
minor court officials, bishops, judges, generals, admirals, priests,
conspirators, and spies. In the unsettled reigns of the later Stuarts
all sorts of persons, who would in calmer times have been merely
spectators, became participants in major political events.
Moreover, the comparatively small scale tended to make politics
intimate and accessible. Government under the Stuarts and
Hanoverians was not something which went on in a separate
sphere, as it seems to do today despite the rapid dissemination
of political news by newspapers and television. Besides, a rapid
increase in the number of private and charity schools, and the
consequent spread of literacy, meant that many more people,
as J. H. Plumb puts it, 'could enjoy vicariously the political
battle'.[3] They could feel they were taking part, for example, in
the running attack on court and government which was kept up
in every available medium of expression during Walpole's long
term of office. 'Has not every body got by Heart Satires, Lampoons, Ballads and Sarcasms against the Administration?' asked
Common Sense; or, the Englishman's Journal (8 October 1737).
Addison described England as 'a Nation of Statesmen'; and

[3] *The First Four Georges* (1956), p. 77.

Goldsmith joked about 'the singular passion of this nation for politics'.[4] Dr. Johnson stated that the publication of small tracts from time to time was especially necessary in England because so many more were written in this country than in any other, and because interest in them was so keen and widespread:

> The *Form* of our *Government*, which gives every Man, that has Leisure, or Curiosity, or Vanity, the Right of enquiring into the Propriety of publick Measures; and, by Consequence, obliges those, who are intrusted with the Administration of *National* Affairs, to give an Account of their Conduct, to almost every Man, who demands it, may be reasonably imagined to have occasioned *innumerable* Pamphlets, which would never have appeared under *arbitrary* Governments, where every Man lulls himself in Indolence under Calamities, of which he cannot promote the Redress, or thinks it prudent to conceal the Uneasiness of which he cannot complain without Danger.[5]

Examples crowd to mind of writers who took an active part in political affairs. Addison was Under-Secretary of State; Prior, chargé d'affaires in the embassy at Paris; and Sheridan, besides being a Member of Parliament for about thirty years, was also at different times Under-Secretary for Foreign Affairs, Treasurer of the Navy and Privy Councillor. Dryden, so the story goes, composed *Absalom and Achitophel*, Part i, at his King's request; Swift wrote in support of Tory policies for some years and, subsequently, for the Irish cause; Addison wrote a tragedy (*Cato*, 1713) upholding Whig principles; Fielding castigated Walpole in *The Champion* (1737), and *Jonathan Wild* (1743); and Swift, Gay, Pope, Chesterfield, Arbuthnot, and others wrote for Bolingbroke in *The Craftsman* (1726–36). Authors so involved in political conflicts could hardly have written on them in an aloof and impersonal manner.

Nor did they, of course. A modern reader can perhaps easily overlook the intensely personal nature of most social and political satire of the Augustan age. The Succession, which is the central question of *Absalom and Achitophel*, was a matter of the most vital concern to Dryden and his contemporaries, and the outcome turned on persons as much as principles. Moreover, the characters in Dryden's poem were real people. Shimei and

---

[4] *The Free-holder*, No. 53, and *Citizen of the World*, Letter v, cited by A. R. Humphreys, *The Augustan World* (1954), p. 127.

[5] Introduction to *The Harleian Miscellany* (1744–6), i. ii.

Bull-fac'd Jonas were not just fanciful creations, but Slingsby
Bethel and Sir William Jones, Sheriff of London and Attorney·
General respectively. *The Beggar's Opera* was applauded at its
opening performances not only for the fresh charm of its songs
and its lively depiction of low characters, but also for its political
allusions.[6] As poems and plays, and literary works generally,
tended to be highly topical and political, their publication frequently caused a great deal of excitement. So Pope remarked in a
letter to Swift that his pleasant pastime in the preceding fortnight
had been watching people's reactions to *Gulliver's Travels*:

> I congratulate you first upon what you call your Couzen's wonder-
> ful Book, which is *publica trita manu* at present, and I prophecy
> will be in future the admiration of all men. That countenance with
> which it is received by some statesmen, is delightful; I wish I could
> tell you how every single man looks upon it, to observe which has
> been my whole diversion this fortnight. I've never been a night in
> London since you left me, till now for this very end, and indeed it
> has fully answered my expectations.[7]

It is tempting to conclude that more personal satire was
written in the late seventeenth and early eighteenth centuries
than in any other period in English history, and that so much
was written because Dryden and Pope and their contemporaries
were comparatively free of the constraints which had inhibited
satirists of a century earlier, and which deter most publishers
today from publishing anything which might be thought to be
libellous. They were not forced to retreat into allegory, as were
Niccols, Drayton, Woodhouse, and Scot, nor to circulate their
satirical pieces anonymously in manuscript, as were the anti-
royalist, anti-Buckingham satirists of the 1620s.[8] They did not
have to contend with such formidable official opposition as the
Order of Conflagration (1 June 1599), or James I's proclamation
of 24 December 1620, which called on writers not to 'intermeddle
by Penne or Speech, with causes of State, and secrets of Empire,
either at home, or abroad, but containe themselves within that
modest and reverent regard, of matters above their reach and
calling, that to good and dutifull Subjects appertaineth'.[9] Nor

---

[6] See John Loftis, *The Politics of Drama in Augustan England* (Oxford, 1963),
pp. 88–91.   [7] 16 November 1726, Swift's *Correspondence*, iii. 181.
[8] See the volume in the Bodleian Library, press-mark Malone 23.
[9] See Arber's *Transcript of the Stationers' Register*, iii. 316; 677–8; and
J. A. Farrer, *Books Condemned to be Burnt* (1892), p. 41.

for that matter did they have to contend with the ready resort to libel action which is common practice today. But the whole question of the relative freedom of the press in Tudor, Stuart, and Hanoverian times is immensely complicated. Undoubtedly, Augustan satirists were aware of constraints. Dryden was given a beating in Rose Alley—allegedly for certain of his satirical writings;[10] Rochester was banished from court for his verses on the King's love-making;[11] Captain Robert Julian was fined and pilloried for 'publishing several scandalous libells';[12] and Stephen College and Algernon Sidney were executed for similar offences.[13] Moreover, as was noted previously,[14] Prior was sufficiently daunted by the dangers of the satirist's life to decide against 'launching into Satyr'. On the other hand, one cannot but suspect that at least some of the talk of danger indulged in by certain other writers, by Swift and Pope for example, was for effect; and that to some extent their paraphernalia of asterisks, dashes, blanks and nicknames, was employed for publicity purposes, rather than to safeguard reputations or persons, or to avoid hurting people's feelings. Certainly it had the result of increasing interest in the personal element of satire and, also sometimes, of widening its application. Atossa could be Sarah, Duchess of Marlborough, or Katherine, Duchess of Buckinghamshire;[15] and more than one person could be fitted in the gap between a 'B' and an 'n', or an 'H' and a 'ley'. The author meanwhile had it both ways: he could plead with some plausibility that he meant to hurt no one, and at the same time privately congratulate himself on having bagged not one but a brace of victims. Besides, the greater the number of people who took his satire personally, the more blandly he could claim generality.

The term 'personal', like the term 'satire' itself, was open to misunderstanding. It could mean simply 'dealing with persons' (instead of issues or principles), or 'identifiable', or *ad hominem*. It usually carried with it associations of pettiness and malice. In this connection one should remember that 'satire' was commonly confused with 'lampoon' and 'libel', and that critics were

[10] Charles E. Ward, *The Life of John Dryden* (1961), p. 143.
[11] *Poems on Affairs of State*, ed. Lord, i. 423–4.
[12] Brice Harris, 'Captain Robert Julian, Secretary to the Muses', *ELH* x (1943), 301.
[13] *Poems on Affairs of State*, ed. Lord, I. xxxvii.   [14] See p. 48.
[15] See 'Who Was Atossa?', Pope's *Poems*, vol. iii, pt. ii, pp. 159–60.

in the habit of calling a satire, which they disliked and which could be taken to refer to living persons, a 'libel' or 'lampoon'.[16] In order to keep the satirical works themselves in perspective one should remember also that, although many of them may be properly described as 'personal', the best of them rise with ease above the ephemeral concerns, the personal antagonisms and political conflicts, which prompted them. To explain this phenomenon we have to turn to neo-classic critical theory, in particular to the insistence of neo-classicists on universality.

Critics from Dryden to Johnson took it as an article of faith that literature must be general in nature and significance. The singular, the bizarre, the unusual, and the improbable were regarded unfavourably because they were 'out of nature', and nature was thought of as all that which accords with common experience. Rapin accordingly refused to believe in Ariosto's women characters, 'which he makes valiant in War, contrary to their Natural timidity';[17] and Addison disliked Cowley's love poems because they failed to express the feelings and thoughts which most men experience when they are in love.[18] Le Bossu carefully argued in his *Traité du poème épique* (1675) that the epics of Homer and Virgil were composed primarily to illustrate universal moral precepts—the *Iliad*, for instance, to show that discord among allies or in families ultimately leads to disaster. Yet, in spite of the importance attached to universality in literature, such were the circumstantial pressures of the age on its imaginative writers, that the mode of literary expression which they found most useful, as well as most congenial, was characteristically personal and particular in its sources and motivation. But—and this is the point—their belief in universality, coupled with their reverence for classical and Biblical myths, provided the leading satirists of the age with both the impetus and the means for raising such works as *Mac Flecknoe* and *The Dunciad* to a level which transcends personal and topical reference. As T. S. Eliot remarked of satire like Ben Jonson's, '[it] is great in the end not by hitting off its object, but by creating it; the satire is merely the means which leads to the aesthetic result, the impulse which projects a new world into a new orbit.'[19] The

---

[16] See pp. 21–4.   [17] Rapin, p. 34.
[18] *The Spectator*, No. 229, 22 November 1711.
[19] *Selected Essays* (1932), pp. 158–9.

contradiction then, which we remarked between the personal focus of Augustan satire and the impersonality of its finest effects, is merely apparent: satire, as is demonstrated by the best Augustan satires, especially the character-portraits, can be personal in its origins, and in some or all of its details, and yet perfectly impersonal in its effects. For a complete artistic response a reader does not need to know exactly who Sporus was in real life, or Mac Flecknoe or Squire Trulliber, any more than he needs to be able to identify the originals of Iago, Holofernes, the Yahoos, or the slithy toves.

Dryden and Pope, and their fellow satirists, however, were less concerned with the immortality of their creatures, than with establishing their right to be born at all. As the satirists frequently ridiculed living persons and were attacked for doing so, they were eager to justify this practice and to establish, as it were, an official rationale for personal satire. For such a rationale they were able to turn to Boileau, who was attacked for his use of contemporary names, as he expected to be. Boileau defended himself mainly in his Satire vii and the *Discours sur la satire* (1668). In the satire just mentioned, Boileau argues that it would be unjust for him to be punished for referring to contemporaries seeing that the Roman satirists did the same thing in their lifetimes with impunity.[20] His argument in the *Discours sur la satire* also rests on precedent. Lucilius, who invented satire, not only attacked other writers, but also men of the highest standing in Rome, even consuls. He spared no one, regardless of wealth or position; but nobody was up in arms as a result. And, if it is urged that Lucilius was able to exercise such liberty because he lived in a republic, the example may be cited of Horace who lived under an emperor in the beginnings of a monarchy, which is a most dangerous time for a satirist, and yet freely named contemporaries. Moreover, he did not merely call people by their names: so fearful was he in some instances that they might not be recognized that he even mentioned their trades and occupation.[21]

Boileau found support for his argument in Persius also, in that this satirist not only attacked other writers, but ridiculed the verses of the Emperor Nero himself, and yet was pardoned by

[20] Boileau's *Satires*, pp. 95–6, lines 73–80.
[21] Ibid., pp. 228–31.

Nero notwithstanding. Juvenal, Boileau admits, did not name the great men of his age, but those of the preceding age instead. None the less he did not (according to Boileau) look beyond his own time for examples of bad writers. It is the freedom to ridicule and censure bad writers which Boileau above all wishes to exercise; and he concludes his survey of the classical Roman satirists with this observation:

Tant il est vrai que le droit de blâmer les Auteurs est un droit ancien, passé en coûtume parmi tous les Satiriques, souffert dans tous les siècles.[22]

He finds precedents also among more recent writers, Virgil, Catullus, Martial, Regnier, and others. Regnier, for instance, though admittedly discreet, does mention names, and Boileau lists some of them. Virgil, in an eclogue, which is otherwise not at all satirical, has in one line made two poets eternally ridiculous—'Qui Bavium non odit, amet tua carmina, Mævi'.[23] Boileau remarks sarcastically that if he were to be banished for his use of contemporary names he would have good company, for a number of great writers would be banished with him. What he feels has vexed readers is his making them aware that they have wasted time and praise on unworthy works. Yet it would clearly be wrong for books to be placed beyond criticism, for them to be treated as 'un azyle inviolable, où toutes les sottises auront droit de bourgeoisie, où l'on n'osera toucher sans profanation'.[24]

English authors of the later seventeenth and the eighteenth centuries knew satire too well at first hand to believe that the personal element could be kept out of it entirely. They were alarmed by the spate of scandalous satire current in their times; and they were offended—the more responsible among them, that is—by the sullying of decent reputations, as well as being more than a little fearful on their own account. But notwithstanding these qualms and misgivings, most of them—and this includes even Addison, the most consistent opponent of libel and slander in the period—knew that satire without particular reference is likely to be vapid and ineffectual. From a literary viewpoint they appreciated that any literary work, satirical or otherwise, must

[22] Ibid., p. 233.
[23] Ibid., pp. 231–4.
[24] Ibid., p. 235.

express the general through the particular, through persons and things, and that those examples strike home best which are the most familiar. As Charles Abbott said, even in satires of a mild and general kind, 'the occasional introduction of known characters gives peculiar force, as they both interest the passions by their familiarity, and convince the judgment by their truth.'[25] From a social viewpoint it was argued that satire's proper function was to drag scoundrels and blockheads into the open. Clearly it could not do this without naming them, or without at least making their identities perfectly plain to themselves and the reader. Moreover, as Gildon pointed out in a letter to a friend who had disparaged the 'personal reflections' in a recently published satirical work, 'if Men must not be told their Faults, they'l never mend 'em; and *general Reflections* will never do the Business, because the Devilish good Opinion ev'ry Man has of himself, furnishes him with an Evasion from the lash of general Characters.' By naming offenders, Gildon states, Aristophanes 'kept many of the *Athenians* in awe, and within moderate bounds . . . and so regulated the City better than the Philosophers, with their empty Sophisms, or the Laws, with their blunted Edge'.[26] In a sane age, satirists are applauded for keeping folly and vice in check. Turning to his own times, which he regards as far from sane, Gildon asks indignantly if it is right that nothing should be done about the fops, fools, and scribblers who are such a pest to society:

Must the Town be always pester'd with their insufferable Impertinences, because, tho' they have been ridicul'd in general Characters a Thousand times, will yet by no means believe themselves touch'd? There is no Remedy for these Public Grievances, but particular Reflections, and tho', as you say; No Man is free from Follies that may be expos'd, yet they will be much diminish'd in them that have any sence, by this means, or at least be made less visible; and then 'tis not much more pains to be Wise, than to play the fool with Secresie, and one might as well shake hands with Vice for good and all, as to be at the fatigue to Sin with discretion.[27]

In William Combe's view it is precisely in order to fulfil its aim of inducing men to practise virtue and deterring them from

[25] Abbott, *Oxford Prize Essays*, i. 186.
[26] *Miscellaneous Letters and Essays, on Several Subjects* (1694), p. 4.
[27] Ibid., p. 5.

vice, that 'Satire directs its shafts to known Persons and Characters, by whom general severities would be scarcely felt'. He grants that general satire may be useful in warning young people in a vague sort of way against moral dangers; but against bad men he has no doubt that personal satire is much more effective:

> General Satire may afford instruction, nay, may give a wholesome alarm to unsophisticated minds. It may convey to Youth the picture of those vices which will assail him, and those Characters which he will meet with in the World, and warn him of its dangers. It may also offer its descriptions to the dubious and varying application of Mankind. But Personal Satire, by pointing out its objects, prevents bad men from flying to any subterfuge, or practising any evasion to elude its exposure. It holds them forth to the immediate and certain odium of their fellow creatures.[28]

It is interesting to note that Dr. Johnson, whose *The Vanity of Human Wishes* stands out as one of the most general of satirical works, did not on the whole much favour general satire. Mrs. Piozzi provides the following testimony:

> Though no man perhaps made such rough replies as Dr. Johnson, yet nobody had a more just aversion to general satire; he always hated and censured Swift for his unprovoked bitterness against the professors of medicine; and used to challenge his friends, when they lamented the exorbitancy of physicians fees, to produce him one instance of an estate raised by physic in England. When an acquaintance too was one day exclaiming against the tediousness of the law and its partiality; 'Let us hear, Sir (said Johnson), no general abuse; the law is the last result of human wisdom acting upon human experience for the benefit of the public'.[29]

Later in her book, after relating an instance of Dr. Johnson tilting at a class of persons, namely attorneys, Mrs. Piozzi comments:

> He did not however encourage general satire, and for the most part professed himself to feel directly contrary to Dr. Swift; 'who (says he) hates the world, though he loves John and Robert, and certain individuals'.[30]

---

[28] Preface to *The Justification*, pp. iv–v.
[29] *Anecdotes of the Late Samuel Johnson, Ll.D.* (1786), p. 111.
[30] Ibid., p. 272.

Dr. Johnson's own written statements on the question support
Mrs. Piozzi's testimony. In *The Idler*, No. 46, for example:

The general lampooner of mankind may find long exercise for his
zeal or wit in the defects of Nature, the temptations of life, the follies
of opinion, and the corruptions of practice. But Falsehood is easier
than Discernment; and most of these Writers spare themselves the
labour of enquiry, and exhaust their virulence upon imaginary
crimes, which, as they never existed, can never be amended.

One may note that Dr. Johnson calls the satirist a 'lampooner'
here to convey his disapproval. In his *Life of Pope*, with the
same practical considerations in mind as in the passage just
quoted, he defends *The Dunciad* for its attack on bad writers,
while fully recognizing that Pope probably wrote it out of
vindictiveness and malice. 'That the design was moral, whatever
the author might tell either his readers or himself, I am not
convinced.' Johnson goes on to say that Pope's first motive was
to revenge himself on Theobald, but as Theobald was not big
enough to fill the whole poem, he had to look round for other
enemies, 'at whose expence he might divert the publick'.

In this design there was petulance and malignity enough; but I
cannot think it very criminal. An author places himself uncalled
before the tribunal of Criticism, and solicits fame at the hazard of
disgrace. Dulness or deformity are not culpable in themselves, but
may be very justly reproached when they pretend to the honour of
wit or the influence of beauty. If bad writers were to pass without
reprehension, what should restrain them? *impune diem consumpserit
ingens Telephus*; and upon bad writers only will censure have much
effect. The satire which brought Theobald and Moore into contempt,
dropped impotent from Bentley, like the javelin of Priam thrown at
Neoptolemus.

All truth is valuable, and satirical criticism may be considered
as useful when it rectifies error and improves judgement; he that
refines the publick taste is a publick benefactor.[31]

Dr. Johnson was frank enough, moreover, to acknowledge the
part played by personal feeling in the composition of satires.
Thus, he admired Dryden's contribution (lines 310–509) to
Absalom and Achitophel, Part II, for the 'poignancy' of its satire,
and was prompted by it to remark: 'Personal resentment, though
no laudable motive to satire, can add great force to general
principles.'[32] But of course this is not to say that he did not set

[31] *Lives* (1779–81), ii. 427.   [32] Ibid. i. 349.

limits to personal satire. He spoke scornfully of Dorset's little personal invectives,[33] and he had no time for the sort of satire which is written merely to gratify spite, or to get a quick laugh:

It is of the nature of personal invectives to be soon unintelligible; and the author that gratifies private malice, *animam in vulnere ponit*, destroys the future efficacy of his own writings, and sacrifices the esteem of succeeding times to the laughter of a day.[34]

In recognizing the need for a personal element in satire, Dr. Johnson was at one with those men of his times who considered the question carefully. At one time or another many Augustans found themselves involved in a discussion of personal satire, if for no other reason than that they had written it or been accused of writing it themselves. Apart from appealing to classical precedent,[35] as Boileau had done so eloquently in the early days of neo-classicism, they emphasized the practical nature of the aims of satire. If, as was accepted on all sides, the satirist should endeavour to reform the present ills of society, then he could hardly avoid saying what these ills were, and who was to blame for them. How could he correct a wrongdoer without telling him what wrong he was doing? 'I am afraid that all such Writings and Discourses as touch no Man, will mend no Man', Pope wrote in his letter to Gay defending the *Epistle to Burlington*. 'Some fancy that to say a Thing is *Personal*, is the same as to say it is *Injust*, not considering, that nothing can be *Just* that is not *Personal* . . .',[36] that is to say, which does not tell the truth about a person's faults, and aim at correcting them. 'But how is it possible, for the most part, to unmask a Hypocrite without entring into the private Concerns of Life?' inquired John Dennis in his postscript to *The Characters and Conduct of Sir John Edgar*.[37]

---

[33] Ibid. 452.

[34] *The Plays of William Shakespeare* (1765), ii. 155.

[35] One of Juvenal's translators provides a typical example of such an appeal: 'I have had, like him, no respect of Persons or Parties, but like a truly Loyal Satyrist have run full tilt at vice and folly, where ever I found it, with a resolution not to give any quarter . . .', [Thomas Wood], Preface to *Juvenalis Redivivus* (1683), sig. A3v.

[36] 16 December 1731, Pope's *Correspondence*, iii. 255.

[37] *Critical Works*, ed. Hooker, ii. 217. By 'the private Concerns of Life' Dennis meant such personal matters as a man's treatment of his wife and his spending habits. In the first two letters of *The Characters and Conduct of Sir John Edgar*, Dennis alluded to Cibber's neglect of his wife and the high debts he had incurred through gambling.

This was a common view: the satirist has to name names because he speaks the plain truth; wrongdoers deserve to be and, in society's interests, have to be exposed. If poets are not allowed to scourge 'the Refuse of the Town', argues Walter Harte, 'Scandal will prevail'. The 'sons of darkness' who attack the weaker sex, the virtuous and the fair, 'must be drag'd to light'.[38] Pope also put forward this pragmatic defence of personal satire in his two replies to Arbuthnot's 'last request' of 17 July 1734, that is his letters dated 2 August [1734], and 26 July 1734.[39] In the former, he advances straightforward, practical arguments in support of personal satire: bad times demand drastic remedies; examples have to be made; punishment by public ridicule is a necessary deterrent.

I thank you dear Sir for making That your Request to me which I make my Pride, nay my Duty; 'that I should continue my Disdain & abhorrence of Vice, & manifest it still in my writings.' I would indeed do it with more restrictions, & less personally; it is more agreeable to my nature, which those who know it not are greatly mistaken in: But General Satire in Times of General Vice has no force, & is no Punishment: People have ceas'd to be ashamed of it when so many are joind with them; and tis only by hunting One or two from the Herd that any Examples can be made. If a man writ all his Life against the Collective Body of the Banditti, or against Lawyers, would it do the least Good, or lessen the Body? But if some are hung up, or pilloryed, it may prevent others. And in my low Station, with no other Power than this, I hope to deter, if not to reform.[40]

In the suppositious reply (26 July 1734), his arguments are loftier and more involved. Here he presents personal satire as the inevitable by-product of a moral nature, as a literary necessity, and as an effective instrument of social reform.

But sure it is as impossible to have a just abhorrence of Vice, without hating the Vicious, as to bear a true love of Virtue, without loving the Good. To reform and not to chastise, I am afraid is impossible, and that the best Precepts, as well as the best Laws, would prove of small use, if there were no Examples to inforce them. To attack Vices in the abstract, without touching Persons, may be safe fighting indeed, but it is fighting with Shadows. General propositions are obscure, misty, and uncertain, compar'd with plain, full,

---

[38] Harte, p. 24.
[39] For the reference to the dating of these two letters see Chapter 6, n. 18.
[40] Pope's *Correspondence*, iii. 423.

and home examples: Precepts only apply to our Reason, which in most men is but weak: Examples are pictures, and strike the Senses, nay raise the Passions, and call in those (the strongest and most general of all motives) to the aid of reformation. Every vicious man makes the case his own; and that is the only way by which such men can be affected, much less deterr'd. So that to chastise is to reform. The only sign by which I found my writings ever did any good, or had any weight, has been that they rais'd the anger of bad men.[41]

Pope's observations in this passage on the need for concreteness, for particular examples, to make ethical instruction effective, are acceptable in themselves; but they beg the question whether the examples have to be of real or imaginary people. If 'every vicious man is to make the case his own', the satire (that is, the personal reference in the satire) presumably has to be explicit and unmistakable.

Swift also appreciated the practical advantages of referring to actual contemporaries. Although he was mostly in favour of general satire, he by no means ruled out the personal element in either practice or theory. Thus, he avowed his high regard for *The Dunciad* ('After twenty times reading the whole, I never in my opinion saw so much good satire, or more good sense, in so many lines') and frankly advised its author not to reduce the number of personal allusions, but instead to make them perfectly plain to the reader. He felt that otherwise the poem might not be understood in Dublin or, for that matter, twenty miles outside London.

I have often run over the *Dunciad* in an Irish edition (I suppose full of faults) which a gentleman sent me. The Notes I could wish to be very large, in what relates to the persons concerned; for I have long observed that twenty miles from London no body understands hints, initial letters, or town-facts and passages; and in a few years not even those who live in London. I would have the names of those scriblers printed indexically at the beginning or end of the Poem, with an account of their works, for the reader to refer to. I would have all the Parodies (as they are called) referred to the authors they imitate—When I began this long paper, I thought I should have filled it with setting down the several passages I had marked in the edition I had, but I find it unnecessary, so many of them falling under the same rule. After twenty times reading the whole, I never in my opinion saw so much good satire, or more

41 Ibid. 419.

good sense, in so many lines. How it passes in Dublin I know not yet; but I am sure it will be a great disadvantage to the poem, that the persons and facts will not be understood, till an explanation comes out, and a very full one. I imagine it is not to be published till towards winter, when folks begin to gather in town. Again I insist, you must have your Asterisks filled up with some real names of real Dunces.[42]

In the ironical preface to *A Tale of a Tub*, Swift implies that general satire is entirely ineffectual and therefore quite acceptable in England. Panegyric, he says, is sure to arouse envy of the few individuals singled out for praise; but general satire is never resented because everyone thinks it applies to everyone but himself. He draws a mocking contrast between ancient Athens and contemporary England. In Athens, he avers, a citizen enjoyed the right of satirizing any other person, no matter how great that person's standing; but he could not make even a slightly unfavourable comment on the general public without stirring them to revenge. In England, on the other hand, you can say as much as you are capable of saying against mankind and, so far from being punished, you will be applauded 'as a Deliverer of precious and useful Truths'. Your criticisms will offend no one: "'Tis but a *Ball* bandied to and fro, and every Man carries a *Racket* about Him to strike it from himself among the rest of the Company.' On the other hand, however, if you tell damaging truths about individuals in England, you should expect the direst consequences.

But on the other side, whoever should mistake the Nature of things so far, as to drop but a single Hint in publick, How *such a one*, starved half the Fleet, and half-poison'd the rest: How *such a one*, from a true Principle of *Love* and *Honour*, pays no Debts but for *Wenches* and *Play*: How *such a one* has got a Clap, and runs out of his Estate: How *Paris* bribed by *Juno* and *Venus*, loath to offend either Party, slept out the whole Cause on the Bench: Or, how *such an Orator* makes long Speeches in the Senate with much Thought, little Sense, and to no Purpose; whoever, I say, should venture to be thus particular, must expect to be imprisoned for *Scandalum Magnatum*: to have *Challenges* sent him; to be sued for *Defamation*: and *to be brought before the Bar of the House*.[43]

---

[42] Swift to Pope, 16 July 1728, Swift's *Correspondence*, iii. 293.
[43] Preface to *A Tale of a Tub* (1704), p. 29.

In Augustan criticism generally, as in this preface of Swift's, one keeps coming back to the view that in a healthy society malefactors are exposed and ridiculed, as they deserve to be. Even those persons who, like Garrick,[44] believed personal satire best avoided, none the less admitted that it had its uses. The trouble was, they felt, that it had been allowed to get out of hand. They were for ever bewailing the 'censoriousness' of the age, and condemning petty tale-bearers and 'scavengers of scandal'. In *The Spectator*, No. 451 (7 August 1712), Addison went so far as to say that, no matter how artful a slander might be, he could only regard it as evil and criminal, and deserving of the severest punishment:

I cannot but look upon the finest Strokes of Satyr which are aimed at particular Persons, and which are supported even with the Appearances of Truth, to be the Marks of an evil Mind, and highly Criminal in themselves. Infamy, like other Punishments, is under the direction and distribution of the Magistrate, and not of any private Person. Accordingly we learn from a Fragment of *Cicero*, that tho' there were very few Capital Punishments in the twelve Tables, a Libel or Lampoon which took away the good Name of another, was to be punished by Death. But this is far from being our Case.

Increasingly personal satire was dismissed out of hand as, for example, by the anonymous author of an attack on Swift, Pope, and Fielding:

> Ingenious general Satire, I can love,
> While all that's Personal I disapprove.[45]

Another anonymous author declared that personal satire offends against every law:

> First then, the Wretch we blame, and *justly* blame,
> Whose frantic Muse attacks a Man by *Name*.
> This is no venial Fault, no trivial Flaw;
> This is offending against ev'ry Law:[46]

Eliza Haywood stated that she was 'as great an Enemy to personal Invectives, as any one can be'. She thought them unjustifiable even if they are true—'their Truth cannot atone for

[44] See Garrick to George Colman [7 April 1765], *The Letters of David Garrick*, edd. David M. Little and George M. Kahrl (1963), ii. 453.

[45] *The Satirists, a Satire* (1739?), p. 11. See Thomas B. Gilmore, jun., 'The Dating of "The Satirists, a Satire"', *N & Q* n.s. xiii (1966), 216–17.

[46] *The Art of Poetry* (1741), p. 7.

their Barbarism'.[47] 'In writing satire,' Newbery advised in *The Art of Poetry on a New Plan*, 'care should be taken that it be true and general, that is, levelled at abuses in which numbers are concerned; for the personal kind of satire, or lampoon, which exposes particular characters, and affects the reputation of those at whom it is pointed, is scarce to be distinguished from scandal and defamation.'[48] In a later passage he drives home the same point much more strongly:

> We have already observed, that personal satire approaches too near defamation, to deserve any countenance or encouragement; for however good in its composition, it must be bad in its tendency, since it is setting a man in a ridiculous point of light, and punishing him (as it were in a pillory) without any form of trial, or hearing the evidence in his behalf. Such satyrists, therefore, are not unlike arbitrary tyrants, who acknowledge no law but what is founded in their own will, and gratify their passions at the expence of public justice.[49]

'It is only the desperate Satyrist', wrote Richard Tickell, 'whose invenomed pen strikes at the character and honour of Individuals, that perverts and disgraces Poetry.'[50]

In addition, it was noted by Abbott, as it had been more than half a century earlier by Gildon, that personal satire was associated primarily with the licentious Old Comedy and with Archilochus, not with the Romans who had taken steps to curb it.[51] It was evidently a kind of writing which a civilized society would seek to restrain, if not to forbid altogether. And restrictions were prescribed for it by a number of Augustans. 'We have no moral right on the reputation of other men', Dryden stated, ''Tis taking from them what we cannot restore to them.' He gave two reasons justifying personal satire, or lampooning, as he called it in this connection. The first was revenge for a serious wrong; and the second that of exposing a public nuisance:

> All those, whom Horace in his Satires, and Persius and Juvenal have mentioned in theirs, with a brand of infamy, are wholly such. 'Tis an action of virtue to make examples of vicious men. They may and ought to be upbraided with their crimes and follies; both for their own amendment, if they are not yet incorrigible, and for the terror of others, to hinder them from falling into those enormities which they see are so severely punished in the persons of others.

---

[47] *The Parrot* (1746), No. 8.   [48] ii. 101.   [49] Ibid. 130.
[50] *The Wreath of Fashion, or, the Art of Sentimental Poetry* (1778), p. iv.
[51] Abbott, *Oxford Prize Essays*, i. 185; Gildon, *Laws of Poetry*, p. 143.

Looking back on his arguments, Dryden concludes: 'The first reason was only an excuse for revenge; but this second is absolutely of a poet's office to perform . . .'[52] Prior ruled that satire should be employed only in self-defence, 'as a shield rather than a Sword to defend yourself but not to wound another'. If a man sees a blow coming he is obliged to strike first, or else be in the unhappy position of not being able to strike at all. In an imperfect world 'this sort of warfare'—the exchange of blow for blow—'has sometimes been necessary . . . even amongst our Divines in Convocation'. One condition, however, should be sedulously observed, 'as Poet Bays said of his Rant, if it is not civil egad it must be sublime'.[53] Trapp thought personal satire justifiable only when aimed at notorious villains such as deserve to be censured by all mankind.[54] Gildon, who was quoted as in favour of personal satire in 1694, approved it only most reluctantly in *The Laws of Poetry* (1721) and only on 'this certain condition, that the crimes and follies they charge any one with, must not only be absolutely true, but known to the public, and prejudicial to others, as well as ignominious to themselves'.[55]

In an effort to disarm their critics, satirists sometimes assured the reader in a preface or the like that they had studiously avoided any reference to individuals. Boileau, for example, remarked of his satire on women that he had made the ridicule so general that he expected women, instead of being offended by it, to be his most avid readers.[56] In *The Spectator*, No. 34 (9 April 1711), Addison promised 'never to draw a faulty Character which does not fit at least a thousand People; or to publish a single Paper, that is not written in the Spirit of Benevolence, with a love to Mankind'. And Fielding claimed in the Preface to *Joseph Andrews* (1752) that he had eliminated all personal satire from his novel:

And here I solemnly protest, I have no intention to vilify or asperse any one: for though every thing is copied from the book of nature, and scarce a character or action produced which I have not taken

---

[52] Dryden's *Essays*, ii. 79–81.
[53] 'Heads for a Treatise upon Learning', *Works*, edd. Wright and Spears, ii. 584.
[54] Trapp, p. 231.
[55] p. 144; cf. *Miscellaneous Letters and Essays* (1694), p. 5.
[56] 'Au lecteur', Satire x, Boileau's *Satires*, p. 142.

from my own observations and experience; yet I have used the utmost care to obscure the persons by such different circumstances, degrees, and colours, that it will be impossible to guess at them with any degree of certainty; and if it ever happens otherwise, it is only where the failure characterized is so minute, that it is a foible only which the party himself may laugh at as well as any other.[57]

The chief argument advanced in support of general satire was the obvious one, namely that it was of wider interest and application than personal satire. As Horace Walpole put it: 'Unfrequent crimes are as little the business of tragedy, as singular characters are comedy; it is inviting the town to correct a single person.'[58] In *The Tatler*, No. 242, Steele pointed out that a satire which deals with a personal quarrel will be dismissed by readers as petty and trivial, it will never be made 'the Cause of Mankind':

There is no Possibility of succeeding in a Satyrical Way of Writing or Speaking, except a Man throws himself quite out of the Question. It is great Vanity to think any one will attend a Thing because it is your Quarrel. You must make your Satyr the Concern of Society in general, if you would have it regarded. When it is so, the Good-Nature of a Man of Wit will prompt him to many brisk and disdainful Sentiments and Replies, to which all the Malice in the World will not be able to repartee.

Steele was arguing here not only that general satire is morally better than personal, but also that it is bound to be more popular. Similarly, Edward Young implied that their freedom from personal reference was the reason for the favourable reception accorded to his seven satires, published under the title, *Love of Fame*: 'These Satires have been favourably received at home, and abroad. I am not conscious of the least malevolence to any particular person thro' all the Characters; tho' some persons may be so selfish, as to engross a general application to themselves.'[59] In *An Essay upon Publick Spirit* (subtitled 'A Satyr in Prose upon the Manners and Luxury of the Times') Dennis put general above particular (which includes personal) satire, but noted that particular satire, provided that it is just, is superior to libel and lampoon. His reasons for preferring general satire were that it

---

[57] *Works*, ed. L. Stephen (1882), iv. xvi.
[58] Walpole to Mason, 11 May 1769, *Walpole's Correspondence*, ed. Lewis, xxviii. 16.
[59] Preface to *Love of Fame, The Universal Passion*, sig. A2r.

is more generous in spirit, that it is free of ill will, that it aims at benefiting more people, and that it is more effective:

As this is a general Satyr, and cannot be the Effect either of Passion or Malice, a general Benefit must be the chief Design of it. The Good which it carries with it, is equally intended to all; even those who happen to be hit by it, are design'd to be oblig'd among the rest, and suffer only by Accident.

And 'tis for this very Reason that a General Satyr is preferable to what is particular, not only because the Design is more generous, of obliging all, and offending none, but because there is a greater probability of its attaining the End to which it directs its Aim, which is the Reformation of the Reader: For the Pleasure which we find that the Generality of Mankind takes in particular Satyr, is a certain Sign that the Publick reaps little Benefit from it; for few are willing to apply those Faults to themselves, for which they see any particular Person expos'd to Contempt and Infamy. Men will more willingly acknowledge Faults, in the committing which they are join'd with Company sufficient to keep them in countenance.[60]

As has already been mentioned in this chapter, neo-classical doctrine favoured general satire in that it placed types before individuals as proper subjects for literature and advocated universality of appeal and application. Swift insisted that *Gulliver's Travels* should be judged by this standard. If the satire refers only to the British Isles, he wrote to l'abbé des Fontaines, then Gulliver must be a very poor writer indeed:

Nous convenons icy que le gout des Nations n'est pas toujours le meme. mais nous sommes portes a croire que le bon gout est le meme par tout ou il y a des gens d'esprit, de judgement et de Scavoir. si donc les livres du Sieur Gulliver ne sont calcules que pour les Isles Britanniques, ce voyageur doit passer pour un tres pitoyable Ecrivain. les memes vices, et les memes follies regnent par tout, du moins, dans tous les pays civilises de l'Europe, et l'auteur qui n'ecrit que pour une ville, une province, un Royaume, ou meme un siecle, merite si peu d'etre traduit qu'il ne merite pas d'etre lû.

Les Partisans de ce Gulliver, qui ne laissent pas d'etre en fort grand nombre chez nous, soutiennent, que son Livre durera autant que notre langage, parce qu'il ne tire pas son merite de certaines modes ou manieres de penser et de parler, mais d'une suite d'observations sur les imperfections, les folies, et les vices de l'homme.[61]

[60] *Critical Works*, ed. Hooker, ii. 396.
[61] July 1727, Swift's *Correspondence*, iii. 226.

As in their discussion of most aspects of satire, Augustan critics changed their minds concerning personal reference according to the needs of the moment and the particular satirical work under discussion. Their dilemma was that they did not really approve of personal satire, yet felt that it alone was effective. 'Satire never can have effect without a personal application', stated T. J. Mathias, but he had noted on the preceding page that 'It is said to be incompatible, if not with the profession, yet certainly with the practice, of Christianity.'[62] A number of writers advocated a compromise. Thus, according to Eliza Haywood, 'A *Satirist*, whose Aim is to reform, will paint the *Offence* in its strongest Colours, but draw, as much as possible, a Veil over the Face of the *Offender*.'[63] And Thomas Blacklock gave the following assurance to readers of his *Address to the Ladies*:

this satire is neither absolutely personal, nor comprehensive of all. To attack any particular character is no less detraction in verse than in prose; or suppose the intention more good-natured, it is confining those moral lessons to one, which may be applicable to a thousand. To attack any sex or species for qualities inseparable from it, is really to write a satire against Nature. So that the business of one who would assume a character so delicate and unwelcome, is neither to confine himself to individuals, nor attempt to include the whole.[64]

Trapp quotes Vossius's argument in favour of personal reference on the ground that it alone can serve the satirist's practical aim of reforming his own times, then goes on to disagree with him. He considers that a satirist may choose either mode, general or personal satire, but if one is to be preferred to the other, in his view it should be general satire, because it is fairer. Personal satire is no doubt necessary in extreme instances; but even here the satirist should employ fictitious names.

He [the satirist] may chuse, indeed, either Way, and it is hard to say which is more peculiarly his Province. But if any Difference is to be made, I should take the Side against *Vossius*, and avoid reproving Particulars. It is undoubtedly fairer to aim our Shafts against the

[62] *The Pursuits of Literature* (5th edn., 1898), pp. vi, vii.
[63] *The Parrot*, No. 8.
[64] *Poems* (1793), p. 165.

Vice, rather than the Man. The latter, indeed, is sometimes justifiable, against some notorious Monsters, that deserve to be the Butts of Mankind: But even here the Poet does not point them out by their real Names, but under fictitious Characters; which is another Particular I have been oblig'd to observe against the foremention'd Author; who, for what Reason I know not, makes it essential to Satire to characterize by Name; a Property which I should much rather leave to the Libeller, than the Poet. *Horace* and *Juvenal*, it is true, sometimes assume this Liberty; but, for the Generality, 'tis Vice they reprove in the Abstract; and when they seem to mention Names, it is to be observ'd, that we, at this Distance of Time, know not whether they are real or borrow'd ones.[65]

Sometimes writers would declare themselves all for general satire, sometimes they would argue the need for personal satire in a degenerate age, and sometimes they wanted to have it both ways. On occasion, a work might be judged too personal by some critics, and too general by others. According to Pope, this was so with *Gulliver's Travels*:

I find no considerable man very angry at the book: some indeed think it rather too bold, and too general a Satire: but none that I hear of accuse it of particular reflections (I mean no persons of consequence, or good judgment; the mob of Criticks, you know, always are desirous to apply Satire to those that they envy for being above them) so that you needed not to have been so secret upon this head.[66]

By and large the position was that, when they wrote as critics on a theoretical level, English writers of the late seventeenth and eighteenth centuries advocated general satire; whereas, when they were taken to task for writing personal satire themselves, they were obliged to offer a defence, or to insist that they had been misinterpreted, that they had not for one moment intended slighting anyone in particular, and so on. We noted a moment ago that, in *An Essay upon Publick Spirit* (1711), Dennis argued the superiority of general to particular satire. Nine years later, however, in *The Characters and Conduct of Sir John Edgar*, we find him going to great lengths to justify the satirical treatment of 'the private Concerns of Life'. He claims not only that they are 'the just and adequate Subjects of Satire', but also that they

---

[65] Trapp, p. 231.
[66] Pope to Swift, 16 November 1726, Swift's *Correspondence*, iii. 181.

'make the chief Beauties of the ancient Satirists'. He states (incorrectly as it happens) that in the lines

> Est Lucilius ausus
> Primus in hunc operis componere carmina morem,
> Detrahere & pellem, nitidus quâ quisque per ora
> Cederet, introrsum turpis[67]

Horace declared the 'unmasking of Hypocrites' to be 'the great business of Satire'. And of Juvenal's famous verses in his first satire—

> Quicquid agunt...
> ... farrago libelli.

he asks: 'Now will anyone pretend that the private Concerns of Life are not included in these Verses?'[68] Undoubtedly Dennis is being disingenuous in his anxiety to excuse his own satirical treatment of Colley Cibber's and Sir Richard Steele's 'private Concerns' in *The Characters*.

A sounder defence than Dennis's is Shadwell's of his own practice in *The Humorists*. He directly confronts his critics:

> But I challenge the most clamorous and violent of my Enemies (who would have the Town believe that every thing I write, is too nearly reflecting upon persons) to accuse me, with truth, of representing the real actions or using the peculiar, affected phrases, or manner of speech of any one particular Man, or Woman living.
>
> I cannot indeed create a new Language, but the Phantastick Phrases, used in any Play of mine, are not appropriate to any one *Fop*, but applicable to many.[69]

Perfectly good and reasonable men, he goes on, can only be represented to their advantage. He insists that his object is not to ridicule worthy people for their trifling faults, but only those people in whom faults so predominate as to turn them 'wholly from the ways of Wisdom or Morality'.

When Pope was attacked on all sides for his depiction of Timon's villa in the *Epistle to Burlington*, he protested[70] his astonishment that a satire treating no Vice, not even folly in general, but only one sort of folly, should cause such an outcry.

---

[67] *Satire*, ii. i. 62–5.

[68] *Critical Works*, ed. Hooker, ii. 217.

[69] Preface to *The Humorists*, sig. A4v.

[70] [William Cleland] to Gay [16 December 1731], Pope's *Correspondence*, iii. 254–7.

Besides, he argued, it ridicules only lack of taste, that is a 'natural' as distinct from a 'moral' defect; and 'Ill Taste employs more Hands, and diffuses Expence more than a Good one.' In the third paragraph he asserts that the *Epistle* is general and then, inconsistently, that a satire must be personal to be just. He beats a retreat, as it were, and then once he is well away, outlines a sound strategy of defence. His poem is not personal, he says, for it describes things: the man's possessions, not the man himself. Then he continues:

Some fancy, that to say a Thing is *Personal*, is the same as to say it is *Injust*, not considering, that nothing can be *Just* that is not *Personal*: I am afraid that all such Writings and Discourses as touch no Man, will mend no Man.[71]

He goes on to explain why good but weak men are disturbed by satire and why vicious men hate it. Then, as part of his rebuttal of 'the malicious Application of the character of Timon' to the Duke of Chandos, he puts forward the standard plea of the author, that he draws composite characters.

Why, in God's Name, must a *Portrait* apparently collected from twenty different Men, be applied to one only? Has it his Eye? No, it is very unlike. Has it his Nose or Mouth? No, they are totally differing. What then, I beseech you? Why, it has the *Mole on his Chin*. Very well: but must the Picture therefore be his, and has no other Man that Blemish? Would to God I had it together with his Magnificence, Beneficence, Generosity and Goodness! Then I would add one Vanity more to the Catalogue, and firmly believe myself the best Man of my Age and Country, because I have *honoured my God* with most Dignity, and done most *Good* to my *Neighbour*.[72]

Scholars now accept that Pope was wrongly accused of personal satire on the Duke of Chandos in the *Epistle to Burlington*.[73] Because the Duke was most unpopular at the time the *Epistle* was published, readers wanted to see him as Timon; but the facts of the poem are against such an interpretation. Also, the Duke of Chandos himself wrote a dignified letter to Pope stating that he would not hold the poet responsible 'for the application the Town has made of Timon's Character'.[74] This was one of the

[71] Ibid. 255.
[72] Ibid. 256.
[73] See Pope's *Poems*, vol. iii, pt. ii, pp. 164–8.
[74] 27 December 1731, Pope's *Correspondence*, iii. 262–3.

occasions, evidently, on which Pope could justly claim that he had been misinterpreted.

I really cannot help smiling at the Stupidity, while I lament the Slanderous Temper of the Town. I thought no Mortal singly could claim that Character of *Timon*, any more than any Man pretend to be Sir *John Falstaff*.

But the Application of it to the D. of Ch. is monstrous; to a Person who in *every particular* differs from it. 'Is his Garden crowded with *Walls*? Are his Trees cut into *Figures of Men*? Do his Basons want *Water*? Are there *ten steep Slopes* of his Terrass? Is he piqued about *Editions* of *Books*? Does he exclude all *Moderns* from his *Library*? Is the *Musick* of his Chappel bad, or *whimsical*, or *jiggish*? On the contrary, was it not the best composed in the Nation, and most suited to grave Subjects; witness *Nicol. Haym's*, and Mr. *Hendel's* noble *Oratories*? Has it the Pictures of Naked Women in it? And did ever Dean Ch— w—d preach his Courtly Sermons there? I am sick of such Fool-Applications.'[75]

It is an easy plea for a satirist to fall back on: that he has been misinterpreted, that his satire has been misapplied. But this is not to say the plea is never genuine. In certain of the circles where satires were passed around in the late seventeenth and the eighteenth centuries, misapplication was a favourite pastime. It went well with the use of dashes and asterisks, aliases and pseudonyms, with the dropping of manuscripts on publishers' doorsteps in the early hours of the morning, with fans held over the lips at the theatre, and with the 'half-shut Eyes' of politicians in coffee-houses.[76] It is possible that sometimes authors were secretly delighted at the way their satires were being taken (or mistaken) even when they protested most vehemently that they had attacked no particular persons. Often, however, their protests were justified. Not only Pope was 'sick of such Fool-Applications'. Mr. Spectator reflects, after leaving a coffee-house one afternoon, on the 'Difficulty of writing any thing in this censorious Age, which a weak Head may not construe into private Satyr and personal Reflection.' He is impatient of the kind of person who smells sedition and treason in every word, and 'never sees a Vice or Folly stigmatized, but finds out one or other of his Acquaintance pointed at by the Writer'.[77] In

---

[75] 27 December 1731, Pope's *Correspondence*, iii. 257.
[76] *The Rape of the Lock*, iii. 118, Pope's *Poems*, ii. 174.
[77] No. 568, 16 July 1714.

The Tatler, No. 41 (14 July 1709), under the motto, '—*Celebrare Domestica Facta*', Steele remarks that he is frequently mortified to receive letters in which people claim to recognize themselves in such and such a passage:

As it is a frequent Mortification to me to receive Letters, wherein People tell me, without a Name they know I meant them in such and such a Passage; so that very Accusation is an Argument, That there are such Beings in Human Life, and our Discourse is not altogether fantastical and groundless.

He goes on to tell a silly story to illustrate his point that some people too readily identify themselves with the characters in a satire. His story is of a boy, who was handing out notices warning against the pox, when he was suddenly knocked down by a passer-by. It seems that the passer-by took what was written on the bills to apply particularly to himself. Steele concludes his reflections on the misapplication of satires by quoting the fine speech of Jaques, which begins

> Why, who cries out on pride,
> That can therein tax any private party?[78]

Comparable to Steele's story of the boy with the 'pocky Bills' is a highly improbable anecdote related by Edward Moore in *The World*, No. 9:

'I am that unfortunate man, madam,' was the saying of a gentleman, who stopt and made a low bow to a lady in the park, as she was calling to her dog by the name of cuckold.

What a deal of good might be expected from these essays, if every man, who should happen to read his own character in them, would as honestly acknowledge it as this gentleman! But it is the misfortune of general satire, that few persons will apply it to themselves, while they have the comfort of thinking that it will fit others as well. It is therefore, I am afraid, only furnishing bad people with scandal against their neighbours: for every man flatters himself, that he has the art of playing the fool or knave so very secretly, that, though he sees plainly how all else are employed, no mortal can have the cunning to find out him.

Moore cites an instance to illustrate the point of his story: a reader has quite fallaciously identified a particular acquaintance of his in the third number of *The World*. In the passage quoted above, Moore repeats Swift's notion that general satire tends to

[78] *As You Like It*, II. vii.

be ineffective because few people apply it to themselves. Further
on, however, he emphasizes with heavy irony that objections can
be advanced against 'personal abuse' also:

If there are objections to general satire, something may also be
said against personal abuse; which, though it is a kind of writing that
requires a smaller portion of parts, and is sure of having almost as
many admirers as readers, is nevertheless subject to great difficulties;
it being absolutely necessary that the author who undertakes it
should have no feeling of certain evils, common to humanity, which
are known by the names of pain and shame. In other words, he must
be insensible to a good kicking, and have no memory of it afterwards.

Conversely, Addison, whose preoccupation was with the evils
of personal satire, expressed misgivings about general satire
also, notably in *The Spectator*, No. 209 (30 October 1711). His
misgivings are such as would be expected of one of the champions of the eighteenth-century 'sentimental' approach to human
nature. He fears the levelling effect of general satire, its tendency
to reduce all human beings, or at least all members of one sex
or species, to a uniformly low level. It is a satirist's duty to discriminate; and, in this respect, he considers Simonides has
satirized women better than Juvenal and Boileau have done:

As the Poet has shewn a great Penetration in this Diversity of
Female Characters, he has avoided the Fault which *Juvenal* and
Monsieur *Boileau* are guilty of, the former in his Sixth, and the other
in his last Satyr, where they have endeavoured to expose the Sex in
general, without doing Justice to the valuable Part of it. Such levelling Satyrs are of no use to the World, and for this reason I have
often wondered how the *French* Author above-mentioned, who
was a Man of exquisite Judgment, and a Lover of Virtue, could
think Human Nature a proper Subject for Satyr in another of his
celebrated Pieces, which is called *The Satyr upon Man*. What Vice
or Frailty can a Discourse correct, which censures the whole Species
alike, and endeavours to shew by some Superficial Strokes of Wit,
that Brutes are the more excellent Creatures of the two?

The Critical Review censured Churchill's *Prophecy of Famine*
(1763) for its indiscriminate satire: 'nor do we think, that indiscriminate satire on whole communities and bodies of men can
be attended with any other effect than the widening national
breaches, and fermenting divisions . . .'.[79] And Charles Abbott
deplored satires in which the whole of mankind is 'treated as a

[79] January 1763, p. 60.

single individual, and involved in general and undiscerning obloquy'. Such calumnies, he maintained, tend 'to contract alike the judgment and the affections, and thus to limit the influence not only of truth and reason, but also of benevolence and humanity'.[80]

The most telling indictment of general satire, however, is Pope's, in the second dialogue of the *Epilogue to the Satires*, where he browbeats his interlocutor into tacit admission that personal reference in satire is not only desirable, but actually inevitable. By making his verse bombastic Pope illustrates how vague and blunt satire becomes when it names categories instead of persons:

> Come on then Satire! gen'ral, unconfin'd,
> Spread thy broad wing, and sowze on all the Kind.
> Ye Statesmen, Priests, of one Religion all!
> Ye Tradesmen vile, in Army, Court, or Hall!
> Ye Rev'rend Atheists!

Writers and critics became increasingly aware, as the eighteenth century went on, of the hazards of all satire—general or particular. They felt that the greatest caution was needed in attempting it at all: the tightrope grew thinner and was placed higher and higher in the air—

> Nice is the Task, be gen'ral if you can,
> Or strike with Caution if you point the Man.[81]

[80] Abbott, *Oxford Prize Essays*, i. 198.
[81] Whitehead, *Essay on Ridicule*, p. 18.

8. Smiling versus Savage Satire

If then any thing will do, it must be *Satyr*, and we may if we observe, find in the dullest apprehensions a quicker resentment of a Jest than of an Argument, the one renders that ridiculous, which the other perhaps cannot make appear to be false, and *Satyrs* are like those *Indian* Apes, of whom I have read, that when *Alexander* came into those parts, They straight rally'd their deformed Squadrons, rank'd themselves in Battalia, camp'd and decamp'd with all the moving Solemnities of a real Army, and brought greater affronts upon that all-conquering Army with their Martial Grimaces, than all the force of *Darius* and *Parus*, I have made the Comparison, let some courteous Reader make out the Application.[1]

SINCE the Augustans considered that delight was the indispensable means through which satire acted, as did all poetry, their preference was for smiling rather than savage satire, for Horace rather than Juvenal, Menander rather than Aristophanes, and Terence rather than Plautus. They felt that smiling satire instructs and reforms more effectively than savage satire because it pleases more readily. It wins more friends and influences more people. As the author of the passage quoted above contends, with the help of his army of improbable monkeys, jesting works better than argument or exhortation, for to reason with fools and knaves is a waste of time. If there is anything which will penetrate dull minds it is smiling satire. The idea is one of the major commonplaces of the great age of English satire:

A Satyr's Smile is sharper than his Frown . . .[2]

there's a sweetness in good Verse, which Tickles even while it Hurts: And, no man can be heartily angry with him, who pleases him against his will.[3]

Of all the means of reform which the wisest men have been able

---

[1] Preface to *A Satyr Against Commonwealths*, [H.P.] (1684), sig. Bir.
[2] Mulgrave, *Essay upon Poetry*, p. 10.
[3] John Dryden, 'To the Reader', *Absalom and Achitophel*, Dryden's *Poems*, i. 215.

to discover, declares Mulgrave, well-written satire has proved the most successful. This is because it pleases as it corrects—it cures, because 'the remedy is lov'd'.[4] In *An Essay on Satyre* he observes that satirists have employed two different methods in the 'great work' of showing us our faults and teaching us to laugh at our 'vain Deeds and vainer Thoughts': first, that of censuring our follies sharply and severely; and second, that of 'laughing and scorning us into shame'. He has no doubts as to which has proved the superior method:

> But of these two, the last succeeded best,
> As men hit rightest, when they shoot in jest.[5]

According to Rapin, Horace expressed his censure 'only by the way of *jest* and merriment because he knew full well that the sporting of wit, hath more effect than the strongest reasons and the most sententious discourse, to render Vice *ridiculous*'.[6] Dryden challenges Barten Holyday's opinion that, as 'chastisement goes farther than admonition', Juvenal and Persius may be said to have changed satire for the better—that is, in following the Lucilian mode of savage satire instead of Horace's milder style. Dryden's quarrel is chiefly with Holyday's statement that 'a perpetual grin, like that of Horace, rather angers than amends a man'. Dryden feels that it does not do justice to the individual merits and uses of Horace's kind of satire: 'Let the chastisement of Juvenal be never so necessary for his new kind of satire, let him declaim as wittily and sharply as he pleases; yet still the nicest and most delicate touches of satire consist in fine raillery.'[7] In his essay on 'true Raillery and Satyr' in *The Tatler*, No. 242, Steele points out that pleasantry is indispensable in satire as a means of showing that the speaker, or author, bears no ill will. If the satire is angry and rude, it will be dismissed as an expression of personal malice and prejudice; but, if it is good-humoured, it will command the attention of readers and listeners, and triumph over adversaries, no matter how malicious they may be. In the words of Edward Young: '*laughing Satire* bids the fairest for success. The world is too proud to be fond of a serious Tutor: And when an Author is in a passion, the laugh,

---

[4] *Essay upon Poetry*, p. 9.
[5] *Works* (1723), i. 114.
[6] Rapin, p. 138.
[7] Dryden's *Essays*, ii. 92.

generally, as in conversation, turns against him.'[8] Elsewhere Young expressed a preference for Addison over Pope and Swift on the ground that Addison's milder satire cures more effectively and pleasantly than the harsh purgatives of Pope and Swift:

> But as good books are the medicine of the mind, if we should dethrone these authors, and consider them, not in their royal, but their medicinal capacity, might it not then be said, that *Addison* prescribed a wholesome and pleasant regimen, which was universally relished, and did much good; that *Pope* preferred a purgative of satire, which, tho' wholesome, was too painful in its operation; and that *Swift* insisted on a large dose of ipecacuanha, which, tho' readily swallowed from the fame of the physician, yet, if the patient had any delicacy of taste, he threw up the remedy, instead of the disease?[9]

Newbery emphasized that the 'Satyrist should always preserve good-humour, and however keen he cuts, should cut with kindness'. Like many other critics he considered that bad temper turns readers against the satirist: 'When he loses temper, his weapons will be inverted, and the ridicule he threw at others will retort with contempt on himself; for the Reader will perceive that he is angry and hurt, and consider his Satire as the effect of malice, not of judgment, and that it is intended rather to wound persons than reform manners.'[10] Cosmetti stated that 'Satyr should give but gentle touches, and should be free, loose and delicate', for if it be written only with 'the pen of animosity and revenge, dipped in gall' it will have only a temporary effect.[11] The same recommendation was succinctly expressed by Gentleman:

> Let us correct, but not with Whips of Steel,
> Feathers more winningly instruct to feel.[12]

In theory at least, the Augustan satirists were anxious to avoid giving offence and to make their writings thoroughly agreeable to their readers, including even their victims—'and he, for whom it was intended, was too witty to resent it as an injury...the jest went round, and he was laught at in his turn who began the frolic.'[13]

---

[8] Preface to *Love of Fame*, sig. A4r.
[9] *Conjectures on Original Composition*, pp. 97–8.
[10] *The Art of Poetry on a New Plan*, ii. 136.
[11] *The Polite Arts. Dedicated to the Ladies* (1767), p. 45.
[12] *The General* (1764), p. 11.
[13] Dryden's *Essays*, ii. 93–4.

The skill was in making a malefactor 'die sweetly', in making a foray, no matter how bloody and fatal its effects might really be, appear an errand of mercy. The weapon of the satirist should glitter in the eyes of its victims, so that they feel compelled to acknowledge themselves 'not butchered . . . but fairly slain':

If the pleasure arising from comedy and satire be either laughter, or some nobler sort of delight, which is above it, no man is so great a master of irony as [Lucian]. That figure is not only a keen, but a shining weapon in his hand; it glitters in the eyes of those it kills; his own gods, his greatest enemies, are not butchered by him, but fairly slain: they must acknowledge the hero in the stroke, and take the comfort which Virgil gives to a dying captain:

> Æneæ magni dextrâ cadis.[14]

Dryden presents his satirist as a light-hearted fellow, a sort of magician who can cut off a man's head and miraculously 'leave it standing in its place'. It was principally a justifiable pride in his own skill and tact that made Dryden so fond of the portrait of Zimri. Only these qualities, he felt, made the personal satire on Buckingham permissible. The satirist must preserve at least the appearance of good temper and good nature—like 'crafty Horace' he must be capable of 'looking his friend in the face while laughing at him'.[15] Salt needs to go into the mixture—Dryden indicates plainly enough in his comments on Juvenal that he considers satire insipid without it—but there must not be any gall.

There is more of salt in all your [Dorset's] verses, than I have seen in any of the Moderns, or even of the Ancients; but you have been sparing of the gall, by which means you have pleased all readers, and offended none.[16]

Similarly, Prior comments in his Dedication of Dorset's *Miscellanies* (1708) that for all the severity of Dorset's satire 'the Gentleman had always so much the better of the Satyrist, that the Persons touched did not know where to fix their Resentments; and were forced to appear rather Ashamed than Angry.'[17]

---

[14] Dryden, *The Life of Lucian* (1711), *Works*, xviii. 73; cf. *The Art of Railing at Great Men: Being a Discourse upon Political Railers, Ancient and Modern*, Anon. (1723), p. iv: 'The great Secret therefore of *Political Railing* is to inveigh without nauseating, and to grumble securely in Defiance of the Secular Arm; which is the Mystery into which I would initiate our modern Authors and political Declaimers.'

[15] See Dryden's translation of Persius, Satire i, in *Works*, xiii. 215.

[16] Dryden's *Essays*, ii. 19.

[17] *Works*, edd. Wright and Spears, i. 250.

Prior believed, however, that such skill and tact as Dorset displayed was exceedingly rare. In *Heads for a Treatise upon Learning* he says that he can recall only one man who practised this art of raillery to perfection:

> I knew one Man, and never but one who had this Talent of Railary in so particular a manner that while he said things severe enough, he rather surprised than hurt the Person, he assailed and brought himself always off so with the Mention of some greater Merit to compensate the Foible he attacked in the same Person, that by a Turn imperceptible his Satyrs slid into Panygeric, which appeared the finer as it seemed less meant; but this is a perfection so hard to attain, and a thing so clumsey if a Man aimes at and misses it, that it is safer and better not to attempt it.[18]

Swift states in his Apology for *A Tale of a Tub* (1710) that any work is the better for having wit and humour, for with these admirable qualities it will offend no one:

> As Wit is the noblest and most useful Gift of humane Nature, so Humor is the most agreeable, and where these two enter far into the Composition of any Work, they will render it always acceptable to the World.[19]

And Pope writes of *The Rape of the Lock*:

> This whimsical piece of work, as I have now brought it up to my first design, is at once the most a satire, and the most inoffensive, of anything of mine. People who would rather it were let alone laugh at it, and seem heartily merry, at the same time that they are uneasy. 'Tis a sort of writing very like tickling.[20]

Pope adds that he is vain enough to believe that the poem gives a pretty complete picture of the life of our modern ladies in this idle town from which his correspondent has 'so happily, so prudently and so philosophically retired', which is to claim that the poem succeeded in being perfectly truthful and yet hurting no one—a singular achievement had it been true. Pope was writing early in his career (1713/14) and gilding the lily into the bargain (*The Rape of the Lock* in fact offended a number of people[21]); nevertheless one should note carefully his linking of the phrases, 'the most inoffensive' and 'the most a satire'. What would have been a contradiction to Hall and Marston and their successors

---

[18] *Works*, edd. Wright and Spears, i. 585.   [19] Swift's *Prose Works*, i. 10.
[20] Pope to Mrs. or Miss Marriott, 28 February [1713/14], Pope's *Correspondence*, i. 211.
[21] See Pope's *Poems*, ii. 88–94; and cf. Spence, *Anecdotes*, ed. Singer, p. 195.

was merely a paradox to the Augustans, for in addition to preferring smiling to savage satire because it is more effective and more
charitable, they preferred it also because it demands a far higher
degree of skill in the writer:

Thus it requires no very shining Abilities to inform our Neighbour of his Oddities, and point out to him his slight Indiscretions;
but to open his Eyes, and let in the Light without rendering it
painful to him; to give a Sense of the Error, without disturbing the
natural Complacence, with which every one is willing to behold
himself, is a Task which requires more Elegance and Refinement
than happens to fall to the Share of every Individual.[22]

This was the new ideal of satire—or rather the old Horatian ideal
of *utile dulci* in new words—and it was propounded not only by
the essayists, Addison and Steele, and by playwrights from
Congreve to Sheridan, but also by practically every satirical poet
and critic of satire from Dryden to Johnson. It is fundamental to
Dryden's *Discourse:* indeed, the principal reason the *Discourse*
is such a landmark in the history of English satire is that it states
authoritatively, for the first time in English, the neo-classic ideal
of satire as mocking rather than abusive, and artful, oblique, and
gentle rather than blunt and punitive. Dryden, however, had
made his preference plain a decade before he wrote the *Discourse.*
In the preface to *Absalom and Achitophel,* he claims he has
written much less severely than he easily might have done, with
the object of pleasing the moderate sort of men:

And, I confess, I have laid in for those, by rebating the *Satyre,*
(where Justice woud allow it) from carrying too sharp an Edge.
They, who can Criticize so weakly, as to imagine I have done my
Worst, may be Convinc'd, at their own Cost, that I can write
Severely, with more ease, than I can Gently. I have but laught at
some mens Follies, when I coud have declaim'd against their Vices;
and, other mens Vertues I have commended, as freely as I have tax'd
their Crimes.[23]

The same sort of claim is made by satirists throughout the
period: they have written for virtuous, and candid readers, for
reasonable men with a sense of justice; they have attacked follies,
not vices and serious crimes; they have studiously avoided giving
offence; they have eschewed personal reflections; they have

---

[22] [Arthur Murphy], *Gray's Inn Journal*, No. 26.
[23] Dryden's *Poems*, i. 215.

sought to reform people without hurting them; and so on. Cambridge, for example, after giving a long and tedious account of his *Scribleriad*, boasts that he has no scruples about putting his name to the work:

> . . . I flatter myself I have shewn throughout my Book that the Follies of Mankind provoke my Laughter and not my Spleen; and so long as they have this effect on me, I cannot have any great quarrel against them. It may plainly be perceiv'd that I have industriously kept clear of much strong satire which naturally presented itself in a work of this nature . . .[24]

How absurd it is after all, Steele argues, to be 'sharp and biting'. The first goal of any writer, as for that matter of any member of society, should be to gain the goodwill of his readers. A man, who has only courage, is 'in a very ill way towards making an agreeable figure in the World', because courage by itself merely makes enemies.

> Your Gentleman of a Satyrical Vein is in the like Condition. To say a thing which perplexes the Heart of him you speak to, or brings blushes into his Face, is a degree of Murder; and it is, I think, an unpardonable Offence to shew a Man you do not care, whether he is pleased or displeased.[25]

We have seen so far that Horatian satire was recommended by the Augustans, in preference to Juvenalian satire, because it is good for the reader. It pleases him and, provided it is sufficiently subtle, may insensibly reform him, too. Some critics pointed out that smiling satire is better for the writer also; or, rather, that a predilection for savage satire may simply indicate ill nature in the writer. So Steele in *The Spectator*, No. 422 (4 July 1712), reproves the satirist who feels ill will towards others; he does not merely advocate the practical advantages of a pleasing manner in order to create a good impression. In his opinion, as he makes clear in the passage quoted above, to hurt a person's feelings is to do him mortal injury; joking is all very well, but it must truly be joking—it is no joke to be publicly humiliated. He proceeds to give examples. There is Callisthenes, 'who rallies the best of any Man', because he chooses as the object of his ridicule an excess of some quality that is in itself laudable. Then there is Acetus, who is 'more generally admired than *Callisthenes*, but not with

---

[24] Preface to *The Scribleriad* (1752), p. xvi.
[25] *The Spectator*, No. 422, 4 July 1712.

Justice', for he has no regard to the modesty or weakness of the person he rallies. He shows no mercy. 'He can be pleased to see his best Friend out of Countenance, while the Laugh is loud in his own Applause.' Besides, his influence, unlike that of Callisthenes, is socially disruptive: 'His Raillery always puts the Company into little Divisions and separate Interests, while that of *Callisthenes* cements it, and makes every Man not only better pleased with himself, but also with all the rest in the Conversation.' Another vicious character is Actius, who deserves to be banished from 'humane Society', because he raises a laugh by hurting someone, which is to say he gains the reputation of a wit by trading on the ill nature of the company. Minutius, on the other hand, is a kindly person and always suggests that he is guilty of the same imperfection he ridicules. In summing up, Steele observes that it is monstrous the lengths to which men, even 'Men of Distinction', go to displease one another, as though contending to see who can be the most disagreeable. Those people whom Steele most admires, 'They who have the true Taste of Conversation, enjoy themselves in a Communication of each others Excellencies, and not in a Triumph over their Imperfections.' William Combe says that he has 'ever considered severe satire as rather a proof of a discontented mind, than, as it is generally termed, a work for the good of the human race'. He then goes on to counter one of the common arguments advanced in favour of the sterner kind of satire:

But it will be argued, that he who scourges vice, certainly shows a rectitude of disposition and morals, in the highest degree commendable. It may be so; but in my opinion much depends on the manner in which it is delivered. The man who seeks to disturb my rest with the basest abuse, and threatens every vengeance that malice can invent, may be my friend; but I take his friendship to be of infinite more value, who by amicable expostulation endeavours to reform my conduct, than his, who strives to terrify me into repentance. The good effects of the one's advice are permanent, of the other's momentary.

> 'Ease would recant
> Vows made in pain, as violent, and void.'
> Milton.[26]

In its capacity to win the reader over, to delight even as it corrected, and to communicate goodwill and good-humour,

[26] Preface to *The Refutation* (1778), pp. 5–6.

Horatian satire was bound to endear itself increasingly to men of the eighteenth century. But of course these were not their only reasons for preferring it to satire of the Juvenalian kind. They admired it for its intrinsic qualities and not only for its effects. It was principally Horace's delicacy, for instance, that impelled Rapin to place Horace above Juvenal as a satirist. For, while it is true that Rapin said Horace's style was chosen for its superior effectiveness—as compared with a 'violent manner of declamation' or 'sententious discourse'—he clearly admires delicacy for its own sake, as something in the work itself, that is to say an artistic quality. So he talks of 'this *delicacy* which properly gives the relish to *Satyr* . . .', and he observes that '*Satyr* [which] takes off the mask, and reprehends Vice too openly, is not very delicate . . .'[27] The same admiration of delicacy and subtlety, as positive qualities in themselves, is the informing spirit of the major part of Dryden's commentary on satirical method in the *Discourse*, as well as of his comments on individual satirists. On Donne and Horace, for example:

Would not Donne's *Satires*, which abound with so much wit, appear more charming, if he had taken care of his words, and of his numbers?[28]

. . . [Horace] had found out the skill of Virgil, to hide his sentences; to give you the virtue of them, without showing them in their full extent: which is the ostentation of a poet, and not his art . . .[29]

It is the art that counts. In the classical tradition of satire hell is chaos, where dullness presides and the dunces declaim their works eternally, and where the devil is *par excellence* the bad writer—Lucilius composing two hundred lines while standing on one leg, Flecknoe still declaiming as he falls through space, his drugget robe, 'Born upwards by a subterranean wind', or Southey throwing the angels into pandemonium by reciting his own poems. The love of order and harmony, and their attendant qualities of clarity, delicacy, subtlety, finesse, and poise, wins for Boileau and Pope the authority to spurn bad writing and chastize bad writers. Without it *Le Lutrin* and *The Dunciad* could be dismissed as essentially trivial. In the major Augustan literary works the literary standards of classicism are elevated into social

---

[27] *Rapin*, pp. 137–8.
[28] Dryden's *Essays*, ii. 102.
[29] Ibid. 83.

and moral values. Perhaps this is to say no more than that eighteenth-century literature, like the literature of any period, was the mirror of its times; yet it is worth stressing that the relationship between life and letters, between the arts of 'conversation' and literature, was peculiarly intimate in the eighteenth century. A man of letters was expected to be, ideally, also a gentleman; and vice versa. Consequently, literary and social values may be mingled in a passage of Augustan literary criticism, or a literary work may be described as though it is a social activity. Steele, in his essay on true and false notions of raillery in *The Spectator*, No. 422, specifically equates the good satirist with the good companion: the good satirist (the good writer, for that matter) makes the reader better pleased with himself, as the good companion makes those about him happier. And Thomas Sprat, in praising Cowley's imitations of Horace, clearly associates Horatian satire with gentlemanly conduct and deportment:

I know some Men disapprove it, because the Verse seems to be loose, and near to the plainness of common Discourse. But that which was admir'd by the Court of *Augustus*, never ought to be esteem'd flat, or vulgar. And the same judgment should be made of Mens styles, as of their behaviour, and carriage: wherein that is most courtly, and hardest to be imitated, which consists of a Natural easiness, and unaffected Grace, where nothing seems to be studied, yet every thing is extraordinary.[30]

Similarly Dryden could be describing almost any aristocratic quality, and not necessarily 'fine raillery', in the following sentences:

'Tis not reading, 'tis not imitation of an author, which can produce this fineness; it must be inborn; it must proceed from a genius, and particular way of thinking, which is not to be taught; and therefore not to be imitated by him who has it not from nature . . .[31]

In literature, as in language and learning, and the conduct of life, the men of Sprat's and Dryden's times, and their successors, were determinedly turning their backs on a barbarous past. They were simplifying language, ordering knowledge, refining literature, making politics scientific and philosophy rational, and

[30] 'Life of Cowley', *Works* (1668), sig. d Ir.
[31] Dryden's *Essays*, ii. 92.

generally civilizing mankind in accordance with the laws of nature and reason. At least, that is how they saw themselves. They felt that even the best of earlier English literature needed to be refined, that even Chaucer and Shakespeare, for all their natural talents, lacked discrimination and taste. It is not at all surprising, then, that they should have turned to Horace as their model, rather than to Juvenal or Persius, or their own English predecessors. However much Horatian satire may have contrasted with their often savage literary practice and the sordid political and social realities of their times, it clearly represented to men of the late seventeenth and eighteenth centuries the kind of satire which they could confidently approve and which they would have liked to live by.

As to English satire of the late sixteenth and early seventeenth centuries, it could be (and in effect *was* by Dryden's essay) swept under the carpet. It was uncouth and barbarous—the antithesis of Horatian. For Hall, Marston, Rowlands, Goddard, and their contemporaries, the phrase, 'smiling satire', was a contradiction in terms—

> . . . in sooth 'tis not my liste
> To make thee laughe; for I'm a Satyrist.[32]

The satirist, in the Elizabethan and Jacobean view, was a malcontent, born under Saturn, calling down on his enemy the 'rotten diseases of the South'. His characteristic manner was violent, rough, explosive:

> Curio, know'st me? why thou bottle-ale,
> Thou barmy froth! O stay me, least I raile
> Beyond Nil ultra . . .[33]

He is liable to take the reader, as well as his victims, by the throat. His chosen weapons are whips, cats-o'-nine-tails, cauterizing irons, bundles of rods, steel flails, knotted ropes, leather thongs, surgeon's scalpels, and strong purgatives and cathartics. His pen may be a knife to cut deep into the patient's body and remove the infected part, or a cloven hoof to drip black aconite or burning copperas on to the victim's skin.[34] Altogether he was

---

[32] William Goddard, A Satyricall Dialogue (Dort?, 1616?), Sig. D2r.

[33] John Marston, The Scourge of Villanie (1598), Satyre vi, lines 1–3.

[34] See M. C. Randolph, 'The Medical Concept in English Renaissance Satiric Theory, SP xxxviii (1941), 125–57.

hardly the type to appeal to men who prided themselves on their refinement. The contrast between the early seventeenth- and early eighteenth-century images of the satirist is startling indeed: a barber-surgeon or torturer-executioner on the one hand, and, on the other, the man of virtue and good sense. The one uses the crude language of plagues and poisons, of hideous diseases and racking tortures, whereas the other employs a milder, more philosophical vocabulary, and retains his poise even when his subject is evil and disgusting—'Yet let me flap this Bug with gilded wings . . .'. The object of his satire is not the body but the mind, the ruling passion instead of the canker in the flesh; and his favourite weapon is not a scourge or a scalpel, but ridicule— 'The best, and indeed the only method to expose vice and folly effectually, is to turn them to ridicule . . .'[35]

Yet one needs to guard against the implication that the change from one sort of satirical writing to the other was sudden and complete. Oldham was respected, though admittedly with reservations, not only immediately after the publication of *Satires on the Jesuits* in 1679, but well into the eighteenth century. 'His satires', stated Giles Jacob in *The Poetical Register* (1720), 'are some of the severest and best, in the English language, tho' sometimes he has taken great liberties . . .'[36] And Oldham stood for savage satire:

> Had I some tame and sneaking author been,
> Whose Muse to love and softness did incline,
> Some small adventurer in song, that whines
> *Chloris* and *Phillis* out in charming lines . . .
>
> Perhaps I might have then forgiven thee,
> And thou had'st 'scaped from my resentments free.
> But I whom spleen and manly rage inspire,
> Brook no affront, at each offence take fire:
> Born to chastise the vices of the age,
> Which pulpits dare not, nor the very stage . . .[37]

Nevertheless, he was a representative of the kind of satire which was going out of favour. Rochester is more to our purpose here, for he was accepted by neo-classical critics and, furthermore, he

---

[35] Newbery, *The Art of Poetry on a New Plan*, ii. 136.
[36] Quoted in *The Poems of John Oldham*, ed. Bonamy Dobrée (1960), p. 1.
[37] Ibid., p. 7.

was held to be superior to Oldham principally on the grounds of his greater delicacy and polish:

> Oldham, écrivit d'une maniere três forte & três severe. *Rochester,* fut plus clairvoyant sur les caractéres des hommes; it eût une force plus penetrante et plus polië.[38]

> Oldham is a very undelicate writer. He has strong rage, but 'tis too much like Billingsgate. Lord Rochester has much more delicacy and more knowledge of mankind.[39]

From these summary comments two inferences may be drawn concerning the Augustan attitude to satire: first, that 'smiling' satire could have much more sting than we might suppose if we take the name too literally; and second, that 'smiling' along with such epithets as 'fine', 'sharp', 'delicate', 'urbane', and 'well-bred', frequently referred to manner alone. After all, Rochester's satire at its finest is fierce and searing—

> Bursting with *Pride,* the loath'd *Imposthume* swells,
> *Prick* him, he sheds his *Venom* strait, and smells;

We have only to read 'My Lord All-Pride', which opens with the lines just quoted (they are by no means the strongest in the poem), to compare *A Satire against Mankind* with Boileau's Satire VIII, which it superficially resembles, or (more significantly) to contrast *An Allusion to Horace* with Horace's *Satires,* I. x, which it professes to 'imitate', in order to appreciate that 'smiling' and 'Horatian' must be interpreted rather freely. They signify a critical ideal rather than the real achievement. But the paradox is that the real achievement was greater than the ideal would have allowed it to be; for it is apparent to us now, at this remove of a couple of centuries, that it is just those under-currents of indignation and disorder in English satire of the late seventeenth and eighteenth centuries—in Dryden, Swift, Pope, Johnson, and Churchill, as well as in Rochester—which constitute the prime source of its power.

For that reason, Dryden's vacillations and inconsistencies regarding the respective merits of Horace and Juvenal, which at first glance might seem at odds with Augustan critical opinion, were in fact entirely representative of the period—that is, the

---

[38] Joseph Spence, 'Quelques remarques hist. sur les poètes anglois' (about 1732–3), quoted in *Pope and His Contemporaries: Essays presented to George Sherburn* (Oxford, 1949), p. 248.

[39] Spence's *Anecdotes,* ed. Osborn, i. 202.

period from Dryden to Johnson, not merely that of Dryden himself. Simply through being in two minds about the merits of Horace and Juvenal, Dryden was reflecting his times, and once again demonstrating his ability to draw together the threads of contemporary opinion and present them as a unified point of view. It was not simply that he was writing early in the period, before Horace had come into his own as the model Augustan satirist, though that had something to do with it: it was also that, as a critic, he was exceptionally sensitive and comprehensive.

The doctrinaire neo-classicist unhesitatingly preferred Horace. Rapin, for instance, after commending Horace's delicacy and merriment, states that Juvenal has little effect because he is always angry, and so cannot write objectively. Furthermore, his morality appeals only to the weaker-minded because it is trite, his rhetoric is ineffectual because it contains 'nothing that is *delicate*, or that is natural' and his motives are suspect in that he appears to write from 'a spirit of vanity and ostentation' and not out of a 'true zeal' for morality.

For indeed that violent manner of declamation which throughout he makes use of, has, most commonly, but very little effect, he scarce persuades at all; because he is alwayes in *choler*, and never speaks in *cold blood*. 'Tis true, he has some *common places* of Morality that may serve to dazzle the weaker sort of apprehension. But with all his strong expressions, *energetick* terms, and great flashes of eloquence, he makes little impression; because he has nothing that is *delicate*, or that is *natural*. It is not a true zeal that makes him talk against the misdemeanors of his Age, 'tis a *spirit* of vanity and ostentation.[40]

Those who insisted that satire should be good-humoured, and that it should ridicule follies rather than vices, naturally leaned towards Horace. So Swift writes in his vindication of Gay:

[Humour] is certainly the best Ingredient towards that Kind of Satyr, which is most useful, and gives the least Offence; which instead of lashing, laughs Men out of their Follies, and Vices, and is the Character which gives *Horace* the Preference to *Juvenal*.[41]

Young praised Horace for appearing to be 'in good humour while he censures', for as a result 'his censure has the more weight, as

[40] Rapin, p. 138.
[41] *The Intelligencer*, No. 3.

supposed to proceed from Judgment, not from Passion'. By con-
trast, '*Juvenal* is ever in a passion; he has little valuable but his
Eloquence, and Morality.' Young goes on to say that he imitated
Juvenal's manner to some extent in his own sixth satire, but
gave it up before long 'as disagreeable to the Writer, and Reader
too'.[42] According to Walpole 'the graces and delicate ironies of
Horace have always found ten Readers for One that frowns with
Juvenal.'[43] 'I find that the generality of critics', wrote James
Beattie, 'are all for the moderation and smiling graces of the
courtly Horace, and exclaim against the vehemence and vindic-
tive zeal of the unmannerly Juvenal.'[44]

Beattie was writing towards the end of the eighteenth century.
Before then the majority of critics were wary of committing
themselves completely to a preference for Horace. They were
inclined rather to argue that certain subjects and times are suitable for Juvenalian as others for Horatian treatment—as Dryden
puts it in his *Life of Lucian*: 'Some diseases are curable by leni-
tives; to others corrosives are necessary.'[45] In the *Epistle to
Henry Higden, Esq.*, Dryden observes that Horace lived in an
age 'Not Bad enough to need an Author's Rage', whereas
Juvenal,

> ... who liv'd in more degen'rate Times,
> Was forc'd to fasten Deep, and woorry Crimes:[46]

In his essay on raillery in *The Tatler*, No. 242, Steele is careful to
recommend both Juvenal and Horace to the young blades of the
town: he points out that each was the right satirist for his times,
and each contributes to a fuller understanding of the nature of
satire and raillery. The most carefully worked-out statement to
the effect that Horace's and Juvenal's satires are of distinguish-
able and equally legitimate kinds was made by Dennis. He
argues that Horatian satire tends towards comedy and Juvenalian
towards tragedy, and that both kinds may be appreciated equally
but by different types of people:

Will not the Tragick Satire, which like Tragedy fetches its Notions
from Philosophy and from common Sense, be in all probability more

[42] Preface to *Love of Fame*, sig. A4r–v.
[43] Introduction to William Mason's *Satirical Poems* (Oxford, 1926), p. 32.
[44] *Essays* (1776), p. 427.
[45] Dryden's *Works*, xviii. 70.
[46] Dryden's *Poems*, i. 351.

acceptable to Universities and Cloisters, and all those Recluse and
Contemplative Men, who pass most of their time in their Closets, all
which Persons are suppos'd to have Philosophy from Study, and Common Sense from Nature? And will not the Comick Satirist, who owes
no small Part of his Excellence to his Experience, that is to the Knowledge of the Conversation and Manners of the Men of the World, be
in all likelihood more agreeable to the discerning Part of a Court,
and a great Capital, where they are qualify'd to taste and discern his
Beauties, by the same Experience which enabled their Authors to
produce them? And above all things, must it not be most agreeable
to a Polite Court, where that dexterous Insinuation, that fine good
Sense, and that true Pleasantry, which are united in the *Horatian*
Satire, are the only shining Qualities which make the Courtier
valuable and agreeable? And will he not take more delight in the
Horatian Satire than in the Tragick Eloquence of *Juvenal*, not only
because he is qualified by Nature and Experience to relish the
Beauties of it, but because the Pleasure which he receives from it,
is subservient to his Interest, which is always his main Design, and
Improves and Cultivates those Talents which are chiefly to
recommend him to those who are to advance him?[47]

William King pointed out that both smiling and savage satire
are necessary for 'although little Vices may be laughed at, yet
enormous Crimes demand a Scourge'.[48] Even Young, although
he preferred Horace to Juvenal, admitted that the term 'satire'
is not 'inapplicable to graver compositions', in that 'Ethics,
Heathen and Christian, and the Scriptures themselves, are, in a
great measure, a satire on the weakness and iniquity of man'.[49]
Trapp was most insistent that there are two quite distinct and
equally legitimate kinds of satire, one of which was brought to
perfection by Horace, and the other by Juvenal.

   They both agree in being pungent and cutting; yet are distinguish'd by very evident Marks: The one is pleasant and facetious;
the other angry and austere: The one smiles; the other storms: The
Foibles of Mankind are the Object of the one; greater Crimes, of the
other: The former is always in the low Style; the latter generally in
the Sublime: That abounds with Wit only; this adds to the Salt
Bitterness and Acrimony. *Horace*'s Satires are of so fine and delicate
a Turn, as may much easier be conceiv'd, than express'd: They are
rightly term'd *Discourses*, for some of them are scarce reducible

[47] *Critical Works*, ed. Hooker, ii. 219–20.
[48] 'Translator's Preface' to *The Toast*, p. xxxvii.
[49] Preface to *Love of Fame*, sigs. A2v–A3r.

under either Species of Satire. *Juvenal's* are all true Satires, except the fifteenth, which is of uncertain Authority. So far is *Vossius* from being in the right, when he makes *Horace* almost the only Satirist, and scarce admits *Juvenal* to the Title of one.[50]

Trapp attacks Vossius for his failure to appreciate Juvenalian satire. Vossius, he says, would have it that the Horatian is the only genuine satire, whereas,

> Satire in *general*, is a Poem design'd to reprove the Vices and Follies of Mankind: It is twofold; either the *jocose*, as that of *Horace*; or the *serious*, like that of *Juvenal*. The former hidden, the latter open. That generally makes Sport with Vice, and exposes it to Ridicule: This probes it to the Bottom, and puts it to Torture: And so far is it from not deserving the Title of Satire, that, in my Opinion, it is the more noble Species of it; and the genteel Jokes of *Horace*, how ingenious soever, are less affecting than the poetic Rage, and commendable Zeal of *Juvenal*.[51]

Unlike many of his contemporaries, Trapp does not balk at the cruelty and malice which he finds in Juvenal. These qualities, he implies, are as essential to Juvenal's kind of satire as are amiability and urbanity to Horace's.[52] Nor does Trapp agree with Vossius that the satirist should restrict himself to colloquial diction. It would be equally absurd, he thinks, to insist that all drama be prosaic and humdrum, and then to disparage Sophocles for departing from this rule. In his praise of Juvenal's style, Trapp in effect pleads, as had Milton and Dryden before him, for satire that 'strikes high and adventures dangerously',[53] that follows the 'majestic way of Persius and Juvenal'. Dryden made the same points as Trapp in protesting against the narrowness of Heinsius's definition of Satire:

> But how come lowness of style, and the familiarity of words to be so much the propriety of satire, that without them a poet can be no more a satirist, than without risibility he can be a man? Is the fault of Horace to be made the virtue and standing rule of this poem? Is the *grande sophos* of Persius, and the sublimity of Juvenal to be circumscribed with the meanness of words and vulgarity of expression? If Horace refused the pains of numbers, and the loftiness of

---

[50] Trapp, p. 232.

[51] Ibid., p. 227.

[52] Ibid., p. 228.

[53] 'Apology against a Pamphlet', *Complete Prose Works of John Milton* (New Haven, 1953), i. 916.

figures, are they bound to follow so ill a precedent? Let him walk afoot, with his pad in his hand, for his own pleasure; but let not them be accounted no poets, who choose to mount, and show their horsemanship.[54]

It is important to realize that Juvenal held his own in the Augustan age, even though Horace was regarded as the more congenial of the two, and the more relevant to the age. Dryden's translation—widely respected as the finest of English verse translations—helped to keep Juvenal's reputation high; and imitations and new translations continued to appear throughout the century.[55] Some critics—a minority, it is true—continued to admire the superior moral force of Juvenal, to feel with the anonymous author of *Mirth in Ridicule: or, A Satyr against Immoderate Laughing* (1708) that 'Horace touch'd the Crimes he ridicul'd, with too gentle a Hand, and only laugh'd at Vices which requir'd the boldest Strokes of Censure and Reprehention.'[56] Moreover, with Johnson's *London* and *The Vanity of Human Wishes* ringing in one's ears, one would not dare suggest that Juvenal ceased to be a force in satire in the eighteeenth century. Yet a change of attitude can be detected: Juvenal continued to be admired, but from a safer distance. 'Juvenalian' came to mean 'severe' rather than 'savage'—as applied to Churchill, for instance. In translations and imitations, Juvenal's *sæva indignatio* was made to sound more august, less specific. In Dryden's translation, for example, the voice is still close to us, that of a commentator excited by an actual scene, caught up in the stream of events; whereas in Johnson's *The Vanity of Human Wishes*, though the voice is amplified to an impressive loudness, as befits the voice of the Preacher, it is heard from afar. There was also some bowdlerizing, in one case at least with unintentionally amusing results. In a version of Juvenal's sixth satire, Edward Burnaby Greene criticizes women not for major vices but for such slight failings as liking Italian music and preferring Barry to Garrick as a stage lover.

---

[54] Dryden's *Essays*, ii. 101.

[55] Dryden's translation was reprinted in 1697, 1702, 1711, 1713, and 1726; and other translations were made by Thomas Sheridan (1739), John Stirling (1760), Edward Owen (1785), and Martin Madan (1789). Wordsworth tried his hand at translating Juvenal in his version of Satire viii (1795). See also R. C. Whitford, 'Juvenal in England, 1750–1802', *PQ* vii (1928), 9–16.

[56] Sig. A2r.

It is difficult in a general account to avoid drawing too sharp contrasts, say, between pairs of satirists like Dryden and Johnson, or between two periods such as Dryden's age and Pope's, or the first and second halves of the eighteenth century. It may be more misleading than helpful, for example, to label Pope's satire 'Horatian', or Churchill's 'Juvenalian', or to say that Dryden, symbolizing his times, was close to Juvenal, while Pope and his contemporaries found Horace a kindred spirit.[57] Churchill rails no doubt but, as has already been suggested, he lacks the immediacy of Juvenal. Pope frequently writes in the Horatian manner and with equally high polish—and, of course, he 'imitated' certain of Horace's poems—but his satire is often more devastating than Horace's. So, after a first reading, one might easily describe his *Epistle to a Lady* as Horatian; on reflection, however, one is likely to adjudge the portrait of Atossa, and the ten lines beginning, 'As Hags hold Sabbaths . . .', not to mention the couplets on Sappho, much closer in spirit to Juvenal than to Horace. With Dryden, distinctions and differences are even harder to determine. *The Medall* is too harsh to conform to his ideal of 'fine raillery'; his satire in *Absalom and Achitophel* is too public and too political to be described as Horatian; and, in his Juvenal translation, he lovingly elaborates some of the more lurid passages—of Satire vi, for example. At the same time, however, it must be remembered that he wrote *Mac Flecknoe* as well as *The Medall*, and that he created Zimri in addition to recreating Messalina. Moreover, though in the *Discourse* he eventually places Horace second to Juvenal as a satirist, we cannot but be amazed at the closeness of the finish.[58]

Inconsistencies of theory in the Augustan age are less numerous than those between theory and practice. In the free-for-all of controversy, political and personal, in the late seventeenth and eighteenth centuries (as has been sufficiently demonstrated in earlier chapters), satirists frequently neglected to don the mask of Horace and swore and spat at each other with abandon. The discrepancy between theory and practice is apparent, too, at higher levels. Thus Swift in theory upheld the Horatian ideal of

---

[57] E. N. Hooker generalizes to this effect in 'Humour in the Age of Pope', *ELH* xi (1948), 367.

[58] For additional comments on eighteenth-century attitudes to Horace and Juvenal, see Jack, *Augustan Satire*, pp. 136–8.

smiling satire, but in practice sometimes put it behind him. In *Cadenus and Vanessa*[59] he advises those who use ridicule to make it perfectly clear that they are joking; in *Verses on the Death of Dr. Swift*[60] he refers to his 'own hum'rous biting way'; in the Apology for *A Tale of a Tub* he makes light of his satire, implying that its humour and wit should ensure that it hurts no one; and in *The Intelligencer*, No. 3, he explicitly states that humour is necessary for satire and that, therefore, Horace is to be preferred to Juvenal. In actual practice, however, Swift was far from being always humorous and inoffensive. 'Swift's intensities are those of negation and rejection'[61] although the severer side of Swift's satire, reflected in this opinion of Dr. Leavis's, is currently being played down by critics, and the lighter side—Swift's exuberance and gaiety—is being emphasized instead,[62] it none the less must be admitted that Swift's satire in *A Tale of a Tub* and book iv of *Gulliver's Travels* is profoundly disturbing in a way that the kind of satire he advocated in his critical writings would never be.

It should be noted also that not all theoretical expressions of opinion on satire in the period call for smiling satire. Just as there were critics, such as Fielding and Goldsmith, who attacked sentimental comedy, so too there were those who protested when satire became anaemic. Dryden, at one point in his *Discourse*, makes it perfectly plain that he does not want mere urbanity in satire. Horace's wit is inclined to be faint, he feels—in Scaliger's words—that '[Horace] only shows his white teeth'. Should there be any doubts as to his demand for fire and strength in satire, they are banished by the eloquent passage which follows on Juvenal's 'more vigorous and masculine wit'.[63] The most thoroughgoing answer to a sentimental approach to satire is given, however, by John Brown in, for example, his description of the harsher operations of satire:

> Well may they dread the Muse's fatal skill;
> Well may they tremble when she draws her quill:
> Her magick quill, that like Ithuriel's spear
> Displays the cloven hoof, or lengthen'd ear;

[59] Swift's *Poems*, ii. 707, lines 664–6.
[60] Ibid., 555, line 54.
[61] F. R. Leavis, 'The Irony of Swift', *Scrutiny*, ii (1934), 371.
[62] See Milton Voigt, *Swift and the Twentieth Century* (Detroit, 1964), p. 123.
[63] Dryden's *Essays*, ii. 84.

> Bids vice and folly take unborrow'd shapes,
> Turns Duchesses to strumpets, beaux to apes,
> Drags the vile whisperer from his dark abode,
> Till all the daemon starts up from the toad.[64]

Later in the *Essay on Satire*, Brown pictures satire in its role of guardian to the state as an Old Testament god of wrath, making the skies grow dark and the mountains tremble, and firing thunderbolts on the guilty. Brown is careful to add, however, that satire (whom, incidentally, he makes feminine despite 'her' strength and severity) is fundamentally gentle and kind.

> Yet SATIRE oft' assumes a gentler mein,
> And beams on virtue's friends a smile serene;
> Reluctant wounds, but pours her balm with joy,
> Pleas'd to commend, where merit strikes her eye.[65]

[64] Brown (1745), pp. 12–13.
[65] Ibid., p. 22.

9. Limitations and Restrictions

In defence, retreat is unavoidable—retreat to a vantage-point, to high ground. The defenders have to establish themselves in as strong a position as possible, determine the limits of their defences, and prepare to surrender that territory which is too difficult to defend or not really worth defending. Without pushing the military metaphor too far, it can be said that the Augustan defence of satire followed this familiar pattern, the high ground being in this instance satire's moral function.

Some satirists and critics were prepared to defend satire of all sorts—of all degrees of vehemence from light raillery to stern censure, and on all manner of subjects from insignificant personal foibles to the gravest crimes against mankind. But those who now appear to have been most militant were the champions of gentle satire and, as we have seen in the previous chapter, they were prepared to defend only that satire which lets its victims off lightly and betrays no malice or anger.

With regard to the subject-matter of satire, Augustan writers were similarly divided, some maintaining that it should be virtually unlimited, and others that it should be restricted to minor misdemeanours and foibles. The former realized that it is in the satirist's interest to claim as wide a field as he can, for then he can imply that his satire is not only necessary, but also inevitable.

In a word, the Opinions and Practices of Men in all Matters, and especially in Matters of Religion, are generally so absurd and ridiculous that it is impossible for them not to be the Subjects of Ridicule.[1]

The world is wider to a Poet than to any other Man, and new follyes and Vices will never be wanting any more than new fashions. Je donne au diable the wrong Notion that *Matter* is exhausted.[2]

Swift, Arbuthnot, and Pope were in the habit of commenting in letters to one another on the abundant supply of subjects for

---

[1] Collins, *Discourse concerning Ridicule and Irony in Writing*, p. 19.
[2] Swift to John Gay (20 November 1729), Swift's *Correspondence*, iii. 360.

M

satire. Thus Arbuthnot remarks in one letter to Swift that 'The ridicule of Medicin is so copious a subject that I must only here & ther touch it', and he proceeds to illustrate his point by citing crazy medical projects. In another letter he comments regretfully on Whetstone's publication of 'his project of longitude', which was evidently a scheme for getting the princes of Europe to build poles for east and west in order to put these two points of the compass on an equal footing with the north and south. Arbuthnot is regretful because he had planned a Scriblerus paper proposing an almost identical scheme. It seems unfair to him that reality should have forestalled his satire. Swift himself in the Preface to *A Tale of a Tub* played at some length with the idea that there is no end to the supply of subjects for satire.

There is a Problem in an ancient Author, why Dedications, and other Bundles of Flattery run all upon stale musty Topicks, without the smallest Tincture of any thing New; not only to the torment and nauseating of the *Christian* Reader, but (if not suddenly prevented) to the universal spreading of that pestilent Disease, the Lethargy, in this Island: whereas, there is very little Satyr which has not something in it untouch'd before. The Defects of the former are usually imputed to the want of Invention among those who are Dealers in that kind: But, I think, with a great deal of Injustice; the Solution being easy and natural. For, the Materials of Panegyrick being very few in Number, have been long since exhausted: For, as Health is but one Thing, and has been always the same, whereas Diseases are by thousands, besides new and daily Additions; So, all the Virtues that have been ever in Mankind, are to be counted upon a few Fingers, but his Follies and Vices are innumerable, and Time adds hourly to the Heap.[3]

Those who accepted both kinds of satirical composition, 'smiling' and 'savage', naturally felt that satire could treat a wide range of subjects, from trivial faults at one extreme to the blackest crimes at the other. Thus Newbery stated that '*the Jocose*' takes 'the foibles of mankind' as its subject, while '*the Serious*' treats 'crimes of a deeper dye'.[4] Trapp refused to countenance the ruling that satire should concern itself only with those vices which are the proper subjects of laughter, because that would exclude Juvenal from a place among the satirists, and Trapp was inclined to consider Juvenal a greater satirist than Horace.[5]

---

[3] Swift's *Prose Works*, i. 30.
[4] *The Art of Poetry on a New Plan*, p. 100.   [5] Trapp, p. 228.

Most eighteenth-century critics, however, were in favour of narrowing the range of subject-matter. They disapproved of indiscriminate satire on both artistic and ethical grounds. Young, for instance, scoffed at those 'Satyrical Wits, and Humorists', who 'like their Father *Lucian*, laugh at every thing indiscriminately; which betrays such a poverty of wit, as cannot afford to part with any thing; and such a want of virtue, as to postpone it to a jest.'[6] Swift himself in a different context advised against treating 'All Subjects like Dan Jackson's Nose', that is against regarding them all as fit subjects for mirth.

> Reproach not tho in jest, a Friend
> For those Defects he cannot mend;
> His Lineage, Calling, Shape or Sense
> If nam'd with Scorn, gives just Offence.
>   What Use in Life, to make Men frett?
> Part in worse humor than they met?[7]

In the lines immediately following these, Swift advised satirists also not to carry jests too far and to discriminate carefully between those they should treat severely and those they should spare. To turn from Swift, however, who was far from being consistent on this question of the proper subject-matter for satire, we should next consider those critics who were fundamentally opposed to the treatment of ugly subjects not just in satire but in all literature. Puritanical moralists, like Allestree and Collier, believed that literature should draw a veil of decency over the nastier aspects of life. They feared that to mention a vice was in a way to condone it, and would probably help to propagate it. Thus Allestree warned that 'the dissecting of putrid Bodies may cast such pestilential fumes, as all the benefits of the scrutiny will not recompence.'[8] In reply to those dramatists who claimed the right to show things as they are, to present a true picture of the life of the town, Collier asked: 'Must we relate whatever is done, and is every Thing fit for Representation? is a Man that has the Plague proper to make a Sight of?' To spread infections deliberately is surely both wicked and absurd. Collier

---

[6] Preface to *Love of Fame*, sig. A5v.
[7] 'To Mr. Delany', lines 67–72, Swift's *Poems*, i. 217.
[8] *The Government of the Tongue*, p. 205.

suggests that it may be better to remain ignorant than to suffer illness or acute displeasure by learning:

> All Experiments are not worth the making. 'Tis much better to be ignorant of a Disease than to catch it. Who would wound himself for Information about Pain, or smell a Stench for the sake of the Discovery?[9]

Thomas Sprat put the same objection at a more general philosophical level. He urged 'the *Wits* and *Railleurs*' of the age to remember that laughter 'proceeds from the observation of the *deformity* of things; but that there is a nobler and more masculine pleasure, which is rais'd from beholding their *Order* and *Beauty*'.[10] In Sprat's historical view, wits and philosophers originally belonged to the same family, Socrates having been both the 'Founder of Philosophy' and 'the famous Author of all Irony'; but the two had gradually drifted apart, until in Sprat's times there was a vast gulf between them—'while *Nature* has only form'd [the Wits] to be pleas'd with its irregularities and monsters, it has given [the Philosophers] the delight of knowing and studying its most *beautiful Works*'. He considered that indiscriminate satire, 'a universal abuse of every thing', is 'inhuman madness'.

> If all things were made the subjects of such humour, all worthy designs would soon be laugh'd out of the World; and for our present sport, our *Posterity* would become barbarous. All good Enterprises ought to find assistance when they are begun, applaus when they succeed, and even pity and prais if they fail. The true *Raillery* should be a defence for *Good* and *Virtuous Works*, and should only intend the derision of extravagant, and the disgrace of vile and dishonourable things. This kind of *Wit* ought to have the nature of *Salt*, to which it is usually compar'd; which preserves and keeps sweet and good and the sound parts of all Bodies, and only frets, dries up, and destroys those humors which putrify and corrupt.[11]

While this general prejudice against satire was widely shared, the practical question remained for comic playwrights and satirical poets as to which exactly are the proper, and which the improper, subjects for satire?

[9] *A Short View*, p. 36.
[10] *History of the Royal Society*, p. 417.
[11] Ibid., pp. 418–19.

> Where then may Censure fall? 'Tis hard to say;
> On all that's wrong it may not, and it may.
> In Life, as Arts, it asks our nicest Care,
> But hurts us more, as more immediate there.[12]

It was agreed by a great number of critics that natural defects and deformities should evoke pity not humour. 'I must confess,' wrote Shadwell, 'it were ill nature, and below a man, to fall upon the natural imperfections of men, as of Lunaticks, Ideots, or men born monstrous.'[13] Whitehead considered that laughter at deformities should be left to the unthinking mob, who are unable to discriminate between objects of pity and those of mirth.

> We pity Faults by Nature's Hand imprest,
> *Thersites'* Mind, but not his Form's the Jest.

But although we should pity natural imperfections, we may 'lash without Controul'

> Acquir'd Ill-nature, ever prompt Debate,
> A Zeal for Slander, and delib'rate Hate:[14]

In *The Tatler*, No. 108 (17 December 1709), Steele tells an anecdote of a recent visit he made to the theatre. When he entered every member of the audience was so quiet and attentive that he 'did not question but some noble Tragedy was just then in its Crisis, or that an Incident was to be unravelled which would determine the Fate of an Hero'. But this was not at all what happened:

> While I was in this Suspence, expecting every Moment to see my old Friend Mr. *Betterton* appear in all the Majesty of Distress, to my unspeakable Amazement, there came up a Monster with a Face between his Feet; and as I was looking on, he raised himself on one Leg in such a perpendicular Posture, that the other grew in a direct Line above his Head. It afterwards twisted it self into the Motions and Wreathings of several different Animals, and after great Variety of Shapes and Transformations, went off the Stage in the Figure of an human Creature.

Even more surprising than the appearance of the Monster itself, however, was the rapture with which he was greeted by the

---

[12] Whitehead, *Essay on Ridicule*, p. 12.
[13] Preface to *The Humorists*, sig. a 1r.
[14] *Essay on Ridicule*, p. 13.

audience. Steele was of course making the point that contemporary taste was depraved, and that a cultivated man prefers to such spectacles as he has described all those scenes in life or passages in books which 'represent human Nature in its Proper Dignity'. Some critics similarly accused the ancients of revealing a crude sense of humour in their comedies. Joseph Warton, for example, stated that 'the grossness, the rudeness, and indelicacy of the ancients will . . . sufficiently appear, even from the sentiments of such critics as CICERO and QUINTILIAN, who mention corporal defects and deformities as proper objects of raillery.'[15]

It was argued too that the misfortunes of worthy people should be exempt from ridicule. Thus Corbyn Morris ruled that Don Quixote 'is not a Subject of Satire, as the Knight is free from all Badness of Heart, and Immorality'. He did not even think he should be a subject of raillery either, 'his Adventures in general being too gross and disastrous'.[16] Great crimes—'Vice too High', in Pope's phrase[17]—were judged unsuitable for satire, or for satirical treatment in comedy. (This is one of the contexts in which 'comedy' and 'satire' are virtually synonymous.)

The business of Comedy being ridicule, those Vices only fall under its correction, that are capable of being made ridiculous, and those only after such a manner as may raise Scorn and Contempt. For this reason Comedy seems to be more naturally disposed for the cure of Mens Follies, than their Vices, those running more naturally into ridicule than these, which are more apt to raise Indignation and Aversion, and are the proper instruments of Tragedy.[18]

Congreve noted Aristotle's ruling that 'there are Crimes too daring and too horrid' for comic treatment; 'the Vices most frequent, and which are the common Practice of the looser sort of Livers, are the subject Matter of Comedy.'[19] A subject is improper for ridicule, Addison said, 'if it is apt to stir up Horrour and Commiseration rather than Laughter'.[20] And Hutcheson solemnly declared: 'The enormous crime or grievous calamity of another, is not of itself a subject which can be naturally turned

[15] The Adventurer, No. 133.
[16] Corbyn Morris, p. 38.
[17] The First Satire of the Second Book of Horace Imitated, line 60, Pope's Poems, iv. 11.
[18] James Drake, The Antient and Modern Stages Survey'd (1699), pp. 232-3.
[19] Amendments of Mr. Collier (1698), p. 7.
[20] The Spectator, No. 446, 1 August 1712.

into ridicule: the former raises horror in us, and hatred; and the latter pity. . . . To observe the contortions of the human body in the air, upon the blowing up of an enemy's ship, may raise Laughter in those who do not reflect on the agony and distress of the sufferers; but the reflecting on this distress could never move Laughter of itself.'[21] In the Preface to *Joseph Andrews*, Fielding said that the ridiculous alone was his province and, furthermore, that only 'affectation' is ridiculous, for vice can arouse in us nothing but disgust. It was his opinion that ridicule has been badly misunderstood even by those who professed it 'for to what but such a mistake, can we attribute the many attempts to ridicule the blackest villainies, and, what is yet worse, the most dreadful calamities?' He asks what could be more absurd than 'the comedy of Nero, with the merry incident of ripping up his mother's belly; or what would give a greater shock to humanity, than an Attempt to expose the Miseries of Poverty and Distress to Ridicule?'[22] Fielding's instance is of course absurd, and the question is by no means as clear-cut as he suggests. In view of his own definition of affectation to include hypocrisy and vanity, which after all cover a wide range of vices and crimes, and in view of his own ironic treatment of crimes of the vilest kind in *Jonathan Wild*,[23] one can hardly take his prescription very seriously.

At this point it is worth while to cast some doubts also on what Dryden had to say about the targets of Horace's satire, in particular on his observation, which became a commonplace of Augustan criticism, that 'Folly was the proper quarry of Horace, and not vice'.[24] The confusion is one of manner with matter: as Horace's manner is light and urbane, especially by contrast with Juvenal's, he may appear to be concerned with relatively unimportant subjects; but, as Nyall Rudd has shown by listing the targets of the two books of satires, Horace's subjects (cruelty, murder, adultery, megalomania, etc.) are certainly serious in themselves. Rudd concludes: 'One shudders to contemplate the moral system of a man to whom these are but "follies".'[25]

---

[21] *Reflections upon Laughter*, p. 30.
[22] *Works*, ed. L. Stephen (1882), iv. xiii.
[23] For further comments, see A. E. Dyson, *The Crazy Fabric* (1965), p. 16.
[24] Dryden's *Essays*, ii. 83.
[25] *University of Toronto Quarterly*, xxxii (1962–3), 157.

Perhaps the nearest we can come to the truth is to say that Horace tends to treat vices as though they are merely follies.

The whole question of the legitimate targets of satire was highlighted by *The Dunciad*. Numerous readers felt that poverty and dullness were neither follies nor vices, and that Pope was wrong to mock them. Ambrose Philips, for example, observed that the great satirists among the ancients, Horace, Persius, and Juvenal, 'well knew that Calamities were not Crimes', and that they refrained from ridiculing anyone on the score of his poverty. Philips's argument is in essence the same as that put forward by those who disapproved of the ridicule of deformities; indeed he avers that it may be no more in a man's power to make his fortune than his person. Poverty and dullness, therefore, which are the twin targets of *The Dunciad*, are unsuitable subjects for satire.

SATIRE was certainly of admirable Use among the Antients, and is of no less among the Moderns; but then they always chose for their Theme some reigning Vice, or growing Folly: But where can you find a *Persius*, a *Juvenal*, or *Horace*, lashing of Personal Defect, or Turns of Providence? These Pious *Heathens* well knew that Calamities were not Crimes; and always exempted such from being the Subject of Satire. They knew it was not in the Power of a Man to make his own Fortune, any more than he could his own Person; and there-fore paid a modest Deference to the Decrees of an over-ruling Power; tho' this enlighten'd Age thinks Scorn to own One. The DUNCIAD is a recent Instance of this, wherein *Dulness*, which in plain *English* is want of *Capacity*, *Deformity*, a want of *Comliness*, and *Poverty*, a want of *Substance*, are the only Subjects he can find to work upon; which how well they become his Pen, has been said already.[26]

Pope's reply to these arguments was that, while the satirist may not be entitled to attack poverty and dullness in themselves, he is perfectly entitled to attack certain of their causes and effects. For example, he is entitled to attack poverty if it is used as an excuse for villainy, or if it is the result of bungling. Those who say that it is uncharitable to ridicule the poor 'mistake the whole matter' for the charitable course is not to encourage people to continue in the way which has kept them poor, 'but to get 'em out of it'; and he added smugly that 'men are not bunglers because they are poor, but they are poor because they are bunglers.'[27] By the same token, he contended that an ugly man may be satirized when he pretends to be a wit.

There remains what in my opinion might seem a better plea for these people, than any they have made use of. If Obscurity or Poverty were to exempt a man from satyr, much more should Folly or Dulness, which are still more involuntary, nay as much so as personal deformity. But even this will not help them: Deformity becomes the object of ridicule when a man sets up for being handsome: and so must Dulness when he sets up for a Wit. They are not ridicul'd because Ridicule in itself is or ought to be a pleasure; but because it is just, to undeceive or vindicate the honest and unpretending part of mankind from imposition, because particular interest ought to yield to general, and a great number who are not naturally Fools ought never to be made so in complaisance to a few who are. Accordingly we find that in all ages, all vain pretenders, were they ever so poor or ever so dull, have been constantly the topicks of the most candid Satyrists, from the Codrus of JUVENAL to the Damon of BOILEAU.[28]

So far we have noted that natural defects and deformities, the misfortunes of worthy people, great calamities and crimes, and poverty and dullness, were regarded by some Augustan critics as unsuitable subjects for satire. To this list must be added serious and lofty matters, obscene jests, members of the nobility and leading members of the government, and persons of very low character.

A 'truly great' object, said Hutcheson, is no matter for jest because it resembles nothing 'mean or base', and he warned that jests so directed rebound on their author and bring him into contempt.[29] According to Kames's theory, 'no object is risible but what appears slight, little, or trifling.'[30] It follows that ridicule should not be employed on serious or lofty subjects, though it can do no great harm: 'Such irregular use made of a talent for wit or ridicule, cannot long impose upon mankind. It cannot stand the test of correct and delicate taste; and truth will at last prevail even with the vulgar.'[31]

---

[27] 'William Cleland', 'A Letter to the Publisher', Pope's Poems, v. 15.
[28] Ibid. 17.   [29] Reflections upon Laughter, pp. 27–8.
[30] Elements of Criticism, i. 339.   [31] Ibid. 56–7.

On the first score, that of obscenity, Rabelais was commonly censured for spoiling his ridicule by his ribaldry and indecency. So Temple, after describing Rabelais as the 'Father of the Ridicule' and 'a Man of Excellent and Universal Learning as well at Wit', observed: 'Yet he must be Confest to have kept up his Vein of Ridicule by saying many things so Malicious, so Smutty, and so Prophane, that either a Prudent, a Modest, or a Pious Man, could not have afforded, tho' he had never so much of that Coyn about him . . .' Cervantes, in Temple's opinion, is 'much more to be admired, for having made up so Excellent a Composition of Satyr or Ridicule, without those Ingredients . . .'[32] Edward Young similarly admitted Rabelais's genius but placed him below Cervantes because of his indecency, for 'Indecency offends our pride, as men, and our unaffected taste, as judges of composition.'[33] And Joseph Warton, in his comparison of the ancients and moderns, put Boileau and Pope above Horace and Juvenal because of the modern poets' greater delicacy: 'That reformers should abound in obscenities, as is the case of the two Roman poets, is surely an impropriety of the most extraordinary kind . . .'[34]

The reasons for avoiding satire of persons of high station were not very clearly stated but, broadly speaking, they were that such satire undermines authority and government and that through picking out small faults in persons who possess great virtues, it brings discredit where this is not deserved. Bayle noted that the Romans had wisely forbidden their comic poets to abuse the magistrates, but left them free to make as much fun as they liked of the gods.[35] The Greeks, who were less wise in this particular respect, for a long while allowed their satirists such licence that even Pericles was ridiculed.[36] Kings, courtiers, prime ministers, and members of parliament were rarely held in high respect in the late seventeenth and eighteenth centuries, however, so this argument was not widely supported. Dennis pointed out that there was ample precedent for ridicule of the nobility, listing the Greek dramatists who had 'not only exposed the chief of the

---

[32] 'Of Poetry', *Miscellanea*, ii. 50–1.
[33] Preface to *Love of Fame*, sig. A5r.
[34] *The Adventurer*, No. 133.
[35] *An Historical and Critical Dictionary* (1710), i. xxiv.
[36] Ibid., xiii.

Athenian Nobility, but mention'd their very Names, and pro-
duc'd their very Persons, by the Resemblance of the Vizors'; and
he emphasized that the Romans too (even Lucilius, 'the Inventor
of Satyr') had attacked consuls and other noble members of
the government.[37] Pope spurned the idea that he should avoid
satire of the great because it is imprudent, and in his *Fourth
Satire of Donne, Versifyed,* and the *Epilogue to the Satires* he
clearly demonstrated his contempt for court favourites.

Steele believed that the satirist should ignore very low or
insignificant characters, that he had the right to lash 'the
reigning Vices' so long as he kept to 'the true Spirit of Satyr,
without descending to rake into Characters below its Dignity'.[38]
And Mulgrave thought he should avoid too great fools or
villains, any too obvious targets in fact. For example, the royal
mistresses were not a fit subject in his opinion because they were
too ugly and too open to blame.[39]

Satirists were constantly claiming that they gave a truthful
picture of the popular vices of the times. But some critics were
afraid that such a picture, instead of checking these popular
vices, might simply enhance their popularity. 'It has been the
common fault of all satirists', Dryden observes in his *Life of
Lucian,* 'to make vice too amiable, while they expose it . . .'[40]
A number of critics expressed the fear that a malefactor, once he
had been publicly exposed, put beyond the pale as it were, might
thereupon give up all thought of reform. Steele, for instance,
argued that the exposing of uncharitable truths may so enrage
the offender as to precipitate him 'into farther Degrees of Ill':

when by a publick Detection he is fallen under that Infamy he
fear'd, he will then be apt to discard all Caution, and to think he
owes himself the utmost Pleasures of Vice; as the Price of his
Reputation. Nay, perhaps he advances farther, and sets up for a
revers'd Sort of Fame, by being eminently wicked, and he who
before was but a clandestine Disciple, becomes a Doctor of Impiety,
&c.[41]

Whitehead gives a lurid picture of the same process at work in a

---

[37] *Critical Works,* ed. Hooker, p. 181.
[38] *The Tatler,* No. 74, 25 September 1709.
[39] 'Essay on Satyre', *Works* (1723), i. 116.
[40] *Works,* xviii. 69.
[41] *The Tatler,* No. 74.

whole society as Steele had described in an individual. Judgement Day turns into a riotous carnival of sin and vice:

> Vices when ridicul'd, Experience says,
> First lose that Horror which they ought to raise,
> Grow by degrees approv'd, and almost aim at Praise.
>
>   .   .   .
>
> Each pictur'd Vice so impudently bad,
> The Crimes turn Frolics, and the Villain mad;
> Rapes, Murders, Incests, Treasons Mirth create,
> And *Rome* scarce hates the Author of her Fate.[42]

In answer to this popular eighteenth-century argument that examples of vicious behaviour tend to set a fashion instead of warning against bad behaviour, and so have a generally depraving effect, Vanbrugh pointed out that to show a vice is not necessarily to recommend it. It is one thing, for instance, to observe that wives cuckold their husbands, but quite another thing to recommend that they should do so.

As to the wider argument that ugly and disgusting subjects should be barred from satire, it is pleasing to be able to record for the honour of Augustan criticism that it was well answered, though by only a few writers. No one put the case for freedom to use any sort of subject-matter more ably than Robert Wolseley, when he defended Rochester's bawdy poems against the attack Mulgrave had made on them in his *Essay upon Poetry*. Wolseley says that 'it never yet came into any man's Head, who pretended to be a Critick, except this *Essayer's*, that the Wit of a Poet was to be measur'd by the worth of his Subject, and that when this was bad, that must be so too: the manner of treating his Subject has been hitherto thought the true Test, for as an ill Poet will depresse and disgrace the highest, so a good one will raise and dignifie the lowest . . .'.[43] The question is clearly a general one, and bears not just on satire, but on all art. Any work of art that shows a horrid or ugly subject is likely to be described as horrid or ugly itself and accused of exaggeration; but as Oldmixon argued with reference to Milton's Sin and Death allegory, when a reader comes, as he does in *Paradise Lost*, 'to the Gates of Hell *wide open*, he certainly should have left his Delicacy behind him'. To drive this point home, Oldmixon remarks a few

---

[42] *Essay on Ridicule*, p. 14.
[43] Preface to *Valentinian*, sig. A3r–v.

sentences further on: it would not be more extravagant to put Perfumes among the Ingredients of a *Stink-Pot*, than to put Delicacy in a Picture of the Devil.'[44] William King mentions that the author (really himself) of *The Toast* has been accused of choosing unsuitable subjects, characters who should have been beneath his notice. King's answer is the same as Wolseley's—that it is the artist's skill, not his subject, which counts: 'The Harlot's Progress by *Hogarth* would purchase an hundred Saints . . .'[45] He ridicules, too, another limitation that is occasionally put forward: *de mortuis nil nisi bonum*. In his opinion there is 'more good Nature than good Sense' in this adage, for if it were adopted 'all History would be confounded'—*Nero* and *Harry* the *VIII*th must be represented as merciful Princes, and *Erostratus* and *Chartres* as honest Men.'[46]

Although some writers, such as Wolseley and William King, spoke up boldly for the freedom of satire, the trend in the eighteenth century was unmistakably in the opposite direction. Dryden, Swift, Pope, and Churchill, or Mathias and Gifford of the later writers, might not have allowed themselves to be much troubled by restrictions, even those they recommended themselves, when they were composing their satirical works; but, as the eighteenth century wore on, the general run of satirists did become increasingly conscious of a set of rules which they were obliged to follow. Propriety, restraint, gentleness, sympathy, and like qualities were, it is true, recommended from the beginning of the period, and by Dryden and Wolseley, as well as by such reformers as Glanvill, Sprat, Allestree, and Collier. In satirical exchanges, 'the Charge should be Powder not Bullets', said Allestree. Dryden and Wolseley used deadlier images—the skilful executioner and the soaring eagle—but they nevertheless agreed with Allestree that the liberty of satire 'is to be bounded with some Cautions'.[47] The number of cautions regarded as necessary multiplied, and satirists became more and more aware of them even though they frequently flouted them in their satirical writings. There is an amplitude about Dryden's appreciation of Juvenal and 'the majestic way' that is lacking in the occasional criticism of satire of even his most distinguished

[44] *An Essay on Criticism* (1728), p. 94.
[45] 'Translator's Preface', p. xxxii.
[46] Ibid., p. xxxviii.   [47] *The Government of the Tongue*, p. 125.

successors; and it comes not from his superior abilities as literary critic and essayist (should these be admitted), but from his greater confidence in the power and standing of satire. Swift and Pope are more defensive; so even is Johnson; and Churchill certainly is, for example in *The Apology* and the *Epistle to Hogarth*. In between Dryden and these latter satirists, there had been Addison and Steele, who, in theory at least, went a long way towards refining satire out of existence. Take, for example, not an attack on satire by either of these writers, but Addison's essay in *The Free-holder*, No. 45, where he is defending satire against the charge of worthlessness made against it by Blackmore in his *Satyr against Wit*. Addison admits that it is practically impossible to produce evidence of the reforms effected by particular satires; but he is prepared to assert with confidence that the *Tatlers* and *Spectators* had at least the good effect of purifying contemporary satire.

They diverted Raillery from improper Objects, and gave a new Turn to Ridicule, which for many Years had been exerted on Persons and Things of a sacred and serious Nature. They endeavoured to make Mirth Instructive, and if they failed in this great End, they must be allowed at least to have made it Innocent.

He goes on to say that persons of discriminating taste now know the rules of raillery. They know, for instance, that it must not be written without a moral, that it must not attack anything that is praiseworthy, and that it must not seek to raise an easy laugh by ridiculing 'serious Objects' simply because these 'are the most capable of Ridicule'. Addison ends the essay with a passage setting out all those faults which a satirical writer may commit if he is more interested in courting popularity than in being a good man:

Scandal and Satyr are never-failing Gratifications to the Publick. Detraction and Obloquy are received with as much Eagerness as Wit and Humour. Should a Writer single out particular Persons, or point his Raillery at any Order of Men, who by their Profession ought to be exempt from it; should he slander the Innocent, or satyrize the Miserable, or should he, even on the proper Subjects of Derision, give the full Play to his Mirth, without regard to Decency and good Manners: he might be sure of pleasing a great Part of his Readers, but must be a very ill Man, if by such a Proceeding he could please himself.

Looked at impartially—without, for example, bringing to them any prejudice about Addison's habitual self-righteousness—these observations seem fair enough. But of course the point one would wish to make about them is not that they can be gainsaid, but rather that they could not but have a constricting effect. In any occupation, once a person starts to worry more about the things he should not do than about getting on with the job, his output is bound to diminish. Moreover, some eighteenth-century critics—Whitehead, for instance, in his *Essay on Ridicule*—hedged the satirist about with so many limitations that they might as well have advised him to steer clear of satire altogether. Even John Brown, whose *Essay* is designed to be a triumphant vindication of satire, carefully prescribes its proper limits:

> Let SATIRE next, her proper limits know;
> And e'er she strike, *be sure* she strikes a foe.
> Nor fondly deem, you spy a real fool
> At each gay impulse of blind *ridicule*;
> Before whose altar virtue oft' hath bled,
> And oft' a fated victim shall be led:[48]

Satire must 'be steady in a noble end', avoid bidding for empty praise or cheap popularity, and refrain from mentioning defects which may not be real. She must never rail, nor lose her temper:

> Let no unworthy rage her form debase,
> But let her smile, and let her frown with grace:[49]

Moreover, her indignation must be proportionate to its object: she must not rage at folly nor laugh at vice. Brown also implies, in his absurdly harsh picture of Dryden, that a satirist should be a man of exceptional integrity. He talks of the extremes of wit and meanness displayed by Dryden, of his talents, which could mount so high, 'Low-creeping in the putrid sink of vice', and alleges that Dryden prostituted satire for personal gain.[50] But these observations comprise the lesser part of the *Essay*: the greater part of it is fulsome enough in its expressions of faith in the satirist's calling and the noble function of satire.

When we turn to Charles Abbott's 'On the Use and Abuse of Satire',[51] however, which serves well as a landmark at the end of

---

[48] Brown (1745), p. 15.
[49] Ibid., p. 19.
[50] Ibid., pp. 28–9.
[51] *Oxford Prize Essays*, i. 179–205.

the period, we are aware of a much more qualified view. He ascribes a secondary role to satire, that of clearing away the rubbish prior to erecting a fine building. Errors and absurdities have to be extirpated 'before just ideas can be introduced'. Accordingly, though 'satire appears to be confined to the lower objects of criticism, it contributes in an eminent degree to the promotion of the highest: and prepares the understanding for those refined and elevated sensations which the perfect comprehension of excellence can alone produce' (i. 200). Abbott is as keenly aware of the dangers of satire as of its uses: it 'may . . . deservedly be numbered among the happiest instructors of mankind' (i. 205); equally it may dazzle readers into accepting untruths and, if it is inspired by malice or immorality, it may give 'a severe and fatal wound . . . to innocence or to virtue' (i. 183). Even when the satirist's choice of subject and his general design cannot be faulted, 'abuse may still arise from the disposition and colouring of the piece':

> When bitterness and severity are employed against men whose failings were venial and light, or ridicule degenerates either into the broad attacks of sarcastic buffoonery, or the unmanly treachery of dark hints and poisonous allusions, not only the particular punishment is excessive and unjust, but also general malice is fostered by new supplies of slander. (i. 188)

Satire can be very useful in the political sphere, as was demonstrated by Butler's ridicule of fanaticism and Addison's 'delicate pleasantry' in support of justice and freedom. Too often, however, it is employed to promote falsehood and inspire sedition. It is interesting to note in this connection that Abbott, while he approves of Swift's scheme of satirizing factions in the 'Voyage to Lilliput', feels that the picture is so depressing that its chief effect must be that of damaging patriotism and inducing dejection and apathy (i. 192). Abbott thinks that religious speculations are too touchy a subject for satire, 'since the mind is thereby taught to regard those subjects with levity which ought only to be contemplated with awful veneration' (i. 198). General satire is suspect because it blackens human nature and encourages misanthropy (i. 199–200). In the fields of science and literature, satire has frequently proved most useful, yet there are grave dangers here also, and serious abuses have been committed. Abbott deplores especially the early attacks on the Royal Society—'all the powers of wit and satire were employed to insult and debase it' (i. 203). Most of all, however, he fears the accidental effects of satire. Whether it singles out for ridicule relatively insignificant failings, or exposes important public figures to shame, it tends to create the sort of climate in which vice flourishes:

> For if they, whose failings were unknown and harmless, be brought forth at once to notice and shame, or if, for the weakness common to human nature, illustrious characters be made objects of contempt, the triumphs of vice are promoted by increasing the number of the vicious, and virtue loses much of its dignity and force, by being deprived of those names which had contributed to its support.
>
> (i. 187)

Those satirical works, which are constantly bewailing the depravity of the times, Abbott believes to be extremely pernicious, because they give the impression that vice is popular and that virtue goes unrewarded (i. 199). It is clear that Abbott is happiest about satire when it is employed for minor tasks. So he commends Horace, Boileau, and Pope for helping to correct literary taste, and Pope for exploding some foolish contemporary notions of landscape gardening (i. 291–2). Satire, in short, is liable to do tremendous damage if it is entrusted with important work—for instance, in the sphere of religion, morals, or even politics. It should be relegated to light duties, a little dusting and tidying: 'If we descend to the minute particularities of domestic elegance, which, though of little independent consequence, are yet rendered interesting by their connection with more important concerns, we shall here find satire perpetually employed with advantage and success' (i. 202).

When all the warnings and prohibitions are listed, as they have been in the preceding paragraphs, satire indeed seems a bed of nails. Any satirist taking all the prohibitions seriously would hardly know which way to turn: he is not allowed to ridicule congenital defects, serious crimes, lofty subjects, human nature, calamities, and sufferings, or very important or very unimportant persons; and he should think twice before meddling in politics; as to religious matters, he had best leave them completely alone. It would be wrong to imply that the decline of satire after the deaths of Pope and Swift was a direct result of these limitations and restrictions; nevertheless, one can understand James Scott's viewpoint when he wrote in 1766 that he was 'more desirous of maintaining the character of a good natured Man, than that of an able Satirist'.[52] When all is said and done, the easiest method of 'whitening the page' is by leaving it blank.

[52] *The Perils of Poetry* (1766), p. v.

10. Conclusion: Inadequacy of the Defence

ARISTOTLE, when he is summoned before Gulliver in Glubb-dubdrib, readily acknowledges his own mistakes in natural philosophy and reveals that he has formed a low opinion of theories generally. He discounts them all as makeshifts and impostures—they are 'but new Fashions, which . . . vary in every Age'.[1] The Augustan 'theory' of satire would have given him no cause to change his mind. Gradually it was supplanted, as the succeeding age turned to a different view of man and society, and of the nature of things generally. The Augustans were predisposed by their historical circumstances towards a satirical outlook on life; that is to say, of all ways of looking at the world the satirist's came to them most easily, and of all modes of artistic expression satire seemed to them to give the sharpest and clearest focus on reality—'a Character of a Splenetick and Peevish *Humour*', Congreve stated, 'Observes and shews things as they are', whereas a character of 'A Jolly and Sanguine *Humour* . . . rather overlooks Nature, and speaks things as he would have them.'[2] For the typical Augustan the satirical was the real. Yet by the late eighteenth century comedy was held to be far truer to human nature than satire; and in the late nineteenth century satire was widely condemned for its gross unreality.[3] The good bishop who was reluctant to credit Gulliver's account of his travels was at least nearer to Swift than Thackeray when he advised against reading book iv on the grounds that it is 'shameful', 'horrible', 'blasphemous', 'obscene', and (perhaps worst of all!) 'unmanly'.[4]

Once a belief in the intrinsic goodness of man overbore the

---

[1] Swift's *Prose Works*, pp. 197–8.
[2] 'Concerning Humour in Comedy', in J. E. Spingarn (ed.), *Critical Essays of the Seventeenth Century*, iii. 244.
[3] See Milton Voigt, *Swift and the Twentieth Century* (Detroit, 1964), pp. 3–27.
[4] *The English Humourists of the Eighteenth Century* (Oxford, 1913), p. 31.

awareness of his imperfections, satire was inevitably diminished in standing and assigned a subsidiary role in the literary hierarchy. 'Point out the good, cease harping on the bad' became increasingly the catch-cry of eighteenth-century critics. Subscribers to the popular periodicals wanted to be mildly entertained and edified: not for them the traumas of retribution and righteous indignation. Heaven moved nearer to home,[5] and hell was kept at a safe distance—even to mention it, as Timon's chaplain appreciated,[6] was a breach of good manners. When ethics is reduced to etiquette, satire loses its sting and humour becomes a sentimental and whimsical tolerance. To his own question, 'why make my Follies publick?' Colley Cibber smugly replies: 'Why not? I have pass'd my Time very pleasantly with them, and I don't recollect that they have ever been hurtful to any other Man living.'[7] How different is this amiable tolerance of personal foibles from the attitudes of Butler and Fielding.[8] Sentimentalists like Colley Cibber appear to have fulfilled the prophecy Swift made in his Preface to A Tale of a Tub that moderns would soon be bragging about their humpbacks and extravagant posteriors. Goldsmith in Retaliation (1774) assures us of his good nature, and he succeeds in creating a poem which, while in impulse satirical, is nevertheless imbued with kindliness and understanding. Even its sharpest observations, so clever is Goldsmith's control of tone, seem to be entirely free of ill will. But so much good nature is not good for satire; at least, hate or righteous indignation, or whatever it may be called, is equally essential. It would appear that satire derives its power from an intense love–hate attitude to its subject, in which the 'love' is rather a kind of guilty fascination, and in which the hate is not nakedly stated but refined in expression to take the form of moral disapproval. If the love–hate relationship is thrown off balance, or if either the 'love' or the 'hate' is reduced in intensity, the satire will be correspondingly weakened. And if the 'love' becomes more nearly 'love' in the everyday sense of the word, the

---

[5] See Carl L. Becker, The Heavenly City of Eighteenth-Century Philosophers (New Haven, 1932), passim.

[6] 'Epistle to Burlington', lines 149–50, Pope's Poems, vol. iii, pt. ii, pp. 151–2.

[7] An Apology for the Life of Mr. Colley Cibber (1740), p. 2.

[8] See Butler's note on the Overdoer, for example, Characters and Passages from Notebooks, ed. A. R. Waller (Cambridge, 1908), p. 273; and for Fielding's attitude see Covent-Garden Journal, Nos. 55 and 56.

result is contradiction and absurdity. That was the error of Addison and Steele, to misunderstand the essential relationship of the satirist to his subject. The sentimental satirist, represented as an ideal by one line of critics from Addison's times to our own,[9] is Thackeray whom Dickens ridicules (under the name of Gowan) in *Little Dorrit*:

It appeared, before the breakfast was over, that everybody whom this Gowan knew was either more or less of an ass, or more or less of a knave; but was, notwithstanding, the most loveable, the most engaging, the simplest, truest, kindest, dearest, best fellow that ever lived. The process by which this unvarying result was attained, whatever the premises, might have been stated by Mr. Henry Gowan thus: 'I claim to be always book-keeping, with a peculiar nicety, in every man's case, and posting up a careful little account of Good and Evil with him. I do this so conscientiously, that I am happy to tell you I find the most worthless of men to be the dearest old fellow too; and am in a condition to make the gratifying report, that there is much less difference than you are inclined to suppose between an honest man and a scoundrel.'[10]

Behind the growing obligation felt by Gowan and his eighteenth-century antecedents to profess sympathy towards wrongdoers was a desire to feel sympathy generally. So, whereas the satirist concentrated on the hurtful actions of the wrongdoer, the sentimental novelist turned his attention to the sufferings of the wrongdoer's victim. There is evidence, too, in eighteenth-century literature of a developing interest in the personality of the wrongdoer, which runs counter to the satirist's natural bent. Characteristically the satirist is concerned with the actions of wrongdoers and the effects of those actions on other people and society. The satirist sees a man for what he does; or, to put the matter another way, the satirist equates what a man does with what he is. He takes it for granted that the wrongdoer's actions are fully conscious and deliberate; that even the fool's acts are the result of a conscious, albeit foolish, choice. It follows, then, that a writer who is interested in what a man is rather than in what he does, in his responses to life, and who explores a character's personality and environment in order to understand and explain why he thinks and feels and acts as he does, will not produce

---

[9] Humbert Wolfe might well stand as the last of the line. See his *Notes on English Verse Satire* (1929).

[10] *Little Dorrit* (Oxford, 1953), pp. 204–5.

satire. Increasingly in eighteenth-century literature the centre of interest shifted from the consequences of characters' actions to the workings, often the obscure workings, of their personalities. And if this is principally apparent in the novel, it is none the less noticeable too in verse satire—in Charles Churchill's 'Dedication to the Sermons' (1765), for example. In this fine poem Churchill does not give a satirical portrait of his subject (William Warburton, Bishop of Gloucester) in the sense in which we use that term in speaking of Dryden's Shaftesbury and Pope's Hervey. Whereas Dryden and Pope display symbolic types in the showcase of satire—Achitophel, or the Devil as Politician; and Sporus, or the Devil in Society—Churchill is not really concerned with Warburton as a type. He is interested rather in the interplay of values exhibited by his relationships with the Bishop and by their contrasting personalities and careers. And, where Dryden and Pope approach their subjects with certainty and present them with objective finality, Churchill appears to be tentative, as though he has found himself grappling with a formidable adversary (or, at any rate, one with a formidable reputation), and who has therefore to use every trick in his repertoire, from ironic feints to thrusts of truth, in order to find out where he is vulnerable and overcome him. Besides, as Yvor Winters has demonstrated by contrasting a section of Churchill's poem with Pope's portrait of Atticus,[11] Churchill employs a more complex and elaborate kind of verse than Pope, one less discrete in its parts and less dogmatic in its effects—one, therefore, better suited to inquiry than to prosecution and condemnation. From Churchill of 'The Dedication' to George Crabbe the progression is clear. Crabbe we think of as a moral psychologist[12] rather than satirist, for behind his penetrating insights into the workings of criminal minds, of Jachin for instance, or even of the dreadful Peter Grimes, there is a reluctance to judge and condemn, an underlying charity that derives from psychological understanding and from a fundamentally sympathetic attitude to the most aberrant of characters. Crabbe illustrates a late stage in the transition we have been following from a literature of strict

[11] 'The Poetry of Charles Churchill', *Forms of Discovery* (Chicago, 1967), pp. 134–5.

[12] R. L. Brett has well described Crabbe's main interest as 'the psychology of moral experience', *George Crabbe* (1968), p. 33.

moral judgement to a literature treating human experience for its own sake. It is significant in this connection that Crabbe turned increasingly to narrative for, as he matured as a writer, he became, like the novelists, increasingly concerned with the development of the individual character and with the interaction of characters on one another.

It is the eighteenth-century novel, more than any other literary form, that reflects the century's changing attitude to satire. For one thing the novel, as its name indicates, is by nature innovative. It sets out to break new ground, whereas satire, by tradition at least, safeguards existing boundaries. Furthermore, in so far as it grew from biography, memoirs, and personal letters, the novel tended to be personal and subjective, thus going against the public stance of the satirist as guardian of the commonweal. But, above all, the novel proved to be compendious, taking to itself all existing sorts of writings and presenting them afresh, in modified forms, to a widening circle of middle-class readers. Romance, epic, epistle, travel book, biography, history, memoirs, letters, comedy, and satire—all were absorbed by this new and rapidly growing organism. Eighteenth-century novels, however, though often satirical in part, were rarely satires, and the tendency of the century was for the satirical elements to grow fewer and the satirical colouring paler. The sentimental novelist sometimes freely employed the satirist's techniques. Henry Mackenzie's cheats and rogues in *The Man of Feeling* (1771), for example, are the stereotypes of preceding satirists. Sterne was delighted by the Earl of Bathurst's comment that he was the successor of Swift and Pope. Modern readers, however, would be much more inclined to see him as illustrating perfectly the radical shift in opinion which took place in his time. The characters of *Tristram Shandy*, especially Shandy Senior, are potential satirical targets, yet with the exception of Dr. Slop they are presented comically rather than satirically. Moreover, Sterne's novel in effect undermines the very foundations of Augustan satire, for its wonderful comic spirit successfully dispels all faith in rational schemes for imposing patterns on the disorder of human experience.

Change in attitudes to satire inevitably occurred; yet the change was more gradual than might be supposed. As Upali Amerasinghe demonstrated in his *Dryden and Pope in the Late*

Eighteenth and Early Nineteenth Centuries (Cambridge, 1962), the zenith of the two greatest Augustan poets' reputations occurred in the 1790s, not earlier, and the question debated in the Dryden–Pope controversy of the 1820s was not whether they were good poets, but which was the better. Nor did satire of high quality in the Augustan style cease to be written after Pope and Johnson. William Gifford, George Canning, and John Frere, for instance, in their contributions to *The Anti-Jacobin* (1797–8), demonstrated that it was still possible at the turn of the century to write satirical verse of high quality in the manner of Dryden and Pope. Some of the most trenchant couplets in their poem *New Morality* are fittingly directed against Candour, the milksop virtue of the late eighteenth century.

> . . . Hail! most solemn Sage,
> Thou driv'ling Virtue of this Moral Age,
> Candour, which softens Party's headlong rage.
> Candour—which spares its foes—nor e'er descends
> With bigot zeal to combat for its friends.
> Candour—which loves in see-saw strain to tell
> Of acting foolishly, but meaning well:
> Too nice to praise by wholesale, or to blame,
> Convinc'd that all men's motives are the same;
> And finds, with keen discriminating sight,
> BLACK's not *so* black—nor WHITE *so very* white.[13]

Before the fire died down completely, it flared up brightly several times—in Churchill, Goldsmith, Pindar, Gifford, and the Byron of *English Bards and Scotch Reviewers*. Yet always with a difference. Churchill and Gifford appear often to be straining for effect; Goldsmith and Pindar substitute pastoral or sentimental mildness for the urbanity and mordancy of Pope; and Byron, who had less critical understanding of his own abilities than most writers, before or since, achieved only a qualified success in *English Bards and Scotch Reviewers*. Pope had so thoroughly exploited the potentialities of the Augustan verse-form that after him imitativeness could be avoided only by the most individual and powerful of satiric writers, like Churchill and Johnson. Significantly, Churchill preferred Dryden to Pope and

---

[13] *English Satiric Poetry, Dryden to Byron*, edd. James Kinsley and James T. Boulton (1966), p. 157.

was inclined to blame Pope for the monotony of much of the satirical verse of the succeeding era. Pope's verse he considered excellent but so uniformly excellent that it ends by creating an effect of tedium—

> But whilst each line with equal beauty flows,
> E'en excellence, unvary'd, tedious grows.[14]

He believed that the example of Pope's verse had encouraged lesser poets to aim at a harmonious smoothness instead of energy and variety which admittedly may produce some roughness of versification. All that Pope's imitators had achieved was 'A happy tuneful vacancy of sense'.[15]

Satire, as Churchill observed, was becoming weaker, less satirical, as though its blood were running thin. Its impulse grew feebler and feebler, and critical doubts about its proper scope and usefulness multiplied. No better example of this weakening process could be cited than Goldsmith's pleasing, humorous, and occasionally witty and perceptive poem, *Retaliation*—no better example because Goldsmith's poem provides such a direct contrast with the biting, retaliatory satires of Dryden's and Pope's times and because, written as it was specifically in response to a challenge from Goldsmith's circle of literary friends—the 'Club of Beaux Esprits', as he calls them in the Preface—it provided him with a wonderful opportunity to get even with Garrick, Cumberland, Burke, and others who had made fun of his speech, appearance, or origins, or had in other ways amused themselves at his expense. *Retaliation* is a prime example of good-natured satire. Addison could have read it with pleasure and could even perhaps, but for its high quality, have given it his unqualified approval. Its movement, in loose twelve-syllable lines with gaily fluttering endings, is light and carefree; its tone is intimate and friendly. Goldsmith is ribbing his friends, and his satire, however pointedly it is turned, never strikes at the heart of his victims. It is directed instead at those personal idiosyncrasies which were no doubt taken by the club as endearing traits, and so, indirectly, as a source of some pride to their possessors. Actually some of the most telling remarks are more in the nature of double-edged

---

[14] *Poetical Works*, ed. Grant, p. 47.
[15] Ibid., p. 46.

compliments than satirical jibes, for example, the couplet on Garrick's penchant for acting more off the stage than on it—

> On the stage he was natural, simple, affecting,
> 'Twas only that, when he was off, he was acting:—[16]

or the famous one on Burke giving up for party what was meant for mankind.[17] In both instances Goldsmith allows the praise in the first line to remain standing alongside the censure of the second line. Garrick is commended on the score that matters most, that is for the moving naturalness of his acting on stage, before he is teased for playing a part off stage, and Burke is described in a glowing phrase as 'born for the Universe' before being censured for devoting his great natural gifts to his political party. The praise in the latter example is expressed in a highly rhetorical but not a mock-heroic way: it is sincere rather than mocking. Similarly, in one of the most delightful parts of the poem, Cumberland's failure to portray characters realistically is presented as evidence of his overwhelmingly generous nature. We read the passage and think, 'What a warm loveable person Cumberland must have been!', and pass over his limitations as a playwright as of only secondary importance. In Dryden's and Pope's satirical couplets the direct ridicule of the second line subverts the praise of the first line. Shadwell may stand out from all of Flecknoe's other sons, but he does so only because he is the most stupid of all of them. His distinction, like Achitophel's and Zimri's, is infinitely dubious. Similarly Sporus's apparently praiseworthy features are revealed as integral parts of his evil nature: his beauty shocks, his wit creeps, and his pride 'licks the Dust'. Dryden and Pope use praise as delayed or concealed censure, whereas Goldsmith makes sure that his subjects are known for their singular merits before putting them sensibly, and without rancour, in human perspective.

> Here Hickey reclines a most blunt, pleasant creature,
> And slander itself must allow him good-nature:
> He cherish'd his friend, and he relish'd a bumper;
> Yet one fault he had, and that one was a thumper:
> Perhaps you may ask if that man was a miser?
> I answer, no, no, for he always was wiser;
> Too courteous, perhaps, or obligingly flat;
> His very worst foe can't accuse him of that.

[16] *Collected Works*, ed. Friedman, iv. 357.   [17] Ibid., p. 353.

> Perhaps he confided in men as they go,
> And so was too foolishly honest; ah, no.
> Then what was his failing? come tell it, and burn ye,
> He was, could he help it? a special attorney.[18]

Peter Pindar also found the milder satiric tone advocated in the latter part of the eighteenth century perfectly suited to his temperament. In one of his 'Expostulary Odes' he smugly boasts that he is 'a melting medlar' whose satire is 'silk' compared to 'the horrid hair-cloth' of Churchill and Junius; his rhyme is 'a rill—a thread of murmuring water' compared to 'their high floods of foaming satire', a whispering zephyr to their whirl-winds, and so on.[19] Pindar's *Epistle to Boswell* (1784) besides providing an additional example of the milder sort of satire, shows also how far the late eighteenth century had turned away from the Augustan conception of the scope and purpose of satire. Pindar, who is obviously enjoying himself no end—as the jaunty rhythm suggests—has no sense of high purpose in his satire. There is no evidence in the poem of his sharing the assumption which would have been taken for granted even by the scribblers of Dryden's and Pope's times, that his satire is serving a social and moral, as well as a literary, purpose. So it is that, whereas Dryden in *Mac Flecknoe* sees a literary figure as not merely literary but as a man of affairs involved in the important public events of his day, and whereas Pope sees a literary enemy (Addison) not just as a bad writer but also as a bad man, Pindar limits his ridicule to Boswell's preoccupation with the trivia of Dr. Johnson's life. Pindar's subjects elsewhere were admittedly more political than literary; yet there too is to be found some restriction in satirical scope. In *Absalom and Achitophel* Dryden is interested primarily in the principles which ensure stability in government. Pindar, on the other hand, in such poems as *The Lousiad*, is interested rather in political topicalities and items of gossip. It is as though he considers a louse in the King's soup as much more the kind of thing that concerns a satirist than, say, a plot to overthrow His Majesty's Government.

The charges of insipidity and triviality cannot be levelled against Churchill. Yet there are indications of a subtler kind in his satires of the uncertainty which, after Pope's times, seriously

---

[18] Ibid., p. 358.
[19] Ode ix, *The Works of Peter Pindar, Esq.* (1830), p. 226.

weakened and diffused the regard for satire of both poets and critics. These danger signs can be perceived, for example, in comparing a passage from Churchill's *Epistle to William Hogarth* with an equivalent passage from Pope's *Epistle to Dr. Arbuthnot*.

> Had I (which Satirists of mighty name,
> Renown'd in rime, rever'd for *moral* fame,
> Have done before, whom Justice shall pursue
> In future verse) brought forth to public view
> A Noble Friend, and made his foibles known,
> Because his worth was greater than my own;
> Had I spar'd those (so *Prudence* had decreed)
> Whom, God so help me at my greatest need,
> I ne'er will spare, those vipers to their King
> Who smooth their looks, and flatter whilst they sting,
> Or had I not taught patriot zeal to boast
> Of Those, who flatter least, but love him most;
> Had I thus sinn'd, my stubborn soul should bend
> At CANDOUR's voice, and take, as from a friend,
> The deep rebuke; Myself should be the first
> To hate myself, and stamp my Muse accurs'd.
>   (*An Epistle to William Hogarth*, lines 141–56)[20]

> 'But why insult the Poor, affront the Great?'
> A Knave's a Knave, to me, in ev'ry State,
> Alike my scorn, if he succeed or fail,
> *Sporus* at Court, or *Japhet* in a Jayl,
> A hireling Scribler, or a hireling Peer,
> Knight of the Post corrupt, or of the Shire,
> If on a Pillory, or near a Throne,
> He gain his Prince's Ear, or lose his own.
>   Yet soft by Nature, more a Dupe than Wit,
> *Sapho* can tell you how this Man was bit:
> This dreaded Sat'rist *Dennis* will confess
> Foe to his Pride, but Friend to his Distress:
> So humble, he has knock'd at *Tibbald*'s door,
> Has drunk with *Cibber*, nay has rym'd for *Moor*.
> Full ten years slander'd, did he once reply?
> Three thousand Suns went down on *Welsted*'s Lye:
>   (*An Epistle to Dr. Arbuthnot*, lines 360–75)[21]

Churchill's sentences are flexible and tentative: they trail side-comments and parentheses, and they go on well beyond the

---

[20] *Poetical Works*, ed. Grant, p. 217.
[21] Pope's *Poems*, iv. 122–3.

couplet in pursuit of a thought. Churchill is willing to start a false hare and run it to earth. Pope, on the other hand, is not at all tentative: he creates the impression that he has been over the same ground many times before and can tell exactly where everything is, so his sentences are neat and precise; they do not deviate and they remain within the couplet. More broadly speaking, the Churchill passage is a soliloquy, while Pope's is a proclamation. Churchill's is introverted, ruminative: Pope's is hortatory and definitive. Churchill is anxious to justify himself to himself; Pope is justifying himself to the world. Such differences, it could be argued, principally reflect the different temperaments of the two writers, and this need not be contradicted. The point that can be made, without any implication of causative connections, is that Churchill's satire can be seen to exhibit the characteristics of post-Augustan satire and to point ahead to Byron's *The Vision of Judgement* as well as back to Pope's *Prologue* and *Epilogue to the Satires*.

It is in his concept of the role of satirist, however, that Churchill most clearly foreshadows the future. He portrays himself as solitary and driven; isolated from society and confined to a garret where he composes furiously when the mood comes on him, not pausing to polish or correct his rude verses. He is a rough-and-tumble poet with a 'poor slattern' of a muse.

> Had I the pow'r, I could not have the time,
> Whilst spirits flow, and Life is in her prime,
> Without a sin 'gainst Pleasure, to design
> A plan, to methodize each thought, each line
> Highly to finish, and make ev'ry grace,
> In itself charming, take new charms from place.
> Nothing of Books, and little known of men,
> When the mad fit comes on, I seize the pen,
> Rough as they run, the rapid thoughts set down,
> Rough as they run, discharge them on the Town.
> Hence rude, unfinish'd brats, before their time,
> Are born into this idle world of rime,
> And the poor *slattern* MUSE is brought to bed
> With all her imperfections on her head.[22]

Churchill admired Dryden and Pope, especially Dryden; but he himself reminds one rather of Oldham, because of the rough

[22] 'Gotham', *Poetical Works*, p. 313.

vigour of his satire and because it is informed by a similar sense of Juvenalian outrage. Yet Churchill's idea of his role is different from that of the Juvenalian satirist, for whereas the latter is impelled to write satire by forces outside himself, by all the wickedness and corruption he sees everywhere about him, Churchill is rather the romantic poet, essentially self-absorbed, driven by an inner force to alienate himself from his fellows.

> But now, *Decorum* lost, I stand
> *Bemus'd*, a Pencil in my hand,
> And, dead to ev'ry sense of shame,
> Careless of Safety and of Fame,
> The names of Scoundrels minute down,
> And Libel more than half the Town.[23]

The pose is Roy Campbell's rather than Juvenal's or Pope's. Campbell is for ever, in his satires, striking the attitude of the misunderstood outsider—'the restive steer', 'the centaur's foal', 'the angry whale'—the natural, honest creature in a world of clever and corrupt fools.[24]

It is to Byron, however, that Churchill may, in the context of the present argument, be most meaningfully related. In distinguishing himself from the painstaking imitators of Pope who, according to him, took infinite trouble to say nothing tunefully, Churchill had passed off the imperfections of his verse as defects of his virtues of naturalness, worldliness, and down-to-earth honesty. Byron's narrator makes much of these same virtues, though of course he wears them in a much more carefree and debonair manner—as befits 'A broken Dandy lately on [his] travels'.[25] He likes life too much to bother to take trouble with his writing—any old reach-me-down simile will do—and if he feels like digressing, then he will digress.

> To turn,—and to return;—the devil take it!
> This story slips for ever through my fingers . . .[26]

Byron revered Pope as 'the moral poet of civilization', and he regarded Dryden and Pope as superior to Wordsworth and Coleridge. Yet he was himself far from being an Augustan. No

---

23 'The Ghost', *Poetical Works*, p. 160.
24 *Collected Poems*, i (1949), 15, 27, and ii (1957), 84–94.
25 'Beppo', *Poetical Works* (Oxford, 1945), p. 629.
26 Ibid., p. 631.

doubt he was more intent on dissociating himself from his contemporaries than with examining carefully his relationship to the Augustan satirists, and was merely using Dryden and Pope as convenient sticks to beat his contemporaries with and not asserting close kinship with them. In retrospect we can now see him as essentially a 'Romantic' satirist, although clearly the connotations of 'Romantic' in this connection are different from those which the term has when it is applied to *Childe Harold* or *The Corsair*. Byron is a 'Romantic' satirist, in the basic sense that he wrote from outside society, against conventional beliefs and practices, against the Establishment. The positive values of his satire are not the Augustan virtues of moderation and order but pleasure—natural, spontaneous worldly pleasure like the love of Don Juan and Haidée—and freedom—the uninhibited *joie de vivre* of the Venetians in *Beppo*, or the undefined liberty which nations may enjoy if they are saved from Tyranny (with a capital 'T'). Byron's narrator has many friends and he enjoys society; nevertheless he is at odds with church and government, and with society, English upper-class society especially. Ostensibly at least, moreover, he is on the Devil's side. Perhaps indeed this provides the most dramatic illustration of the gap between Byron and the Augustans. Dryden was on God's side, of the King's party, and his chief target was the rebel who plotted against his King and conspired to overthrow His Majesty's Government. Dryden accepted the order of society and government as embodied in king, church, and parliament and, at the King's request, so it is believed, he wrote a satire in which the rebel is portrayed as Satan, the cosmic rebel, and the King as God's anointed representative on earth. How radically different is the fiction which Byron found suitable to his temperament and times. In *The Vision of Judgement* (like Bernard Shaw later in *The Devil's Disciple*) he presents the Devil as hero, for it is Mephistopheles who speaks the truth and establishes the foundations of the satire. The fashion is still with us: the satirical protagonist is still an outsider, in fact he has moved further and further outside society. Dick Dudgeon is not such a misfit as Waugh's Paul Pennyfeather, and not nearly so hopeless a misfit as Joseph Heller's Yossarian. The protagonist of satire may indeed be so far outside that he is, or at any rate goes, mad. Tod Hackett in Nathanael West's *The Day of the Locust* is carried away from a riot in Los Angeles, shrieking like the siren of a police car. The twentieth-century satirist sees himself as completely alienated from society and, for this and other reasons, he is fundamentally unsure of himself and his standards—less reasonable and judicial than Dryden or Johnson, more pessimistic than Juvenal or Swift. His tone may be cynical, or hysterical, but it is unlikely to be hortatory, and for *sæva indignatio* he may substitute a despairing nihilism. As Nathanael West put it, 'there is nothing to root for in my work and what is even worse, no rooters.'[27]

It follows that the modern critic will have a very different view of satire from that of the Augustans, for an age's idea of the role of the satirist is fundamental to its conception of the nature and function of satire. In the opening chapter it was suggested that 'theory' is hardly the right word to apply to the miscellaneous opinions on satire expressed in the late seventeenth and eighteenth centuries, if by 'theory' we mean 'the systematic statement of a point of view'. Yet, as subsequent chapters have attempted to demonstrate, a pattern is discernible in these miscellaneous opinions, an underlying consensus of belief, which can be appraised at a theoretical level.

From this standpoint a modern reader may find little in it with which he can agree. For instance, he would surely not accept the notion that satire should avoid inherently disgusting subjects, unless (like Richardson and Johnson) he were prepared to reject large sections of *Gulliver's Travels*, or unless he were to rule that George Orwell should not have included descriptions of torture in *Nineteen Eighty-Four*—and it would be an odd critic nowadays who would go so far. Nor could he dismiss the English satirists of the late sixteenth and early seventeenth centuries as blithely as the Augustans appear to have done. The satires of Hall, Marston, and Donne have one advantage over even the finest Augustan satires: by their very bluntness and vigour they are able to make the reader feel directly involved in the satire; with Augustan satire the effect is rather that of witnessing an expert performance from a safe distance. Then again, the modern reader would attach much less importance than the Augustans did to such considerations as the ethics of personal

---

[27] Unpublished letter, quoted in *The Day of the Locust* (New York, 1957), p. xx.

satire, and the relative merits of personal and general satire. From a strictly literary point of view, what we now consider important is not whether the satirist has drawn living persons, but whether he has made them live in his satires. For even if they are real people, in the sense of being drawn from real life, they still have to be imaginatively realized; and once this has been achieved, worries over personal reference recede into the background. At the moment of their creation, Zimri, Babbitt, and Snowball leave the real world behind.

In the areas which have just been mentioned, our modern approach to satire appears more resilient and comprehensive than the Augustan one. It would be rash to suggest, however, that it is any more clearly defined. Our idea of 'satire' is indeed probably even vaguer and more confused than that of the Augustans, if only because the area of confusion is now larger. 'Satire' continues to be the most variable of critical terms, appearing in a wide variety of contexts and changing from one context to another. It is associated with such different writers as Aristophanes, Horace, Skelton, Marston, Swift, Byron, Orwell, and Waugh, and applied to forms of such diverse origins and histories as mock-heroic poems, allegorical novels, beast-fables, and comedies of manners. It may be applied also to paintings, to mime, and (in the instance of musical parody) to music. In ordinary critical usage it may indicate almost anything which combines censure and humour, in whatever proportions, from a *jeu d'esprit* to a masterpiece. We have no working definition of the term; and the stock one which has been handed down to us, 'a composition (or the kind of composition) which holds up follies and vices to ridicule and scorn', has a hollow ring. In particular the terms 'folly' and 'vice' now seem unsatisfactory: 'folly' implies a deliberateness, a degree of volition, which may make us uneasy with it as a critical term, for we look on people as less responsible for their foolish actions than did Boileau and Pope: and 'vice' involves reference to absolutes of good and evil (except in its popular sense of 'a degrading, illegal pastime') which are no longer taken for granted. As Donald Davie comments in his poem 'Too Late For Satire':

> I might have been as pitiless as Pope
> But to no purpose; in a tragic age

> We share the hatred but we lack the hope
> By pinning follies to reform the age.
> To blame is lame, and satirists are late.
> No knife can stick in history or the id,
> No cutlass carve us from the lime of fate.[28]

Here is the crux of the matter. The fundamental difference between the Augustan and modern approaches to satire is that whereas Pope and his contemporaries saw man as a free and responsible agent, capable of ordering his life and society in the light of reason, we tend to think of him instead as impelled by all sorts of forces from within and without, from his own personality and society, which he is powerless to control—at best he may slightly alter their direction. It is sometimes suggested with regard to Augustan satire that the crucial change which took place in the eighteenth century was the substitution of humour for wit and of the comic for the satiric vision. 'Satire was killed with kindness', A. M. Wilkinson states.[29] This is a telling remark. But we need to go deeper, to explain that it was only the notion of 'corrective' satire that was killed, and that 'kindness' in this connection must be taken to imply not only a more sympathetic understanding of men as individuals, but also the realization that they are not reasoning beings capable of running their lives to rule. When the writer ceases to have faith in the ascendancy of reason, or in free will, he no longer instructs his fellow human beings: he depicts them. After Cervantes, Flaubert. Emma Bovary is as suitable a subject for satirical treatment as Don Quixote—at all events, she is equally deluded—but in Flaubert the satiric vision is replaced by realism.[30]

Yet satire is not, as the Augustans believed, in essence 'corrective'. Only a very gullible person thinks that it can 'wonderfully mend the world'. But no doubt we should take more care than we ordinarily do to avoid defining satire in terms of its reformative effects, and to avoid defending it on the grounds of its moral function. If we are to claim moral value for satire, it must be because it brings to light truths about human nature and society, not because it effects practical reforms. 'Je n'impose rien:

---

[28] *New Lines*, ed. Robert Conquest (1956).

[29] 'The Decline of English Verse Satire in the Middle Years of the Eighteenth Century', *RES* n.s. iii (1952), 228.

[30] For comments along these lines see John Lawlor, 'Radical Satire and the Realistic Novel', *E & S* n.s. viii (1955), 58–75.

j'expose.' The 'true end of satire' in modern terms is not 'reformation' (as it was for Defoe), nor 'the amendment of vices by correction' (as it was for Dryden), but the revelation of incongruities, absurdities, fallacies, and anomalies. Satire is a catalytic agent rather than an arm of the law or an instrument of correction: its function is less to judge people for their follies and vices than to challenge their attitudes and opinions, to taunt and provoke them into doubt, and perhaps into disbelief; its function is to make them at least *see* the world's enormities and absurdities.

If in one way the Augustan defenders of satire claimed too much for it—the claims of John Brown, for example, regarding its moral function and social effects now seem absurdly grandiose—in another way they claimed too little. They were too anxious to prescribe limits, whether of form, style, or subject-matter, and to push satire into one or another of a set of exclusive and opposed categories—Roman and Greek, Horatian and Juvenalian, 'smiling' and 'savage'. The danger in these white-black contrasts is not simply that of failing to notice sufficiently the shades in between, but of failing to realize that there are other colours as well. Even the latitude granted to satire by Dryden and Johnson, by the most far-seeing of the Augustan satirists and critics, can be shown to be inadequate by reference to one satirical work or another. For that matter it was proved inadequate by their own practice. Satire is the genie in the bottle: until he shows himself we cannot be quite sure which bottle he is in, or what shape he will take.

The variety and range of its meaning in the period may be illustrated by the following examples:

(*a*) 'Ridicule':

> Then decent pleasantry and sterling sense
> That never gave nor would endure offence,
> Whipp'd out of sight with satyr just and keen,
> The puppy pack that had defil'd the scene.
>
> (William Cowper, 'Table Talk', *Poems* (1782), i. 33)

(*b*) 'Censure' or 'sharp rebuke':

I know not, Orontes, how I shall escape your satyr, for venturing to be thus free with a science [verbal criticism] which is sometimes, I know, admitted into a share of your meditations . . .

> (Sir Thomas Fitzosborne [William Melmoth],
> *Letters on Several Subjects* (1748), p. 174)

(*c*) 'The subjecting of foolish and evil people to ridicule':

I have long been against my Inclination employ'd in Satyr, and that in Prosecution of such Persons who are below the Dignity of the true Spirit of it; such who I fear are not to be reclaim'd by making 'em only Ridiculous.

> (Sir Richard Steele, *The Tatler*, No. 71,
> 22 September 1709)

(*d*) 'A piece of light-hearted mockery':

This whimsical piece of work [*The Rape of the Lock*], as I have now brought it up to my first design, is at once the most a satire, and the most inoffensive, of anything of mine. People who would rather it were let alone laugh at it, and seem heartily merry, at the same time that they are uneasy. 'Tis a sort of writing very like tickling.

> (Pope to Mrs. or Miss Marriott, 28 February
> [1713/14], Pope's *Correspondence*, i. 211)

(*e*) 'A literary work exposing people and institutions to ridicule and censure':

As for those who condemn our author for the too much gall and virulency of his satires, it is to be suspected, says Dr. Mayne, that they themselves are guilty of those hypocrisies, crimes, and follies, which he so sharply exposes, and at the same time endeavours to reform.

> (Dryden, 'Life of Lucian' (1711),
> Dryden's *Works*, xviii. 70)

(*f*) 'The kind of literature which consists predominantly of ridicule and censure':

The most remarkable species of satire are, the narrative, dramatic, and picturesque . . .

> (George A. Stevens, 'An Essay on Satire', appended
> to *A Lecture on Heads* (1787), p. 119)

(g) 'A satirist):

> Leave dang'rous *Truths* to unsuccessful *Satyrs*,
> And *Flattery* to fulsome *Dedicators*,
>
> (Pope, *An Essay on Criticism*, lines 591–2,
> Pope's *Poems*, i. 307)

Bibliography

(The place of publication is London, unless otherwise specified)

A. BEFORE 1800

ABBOTT, CHARLES, Lord Tenterden, 'On the Use and Abuse of Satire' (1786), *Oxford English Prize Essays* (Oxford, 1836), i. 179–205.

ABERCROMBY, DAVID, *A Discourse of Wit* (1686).

ADDISON, JOSEPH, *The Tatler*, 1709–11. Revised and Corrected (5 vols., 1716).

—— *The Spectator*, Nos. 1–635, ed. D. F. Bond (5 vols., Oxford, 1965).

—— *The Free-Holder*, December 1715–June 1716 (1716).

The Adulteress (1773).

The Adventurer (1752–4).

AIKIN, JOHN, *Essay on the Application of Natural History to Poetry* (1777).

[ALLESTREE, RICHARD,] *The Government of the Tongue* (Oxford, 1674).

The Art of Poetry (1741).

The Art of Railing of Great Men: being a Discourse upon Political Railers Ancient and Modern (1723).

BAILEY, NATHAN, *Universal Etymological English Dictionary* (1st edn., 1721; 2nd edn. enlarged, 1724).

BARKER, HENRY (trans.), *The Polite Gentleman; or, Reflections Upon the Several Kinds of Wit* . . . (1700).

BARROW, ISAAC, *Against Foolish Talking and Jesting* (1678).

—— *Several Sermons Against Evil-Speaking* (1678).

BAYLE, PIERRE, *An Historical and Critical Dictionary*. Translated into English . . . (4 vols., 1710).

BEATTIE, JAMES, *Essays: on Poetry and Music as they affect the Mind; on Laughter and Ludicrous Compositions; on the Utility of Classical Learning* (Edinburgh, 1776).

BELLEGARDE, J. B. MORVAN DE, *Reflexions upon Ridicule* (1706).

[BENTLEY, RICHARD,] *Patriotism* (1763).

BLACKLOCK, THOMAS, *Poems* (1793).

BLACKMORE, SIR RICHARD, Preface to *Prince Arthur, an Heroick Poem* (1695).

[——] *A Satyr Against Wit* (1700).

BLACKWELL, T., *Letters Concerning Mythology* (1748).

BLAIR, H., *Lectures on Rhetoric and Belles Lettres* (2 vols., 1783).

BLOUNT, SIR THOMAS POPE, *De Re Poetica* (1694).

[——] *Glossographia Anglicana Nova* (1707).

BOILEAU-DESPRÉAUX, N., *Satires*, ed. Albert Cahen (Paris, 1932).
—— *Boileau's Lutrin: A Mock-Heroic Poem* (1708).
—— *Works*, trans. John Ozell (2 vols., 1712).
BOSCAWEN, WILLIAM, *The Progress of Satire* (1798).
BOSWELL, JAMES, *Letters between A. Erskine and J. Boswell* (1763).
—— 'On Ridicule', *The Hypochondriack*, No. lxii (1782).
—— *Life of Samuel Johnson* and *Journal of a Tour to the Hebrides*, ed.
   G. B. Hill, rev. L. F. Powell (6 vols., Oxford, 1934–64).
BOUHOURS, D., *Les Entretiens d'Ariste et d'Eugene* (Amsterdam, 1671).
BRAMSTON, J., *The Man of Taste* (1733).
BROWN, JOHN, *An Essay on Satire* (1745).
—— 'Essay on Ridicule', *Essays on the Characteristics of the Earl of
   Shaftesbury* (1751).
BROWN, TOM, 'An Essay upon Satyr', *The Works of Mr. Thomas Brown*
   (1707).
BRUYÈRE, JEAN DE LA, *The Character, or the Manners of the Age* . . .
   Made English by several hands (1699).
BULKELEY, CHARLES, *A Vindication of my Lord Shaftesbury on the
   Subject of Ridicule* (1751).
BULSTRODE, RICHARD, *Miscellaneous Essays* (1715).
BURNET, GILBERT, *A Discourse of the Pastoral Care* (1692).
BUTLER, SAMUEL, 'A Humorist', *Characters*, ed. A. R. Waller (Cambridge,
   1908).
CAMBRIDGE, RICHARD OWEN, *The Scribleriad* (1752).
CAMPBELL, GEORGE, *Philosophy of Rhetoric* (1776).
CASAUBON, ISAAC, *De Satyrica Græcorum Poesi et Romanorum Satira
   libri duo* . . . (Paris, 1605).
CHAMBERS, [EPHRAIM], *Cyclopaedia: or, An Universal Dictionary of Arts
   and Sciences* (2 vols., 1728).
The Champion, 1739–43 (2nd edn., 2 vols., 1743).
CHARLETON, WALTER, *A Brief Discourse Concerning the Different Wits
   of Men*: Written . . . In the Year 1664 (1669).
CHURCHILL, CHARLES, *Poetical Works*, ed. D. Grant (Oxford, 1956).
Churchill Defended (1765).
Churchill Dissected (1775).
CIBBER, THEOPHILUS, *An Apology for the life of Mr. Colley Cibber*
   (1740).
—— *Lives of the Poets of Great Britain and Ireland* (5 vols., 1753).
COCKER, EDWARD, *Cocker's English Dictionary* (1704).
COLES, E[LISHA,] *An English Dictionary* (1676).
COLLIER, JEREMY, *A Short View of the Profaneness and Immorality of the
   English Stage* (1698).
COLLINS, ANTHONY, *A Discourse concerning Ridicule and Irony in
   Writing* (1729).
[COMBE, W.,] *The Justification* (1777).
[——] *The Refutation* (1778).
Common Sense: or, The Englishman's Journal (1737–43).
CONGREVE, WILLIAM, *Comedies*, ed. B. Dobrée (1929).

CONGREVE, WILLIAM, *Amendments of Mr. Collier* (1698).
COOKE, THOMAS, *A Tryal of Hercules, an Ode on Glory, Virtue, and Pleasure* (1752).
—— *A Prologue on Comic Poetry* (1753).
COOPER, ANTHONY ASHLEY, Third Earl of Shaftesbury. *A Letter Concerning Enthusiasm* (1708).
—— *Advice to an Author* (1710).
—— *Characteristicks of Men, Manners, Opinions, Times* (1711).
COOPER, JOHN G., *Socrates* (1750).
COSMETTI, *The Polite Arts, Dedicated to the Ladies* (1767).
COTGRAVE, RANDLE, *A Dictionarie of the French and English Tongues* (1632).
The Covent-Garden Journal. See Fielding, Henry.
The Craftsman (1726–50).
The Critical Review (1756–90).
COWPER, WILLIAM, *Poetical Works*, ed. H. Milford (Oxford, 1905).
—— *Poems* (1782–5).
—— *Letters*, ed. T. Wright (4 vols., 1904).
DACIER, ANDRÉ, 'Préface sur les satires d'Horace', *Œuvres d'Horace*, 1681–9, vi (1687).
Dedication to the Author of the Dunciad, A Compleat Collection of all the Verses, Essays, Letters and Advertisements which Have been occasioned by the Publication of Three Volumes of Miscellanies, by Pope and Company (1728).
DEFOE, B. N., *A Compleat English Dictionary* (1735).
DEFOE, DANIEL, *Works*, ed. G. H. Maynadier (16 vols., New York, 1903–4).
—— *The True-Born Englishman* (1701).
—— *Letters*, ed. G. H. Healey (Oxford, 1955).
DENNIS, JOHN, *Critical Works*, ed. E. N. Hooker (Baltimore, 1939).
DESCARTES, RENÉ, *Passiones Animae* (Amsterdam, 1650).
DRAKE, JAMES, *The Antient and Modern Stages survey'd* (1699).
DRAKE, JUDITH, *An Essay in Defence of the Female Sex* (1696).
DRANT, THOMAS, *Medicinable Morall* (1566).
DRYDEN, JOHN, *Works*, ed. Walter Scott (18 vols., 1808).
—— *Essays*, ed. W. P. Ker (2 vols., Oxford, 1900).
—— *Letters*, ed. C. E. Ward (Durham, N.C., 1946).
—— *Poems*, ed. J. Kinsley (4 vols., Oxford, 1958).
—— *Of Dramatic Poesy, and Other Critical Essays*, ed. George Watson (2 vols., 1962).
D'URFEY, THOMAS, *A Fool's Preferment* (1688).
DYCHE, THOMAS, *A New English Dictionary*. Originally begun by the late . . . Thomas Dyche, And now finish'd by William Pardon (1740).
EACHARD, JOHN, *The Grounds and Occasions of the Contempt of the Clergy and Religion Enquired into* (1670).
An Essay on Laughter, wherein are Displayed its Natural and Moral Causes . . . (1769).

An Essay on Polite Behaviour, wherein The Nature of Complaisance and True Gentility is consider'd and Recommended (1740).
An Essay on Wit (1748).
An Essay upon the Taste and Writings of the Present Times (1728).
FARQUHAR, GEORGE, *A Discourse upon Comedy, in reference to the English Stage* (1702).
FIELDING, HENRY, *Works*, ed. L. Stephen (10 vols., 1882).
―― *The Historical Register for the Year 1736* (1736).
―― *The Champion* (1739–43).
―― *The Covent-Garden Journal*, 4 January 1752–25 November 1752.
FLECKNOE, RICHARD, 'Of Raillerie', *Enigmaticall Characters* (n. pl., 1658).
FLORIO, JOHN, *A Worlde of Words* (1598).
FORRESTER, JAMES, *The Polite Philosopher* (Edinburgh, 1734).
The Free-Holder, December 1715–June 1716 (1716).
GARRICK, DAVID, *The Letters of David Garrick*, edd. David M. Little and George M. Kahrl (3 vols., 1963).
GAY, JOHN, *Poetical Works*, ed. G. C. Faber (1926).
―― *The Present State of Wit* (1711).
GENTLEMAN, F., *The General* (1764).
GERARD, ALEXANDER, *Essay on Taste* (1759; 2nd edn., Edinburgh, 1764).
GIBBON, EDWARD, *Letters*, ed. J. E. Norton (3 vols., 1956).
GILBERT, THOMAS, *The First Satire of Juvenal Imitated* . . . (1739), in *Poems on Several Occasions* (1747).
GILDON, CHARLES, *A Letter to Mr. d'Urfey, Occasioned by his Play Called the Marriage-Hater Matched* (1692).
―― *Miscellaneous Letters and Essays* (1694).
―― *The Complete Art of Poetry* (2 vols., 1718).
―― *The Laws of Poetry* (1721).
[GLANVILL, JOSEPH,] *Reflections on Drollery and Atheism; in a Blow at Modern Sadducism* (1668).
GODDARD, WILLIAM, *A Satyricall Dialogue* ([Dort ?, 1615?]).
GOLDSMITH, OLIVER, *Collected Letters*, ed. K. C. Balderston (Cambridge, 1928).
―― *Collected Works of Oliver Goldsmith*, ed. Arthur Friedman (5 vols., Oxford, 1966).
[GORDON, THOMAS,] *The Humourist* (1720–5).
GREENE, SIR EDWARD BURNABY. *See* Juvenal.
The Grub-Street Journal (1730–7).
The Guardian (1713).
HACKET, JOHN, *A Century of Sermons Upon Several Remarkable Subjects* (1675).
HALL, JOSEPH, *Poems*, ed. A. Davenport (Liverpool, 1949).
The Harleian Miscellany: or, a Collection of Scarce, Curious, and Entertaining Pamphlets and Tracts (10 vols., 1744–6).
HARTE, WALTER, *An Essay on Satire, Particularly on the Dunciad. To which is added A Discourse on Satires, Arraigning Persons by Name. By Monsieur Boileau* (1730).

HARTLEY, DAVID, *Observations on Man, His Frame, His Duty, and His Expectations* (1749).

HAYWOOD, ELIZA, *The Parrot*, No. 8 (1746).

HEAD, RICHARD, *Proteus Redivivus* (1675).

HEINSIUS, DANIEL, *De Satyra Horatiana Libri Duo* (Elzevir edn., Leyden, 1629).

HERVEY, LORD JOHN, *A Satire in the Manner of Persius* (1739).

HOBBES, THOMAS, *Leviathan, Or the Matter, Forme and Power of a Commonwealth Ecclesiasticall and Civil* (1651).

HOME, HENRY, Lord Kames, *Elements of Criticism* (2 vols., Edinburgh, 1762).

HORACE, Q. *Horati Flacci Opera*, ed. H. W. Garrod (Oxford, 1912).

HUGHES, JOHN, *Poems on Several Occasions. With some Select Essays in Prose* (1735).

HURD, RICHARD, *A Discourse Concerning Poetical Imitation; Q. Horati Flacci Epistola ad Augustum* (1751).

HUTCHESON, FRANCIS, *Reflections upon Laughter* (Glasgow, 1750).

The Intelligencer (Dublin, 1728).

JACOB, GILES, *An Historical Account of the Lives and Writings of Our Most Considerable English Poets* (1720).

—— *The Poetical Register* (1723).

The Jacobite's Journal, 5 December 1747–5 November 1748.

JEMMAL, C., *Miscellanies in Prose and Verse* (1766).

JOHNSON, SAMUEL, *The Rambler*, 1750–2 (2nd edn., 6 vols., 1752).

—— *The Idler* (2 vols., 1761).

—— *The Plays of William Shakespeare* (8 vols., 1765).

—— *The Lives of the English Poets* (3 vols., Dublin, 1779–81).

—— *Poems*, edd. D. N. Smith and E. L. McAdam (Oxford, 1941).

—— *Letters*, ed. R. W. Chapman (3 vols., Oxford, 1952).

JUVENAL, *A Persi Flacci et D. Junii Juvenalis Saturae*, ed. W. V. Clausen (Oxford, 1959).

—— *D. J. Juvenal and A. Persius Flaccus*, trans. Barten Holyday and William Dewey (Oxford, 1673).

—— *Juvenalis Redivivus*, [*Thomas Wood*] (1683).

—— *The Satires of Decimus Junius Juvenalis*, Translated into English Verse by Mr. Dryden and Several Other Eminent Hands, Together with the *Satires of Aulus Persius Flaccus* (1693).

—— *The Satires of Juvenal Paraphrastically Imitated and Adapted To the Times*, trans. Sir Edward Burnaby Greene (1763).

—— *The Satires of Juvenal with . . . An essay on the Satire of the Ancients and the Abuses of Modern Satire*, trans. E[dward] Owen (2 vols., 1785).

K., J., [JOHN KERSEY?] *A New English Dictionary* (1702).

[KING, WILLIAM,] *Some Remarks on the Tale of a Tub* (1704).

[——] *The Toast, An Heroick Poem* (1736).

KNOX, VICESIMUS, 'Cursory Thoughts on Satire and Satirists', *Essays, Moral and Literary* (2 vols., 1778–9).

LANGBAINE, GERARD, *An Account of the English Dramatick Poets* (Oxford, 1691).

LENNOX, CHARLOTTE, *The Female Quixote* (2 vols., 1752).

L'ESTRANGE, ROGER, *Tully's Offices* (1681).

LOVELING, BENJAMIN, *The First Satire of Persius Imitated* (1740).

LYTTLETON, GEORGE, BARON, *Dialogues of the Dead* (1760).

—— *Works* (1774).

MANDEVILLE, BERNARD, *The Fable of the Bees: or, Private Vices, Publick Benefits* (1714).

—— *The Fable of the Bees*, ed. F. B. Kaye (2 vols., Oxford, 1924).

MARSTON, JOHN, *The Scourge of Villanie* (1598).

MASON, WILLIAM, *Works* (4 vols., 1811).

—— *Poems* (1764).

—— *Satirical Poems*. With Introduction by Horace Walpole (first published, 1779; repr. Oxford, 1926).

[MATHIAS, T. J.,] *The Pursuits of Literature, A* Satirical Poem in Four Dialogues (5th edn., 1798).

MEIER, GEORG FRIEDRICK, *The Merry Philosopher; or Thoughts on Jesting* (1765).

[MELMOTH, WILLIAM,] *Letters of Several Subjects by the late Sir Thomas Fitzosborne* (1748; 2nd edn., 1776, expanded [especially on the function of satire]).

MILTON, JOHN, *Complete Prose Works*, 7 vols., i (1624–41), ed. D. M. Wolfe; ii (1643–8), ed. E. Sirluck; iii (1648–9), ed. M. Y. Hughes (1953–9).

Mirth in Ridicule: or, a Satyr against Immoderate Laughing (1708).

MONTAGU, LADY MARY WORTLEY, *The Complete Letters*, ed. R. Halsband (Oxford, 1965).

The Monthly Review, 1749–89).

[MOORE, E., and others,] *The World*, 4 January 1753–30 December 1756.

MORERY, LEWIS, *The Great Historical, Geographical and Poetical Dictionary*, trans. 'by several Learned Men' (1694).

[MORRIS, CORBYN,] *An Essay Towards Fixing the True Standards of Wit, Humour, Raillery, Satire, and Ridicule* (1744).

[MURPHY, ARTHUR,] *The Gray's-Inn Journal*, September 1753–September 1754 (1754).

NEWBERY, J., *The Art of Poetry on a New Plan* (2 vols., 1762).

OLDHAM, JOHN, *The Works of Mr. John Oldham, Together with his Remains* (1684).

—— *The Poems of John Oldham*, ed. Bonamy Dobrée (1960).

—— *Satyrs upon the Jesuits: Written in the Year 1679* ('corrected' edn., 1682).

OLDMIXON, JOHN, *Essay on Criticism* (1728).

OTWAY, THOMAS, *Works* (2 vols., 1712).

OWEN, E[DWARD,]. See Juvenal.

[P., H.,] *A Satyr Against Commonwealth* (1684).

PHILIPS, AMBROSE, *A Reflection on our Modern Poesy* (1695).

—— *Codrus: or, The Dunciad Dissected* (1728).

PARKER, SAMUEL, *A Free and Impartial Censure of the Platonick Philosophie* (Oxford, 1666).

PERSIUS. *See* Juvenal.

P[HILLIPS,] E[DWARD,] *The New World of English Words* (1658).

PHILLIPS, EDWARD, *Preface to Theatrum Poetarum* (1675).

PIOZZI, HESTER LYNCH, *Anecdotes of the Late Samuel Johnson, LL.D.* (1786).

A Pocket Dictionary or Complete English Expositor (1753).

Poems on Affairs of State (1679 et seq.).

Poems on Affairs of State: Augustan Satirical Verse, 1660–1714; vol. i, 1660–78 (Yale, 1963).

POOLE, JOSHUA, *The English Parnassus: or, A Helpe to English Poesie* (1657).

POPE, ALEXANDER, *Poems*, Twickenham edn., edd. J. Butt and others (6 vols., 1954–63).
  I. *Pastoral Poetry and Essay on Criticism*, edd. E. Audra and A. L. Williams (1961).
  II. *The Rape of the Lock and Other Poems*, ed. G. Tillotson (3rd edn., 1962).
  III. (i) *Essay on Man*, ed. M. Mack; (ii) *Epistles to several Persons*, ed. F. W. Bateson (2nd edn., 1961).
  IV. *Imitations of Horace*, ed. J. Butt (rev. edn., 1953).
  V. *The Dunciad*, ed. J. Sutherland (rev. edn., 1963).
  VI. *Minor Poems*, edd. N. Ault and J. Butt (1954).
—— *Correspondence*, ed. G. Sherburn (5 vols., Oxford, 1956).

PRIESTLEY, J., *A Course of Lectures on Oratory, and Criticism* (1777).

PRIOR, MATTHEW, *The Literary Works of Matthew Prior*, edd. H. Bunker Wright and Monroe K. Spears (2 vols., Oxford, 1959).

PUTTENHAM, GEORGE, *The Arte of English Poesie* (1589).

Raillerie a la Mode Consider'd or the Supercilious Detractor (1673).

The Rambler (1750–2).

RAMSAY, ALLAN, *An Essay on Ridicule* (1753).

RAPIN, RENÉ, *Reflections on Aristotle's Treatise of Poesie*, trans. Thomas Rymer (1674).

RICHARDSON, SAMUEL, *Works*, ed. L. Stephen (12 vols., 1883).
—— *Selected Letters of Samuel Richardson*, ed. John Carroll (1964).

RIGALTIUS, NICOLAUS, *De Satyra Juvenalis* (Leyden, 1616).

ROWE, N., 'Some account of Boileau's Writings, And this Translation', *Boileau's Lutrin*, trans. John Ozell (1708).

RUFFHEAD, OWEN, *Life of Pope* (1769).

SACKVILLE, CHARLES, Earl of Dorset, *The Works of the Earls of Rochester, Roscommon, Dorset*, etc. (2 vols., 1714).

[SACKVILLE, GEORGE, Marquis of Halifax] *The Character of a Trimmer* (1688).

The Satirists, A Satire . . . [1739?].

SCOTT, JAMES, *The Perils of Poetry* (1766).

S.[ERGEANT,] J.[OHN,] *Raillery Defeated by Calm Reason* (1699).

SHADWELL, THOMAS, *The Humorists* (1671).

SHEFFIELD, JOHN, Earl of Mulgrave, *Works* (1721).
—— *Essay on Satyre* (1679).
—— *An Essay Upon Poetry* (1682).
SHENSTONE, WILLIAM, *Works* (2 vols., 1764).
SHERIDAN, RICHARD BRINSLEY, *Plays and Poems*, ed. R. C. Rhodes (3 vols., Oxford, 1928).
SMART, CHRISTOPHER, *The Hilliad* (1753).
SMITH, EDMUND, *A Poem on the Death of Mr. John Philips* (n.d. [1710]).
SMOLLETT, TOBIAS, *Works*, ed. G. Saintsbury (11 vols., Oxford, 1925–6).
The Spectator. See Addison, J.
SPENCE, JOSEPH, *Observations, Anecdotes, and Characters of Books and Men*, ed. James M. Osborn (2 vols., Oxford, 1966).
SPRAT, THOMAS, *History of the Royal Society* (1667).
—— *An Account of the Life and Writings of Mr. Abraham Cowley. Prefixed to Cowley's Works* (1668).
STANHOPE, PHILIP D., 4th Earl of Chesterfield, *Letters to his Son* (2 vols., 1774).
STEELE, SIR RICHARD, *The Tatler*. See Addison, J.
—— *The Spectator*. See Addison, J.
STERNE, LAURENCE, *Works*, ed. G. Saintsbury (7 vols., Oxford, 1926–7).
STEVENS, GEORGE ALEXANDER, *A Lecture on Heads . . . To Which is added an Essay on Satire* (1787).
STILLINGFLEET, BENJAMIN, *An Essay on Conversation* (1737).
The Student, or, the Oxford and Cambridge Monthly Miscellany (Oxford, 1750–1).
SWIFT, DEANE, *An Essay Upon the Life, Writings and Character of Dr. Jonathan Swift* (1755).
SWIFT, JONATHAN, *Prose Works*, ed. H. Davis (14 vols., Oxford, 1939–63).
—— *Poems*, ed. H. Williams (3 vols., Oxford, 1937; 2nd edn., 1958).
—— *Correspondence*, ed. H. Williams (5 vols., 1963–5).
SWIFT, T., *The Temple of Folly* (1787).
The Tatler, 1709–11. See Addison, J.
TEMPLE, WILLIAM, 'Upon Poetry', and 'Upon Ancient and Modern Learning', *Miscellanea*, Second Part (1690).
TICKELL, RICHARD, *The Wreath of Fashion, or, the Art of Sentimental Poetry* (1778).
TILLOTSON, JOHN, *Works* (3 vols., 1728).
TRAPP, JOSEPH, *Praelectiones Poeticae* (1711–15).
—— *Lectures on Poetry*, trans. W. Clarke and W. Bowyer (1742).
TRUSLER, JOHN, *The Distinction Between Words Esteemed Synonymous*, (1766; 2nd edn., 1783).
VANBRUGH, SIR JOHN, *The Provok'd Wife* (1697).
The Vanity of Scoffing: or a Letter to a Witty Gentleman, Evidently Shewing the Great Weakness and Unreasonableness of Scoffing at the Christian's Faith, on Account of its Supposed Uncertainty, [Clement Ellis and John Fell?] (1674).
VICTOR, BENJAMIN, *An Epistle to Sir Richard Steele, On His Play call'd The Conscious Lovers* (1722).

VILLIERS, GEORGE, Duke of Buckingham, *The Rehearsal* (1671).

A Vindication of the Stage (1698).

VOLTAIRE, FRANÇOIS MARIE AROUET DE, 'Memoire sur la satire', *Œuvres complètes de Voltaire*, iii (1785), 480–503.

WALPOLE, HORACE, Earl of Orford, *Correspondence*, ed. Mrs. P. Toynbee (16 vols., Oxford, 1903–5; supplement, ed. P. Toynbee, 3 vols., Oxford, 1918–25). Yale Edition, edd. W. S. Lewis and others, 1937– (vols. 1–22, 28–31 published).

WALWYN, B., *An Essay on Comedy* (1783).

WARTON, JOSEPH, *The Adventurer* (1752–4).

—— *The World*, No. 26 (1753).

—— *An Essay on the Writings and Genius of Pope* (1756).

WEBB, D., *Remarks on the Beauties of Poetry* (1762).

WELSTED, LEONARD, *A Dissertation Concerning the Perfection of the English Language, the State of Poetry*, etc. (1724).

[WELSTED, L., and SMYTHE, J. M.,] *One Epistle to Mr. Pope Occasion'd by two Epistles Lately Published* (?1730).

WHICHCOTE, BENJAMIN, *The Work of Reason* (1660).

WHITEHEAD, WILLIAM, *An Essay on Ridicule* (1743).

WILKES, THOMAS, *A General View of the Stage* (1759).

WILMOT, JOHN, Earl of Rochester, *Poems*, ed. V. de S. Pinto (1963).

WOLSELEY, ROBERT, Preface to *Valentinian* (1685).

WOOD, ANTHONY A, *Athenae Oxonienses*, ed. Philip Bliss (4 vols., 1813–20).

[WOOD, THOMAS,]. *See* Juvenal.

The World, 4 January 1753–30 December 1756.

WYCHERLEY, WILLIAM, *The Plain Dealer* (1677).

[YOUNG, EDWARD,] *Love of Fame, the Universal Passion, in Seven Characteristical Satires* (2nd edn., corrected, 1728).

[——] *Two Epistles to Mr. Pope, concerning the Authors of the Age* (1730).

[——] *Conjectures on Original Composition* (1759).

B. AFTER 1800

ABERCROMBIE, NIGEL, 'Cartesianism and Classicism', *MLR* xxi (1936), 358–76.

ALDEN, RAYMOND M., *The Rise of Formal Satire in England under Classical Influence* (Philadelphia, 1899).

ALDRIDGE, ALFRED OWEN, 'Shaftesbury and the Test of Truth', *PMLA* lx (1945), 129–56.

AMERASINGHE, UPALI, *Dryden and Pope in the Early Nineteenth Century, a Study of Changing Literary Taste, 1800–1830* (Cambridge, 1962).

ARMENS, S. M., *John Gay: Social Critic* (Oxford, 1954).

ATKINS, J. W. H., *English Literary Criticism: The Renascence* (1947).

AUDRA, EMILE, *L'Influence Française dans l'œuvre de Pope* (Paris, 1931).

BARNES, ARTHUR G., *A Book of English Verse Satire* (1926).

BARRETT, WILLIAM, 'Writers and Madness', *Partisan Review*, xiv (1947), 5–22.

BEATTY, J. M., 'Churchill's Influence on Minor Eighteenth Century Satirists', *PMLA* xlii (1927), 162–76.

BECKER, CARL L., *The Heavenly City of Eighteenth-Century Philosophers* (New Haven, Conn., 1932).

BELJAME, ALEXANDRE, *Men of Letters and the English Public in the Eighteenth Century, 1660–1744*, ed. Bonamy Dobrée, trans. E. O. Lorimer (1948).

BERGSON, HENRY, *Le Rire. Essai sur la signification du comique* (Paris, 1900).

—— *Laughter. An Essay on the Meaning of the Comic*, trans. C. Brereton and F. Rothwell (1911).

BOND, RICHMOND P., *English Burlesque Poetry, 1700–1750* (Harvard, 1932).

BRAY, RENÉ, *La Formation de la doctrine classique en France* (Paris, 1927).

BREDVOLD, LOUIS I., 'Dryden, Hobbes and the Royal Society', *MP* xxv (1928), 417–38.

—— *The Intellectual Milieu of John Dryden* (Ann Arbor, Mich., 1934).

—— 'A Note in Defence of Satire', *ELH* vii (1940), 253–64.

BRETT, R. L., *The Third Earl of Shaftesbury: A Study in Eighteenth Century Literary Theory* (1951).

BROOKS, HAROLD F., 'Imitation in English Poetry', *RES* xxv (1949), 124–40.

CANNAN, GILBERT, *Satire* [1914].

CARROLL, JOHN, 'Richardson on Pope and Swift', *University of Toronto Quarterly*, xxxiii (1963–4), 19–29.

CHESTERTON, G. K., *Varied Types* (New York, 1903).

CLARK, A. F. B., *Boileau and the French Classical Critics in England* (Paris, 1925).

CLIFFORD, J. L., and LANDA, L. A., *Pope and His Contemporaries, Essays Presented to George Sherburn* (1949).

CONQUEST, ROBERT (ed.), *New Lines* (1956).

'Considerations in the Similitude of Genius between Horace, Boileau and Pope', *British Magazine*, i (1960), 467–8.

DAVIS, HERBERT, *The Satire of Jonathan Swift* (New York, 1947).

DITCHFIELD, P. H., *Books Fatal to their Authors* (1895).

DRAPER, JOHN W., *Eighteenth Century English Aesthetics: A Bibliography* (Heidelberg, 1931).

—— 'The Theory of the Comic in Eighteenth Century England', *JEGP* xxxvii (1938), 207–23.

DURHAM, W. H., *Critical Essays of the Eighteenth Century 1700–1725* (New Haven, 1915).

DYSON, A., *The Crazy Fabric: Essays in Irony* (1965).

EASTMAN, MAX, *Sense of Humour* (New York, 1922).

EINSTEIN, LEWIS, *The Italian Renaissance in England* (New York, 1902).

ELIOSEFF, LEE ANDREW, *The Cultural Milieu of Addison's Literary Criticism* (Austin, 1963).

ELLEDGE, SCOTT, *Eighteenth Century Critical Essays* (Cornell and O.U.P., 1961).

ELLIOTT, ROBERT C., 'The Satirist and Society', *ELH* xxi (1954), 237–48.

—— *The Power of Satire* (Princeton, N.J., 1960).

ELLIS, AMANDA M., 'Horace's Influence on Dryden', *PQ* iv (1925), 39–60.

ELTON, O., *A Survey of English Literature 1730–1780* (2 vols., 1928).

FAIRCLOUGH, H. RUSHTON, 'Horace's View of the Relations Between Satire and Comedy', *American Journal of Philology*, xxxiv (1913), 183–93.

FARRER, J. A., *Books Condemned to be Burnt* (1892).

FEINBERG, LEONARD, *The Satirist* (Iowa, 1963).

FOX, W. SHERWOOD, 'Cursing as a Fine Art', *Sewanee Review* xxvii (1919), 460–77.

FRENCH, J. MILTON, 'Milton as Satirist', *PMLA* li (1936), 414–29.

FRYE, NORTHROP, 'The Nature of Satire', *University of Toronto Quarterly*, xiv (1944), 75–89.

—— *Anatomy of Criticism* (Princeton, N.J., 1957).

GIFFORD, H., 'The Vanity of Human Wishes', *RES* n.s. vi (1955), 157–65.

GILMORE, THOMAS B. JUN., 'The Dating of "The Satirists, A Satire"', *N & Q* n.s. xiii (1966), 216–17.

GOAD, CAROLINE MABEL, *Horace in the English Literature of the Eighteenth Century* (New Haven, Conn., 1918).

GRANSDEN, K. W., *Tudor Verse Satire* (1970).

GRANT, MARY A., *The Ancient Rhetorical Theories of the Laughable: The Greek Rhetoricians and Cicero*, University of Wisconsin Studies in Language and Literature, No. 21 (Madison, Wisconsin, 1924).

GREENE, D. J., 'Logical Structure in Eighteenth-Century Poetry', *PQ* xxxi (1952), 326–36.

HANNAY, JAMES, *Satire and Satirists, Six Lectures* (1854).

HARRIS, BRICE, 'Captain Robert Julian, Secretary to the Muses', *ELH* x (1943), 294–309.

HARRISON, G. B., *Introduction to John Marston: The Scourge of Villainie, 1599* (Bodley Head Quarto, 1925).

HENDRICKSEN, G. L., 'The Dramatic Satura and the Old Comedy at Rome' *AJP* xv (1894), 1–30.

—— 'Are the Letters of Horace Satires?' Ibid. xviii (1897), 313–24.

—— 'The Present Status of the Satura Question', *SP* xvii (1920), 379–401.

HIGHET, GILBERT, *Juvenal the Satirist* (Oxford, 1954).

—— *The Anatomy of Satire* (Princeton, N.J., 1962).

HODGART, MATTHEW, *Satire* (1969).

HOLDEN, WILLIAM P., *Anti-Puritan Satire 1572–1642* (Hamden, 1968).

HOOKER, E. N., 'Humour in the Age of Pope', *HLQ* xi (1948), 361–85.

HOPKINS, K., *Portraits in Satire* (1958).

HUMPHREYS, A. R., *The Augustan World* (1954).

HUXLEY, ALDOUS, 'Forgotten Satirists', *London Mercury*, i (1920), 565–73.

IRVINE, MAURICE, 'Identification of Characters in Mulgrave's "Essay Upon Satyr" ', *SP* xxxv (1937), 533–51.

IRWIN, W. R., 'Satire and Comedy in the Works of Henry Fielding', *ELH* xiii (1946), 168–88.

JACK, IAN, *Augustan Satire: Intention and Idiom in English Poetry, 1660–1750* (Oxford, 1952).

JOHNSON, JAMES WILLIAM, 'The Meaning of "Augustan" ', *JHI* xix (1958), 507–22.

JONES, W. A., 'Political Satire', *Essays upon Authors and Books* (New York, 1849).

KENNER, HUGH, 'The Man of Sense as Buster Keaton', *Virginia Quarterly*, xli (Winter, 1965), 77–91.

KERNAN, ALVIN B., *The Cankered Muse* (New Haven, 1959).

—— *The Plot of Satire* (New Haven, 1965).

KINSLEY, JAMES, and BOULTON, JAMES T. (edd.), *English Satiric Poetry, Dryden to Byron* (1966).

KITCHEN, G., *A Survey of Burlesque and Parody in English* (1931).

KNOX, NORMAN, *The Word IRONY and Its Context, 1500–1755* (Duke, 1961).

KNOX, RONALD, *Essays in Satire* (1928).

KRUTCH, JOSEPH WOOD, *Comedy and Conscience After the Restoration* (New York, 1924).

LANDA, L., and CRANE, R. S., *English Literature 1600–1800: A Bibliography of Modern Studies* (Princeton, N.J., 1962).

LASCELLES, MARY, 'Johnson and Juvenal', *New Light on Dr. Johnson: Essays on the Occasion of his 250th Birthday*, ed. Frederick W. Hilles (Yale, 1959).

LAWLOR, JOHN, 'Radical Satire and the Realistic Novel', *E & S*, n.s. viii (1955), 58–75.

LEAVIS, F. R., 'The Irony of Swift', *Scrutiny*, ii (1934), 364–78.

—— *Revaluation: Tradition and Development in English Poetry* (1936).

LECOCQ, LOUIS, *La Satire en Angleterre de 1588 à 1603* (Paris, 1969).

LEEDY, P. F., 'Genres Criticism and Warton's Essay on Pope', *JEGP* xlv (1946), 140–6.

LEWIS, WYNDHAM, *Men Without Art* (1934).

—— 'Studies in the Art of Laughter', *London Mercury*, xxx (1934), 509–15.

LEYBURN, ELLEN DOUGLASS, *Satiric Allegory: Mirror of Man* (Yale, 1956).

LOFTIS, JOHN, *The Politics of Drama in Augustan England* (Oxford, 1963).

LOVEJOY, ARTHUR O., ' "Nature" as Aesthetic Norm', *MLN* xlii (1927), 444–50.

MacCLINTOCK, W. D., *Joseph Warton's Essay on Pope: A History of the Five Editions* (Chapel Hill, 1933).

McDONALD, CHARLES O., 'Restoration Comedy as Drama of Satire: An Investigation into Seventeenth Century Aesthetics', *SP* vol. lxi, no. 3 (July 1964), 522–44.

MACK, MAYNARD, 'The Muse of Satire', *Yale Review*, xl (1951), 80–92.

MACKIN, R. COOPER, 'The Satiric Technique of John Oldham's Satyrs Upon the Jesuits', *SP* vol. lxii, no. 1 (January 1965), 78–90.

MACLEAN, KENNETH, *John Locke and English Literature of the Eighteenth Century* (New Haven, Conn., 1936).

MARBURG, CLARA, *Sir William Temple* (New Haven, 1932).

MARESCA, THOMAS E., 'Pope's Defense of Satire: The First Satire of the Second Book of Horace, Imitated', *ELH* xxxi (1964), 366–94.

MARIOTT, J. W., 'Satire and Satirists', *Papers of the Manchester Literary Club*, xliv (1918), 99–100.

MENDELL, C. W., 'Satire as Popular Philosophy', *CP* xv (1920), 138–57.

MEREDITH, GEORGE, *An Essay on Comedy and the Uses of the Comic Spirit* (1897).

MILLER, HENRY KNIGHT, *Essays on Fielding's Miscellanies* (Princeton, 1961).

MOORE, C. A., 'Shaftesbury and the Ethical Poets in England, 1700–1760', *PMLA* xxxi (1916), 264–325.

NEFF, T. L., *La Satire des femmes dans la poésie lyrique française du moyen age* (Paris, 1900).

NETTLESHIP, H., 'The Original Form of the Roman Satura', *Lectures and Essays* (2nd series, Oxford, 1895).

NICOLL, ALLARDYCE, *The Theory of Drama* (1931).

PARKER, DE WITT, *The Principles of Aesthetics* (New York, 1947).

PAULSON, RONALD, *Satire and the Novel in Eighteenth-Century England* (Yale, 1967).

—— (ed.), *Satire: Modern Essays in Criticism* (1971).

PLUMB, J. H., *Sir Robert Walpole* (1956).

—— *The First Four Georges* (1956).

POUND, EZRA, 'Horace', *Criterion*, ix (1930), 217–27.

PREVITÉ-ORTON, C. W., *Political Satire in English Poetry* (Cambridge, 1910).

RALEIGH, SIR WALTER, *Some Authors, a Collection of Literary Essays, 1896–1916* (Oxford, 1923).

RAND, BENJAMIN, *The Life, Unpublished Letters and Philosophical Regimen of Anthony, Earl of Shaftesbury* (1900).

RANDOLPH, MARY CLAIRE, 'The Medical Concept in English Renaissance Satiric Theory', *SP* xxxviii (1941), 125–57.

—— 'The Structural Design of the Formal Verse Satire', *PQ* xxi (1942), 368–84.

—— 'Candour in Eighteenth Century Satire', *RES* xx (1944), 45–62.

ROBINSON, F. N., 'Satirists and Enchanters in Early Irish Literature', *Studies in the History of Religions* (New York, 1912).

ROGERS, A. K., 'The Ethics of Mandeville', *International Journal of Ethics*, xxxvi (1925), 1–17.

ROSENHEIM, EDWARD W., JUN., *Swift and the Satirist's Art* (Chicago, 1963).

RUDD, NYALL, 'Dryden on Horace and Juvenal', *University of Toronto Quarterly*, xxxii (1962–3), 155–69.

RUSSELL, FRANCES T., *Satire in the Victorian Novel* (New York, 1920).

SCHEFFAUER, HERMAN, 'The Death of Satire', *Fortnightly Review*, xcix (1913), 1188–99.

SHERBURN, G., 'The Restoration and Eighteenth Century', *A Literary History of England*, ed. A. C. Baugh (1950).

SHERO, LUCIUS ROGERS, 'The Satirist's Apologia', *Classical Studies*, Series II, University of Wisconsin Studies (1922), 148–67.

SMEATON, OLIPHANT (ed.), *English Satires* (1924).

SMITH, G. GREGORY (ed.), *Elizabethan Critical Essays* (2 vols., Oxford, 1904).

SPACKS, PATRICIA M., 'Recent Studies in the Restoration and the Eighteenth Century', *Studies in English Literature 1500–1900*, vol. iv, no. 3 (Summer, 1964), 497–517.

SPINGARN, J. E. (ed.), *Critical Essays of the Seventeenth Century* (3 vols., 1908).

STARNES, DE WITT T., and NOYES, GERTRUDE E., *The English Dictionary from Cowdrey to Johnson* (Chapel Hill, 1946).

STRACHEY, LYTTON, *Pope* (Cambridge, 1925).

SULLY, JAMES, *An Essay on Laughter* (1902).

SUTHERLAND, J. R., *A Preface to Eighteenth Century Poetry* (1948).

—— *English Satire* (Cambridge, 1958).

SUTHERLAND, W. O. S., JUN., *The Art of the Satirist* (Texas, 1965).

TATE, J., 'Horace and the Moral Function of Poetry', *Classical Quarterly*, xxii (1928), 65–72.

TAVE, STUART M., *The Amiable Humourist* (Chicago, 1960).

THACKERAY, WILLIAM MAKEPEACE, *English Humourists of the Eighteenth Century* (1853).

THOMPSON, E. N. S., 'Tom Brown and Eighteenth-Century Satirists', *MLN* xxxii (1917), 90–4.

THORPE, CLARENCE DE WITT, *The Aesthetic Theory of Thomas Hobbes* (Ann Arbor, Mich., 1940).

TIDDY, R. J. E., *English Literature and the Classics* (Oxford, 1912).

TRICKETT, R., 'The Augustan Pantheon', *E & S* N.S. vi (1953), 71–86.

—— *The Honest Muse* (Oxford, 1967).

TUCKER, SAMUEL MARION, *Verse Satire in England before the Renaissance* (New York, 1908).

TUPPER, JAMES W., 'A Study of Pope's Imitations of Horace', *PMLA* xv (1900), 181–215.

ULLMAN, B. L., 'Horace on the Nature of Satire', *Transactions of the Amer. Philological Assoc.*, xlviii (1917), 111–32.

—— 'Q. Horatius Flaccus, Ph.D., Professor of Ethics', *Classical Journal*, xiii (1917), 258–66.

—— 'The Present Status of the *Satura* Question', *SP* xvii (1920), 379–401.

VAN ROOY, C. A., *Studies in Classical Satire and Related Literary Theory* (Leiden, 1965).

VOIGT, MILTON, *Swift and the Twentieth Century* (Detroit, 1964).

WALKER, HUGH, *English Satire and Satirists* (1925).

WARD, CHARLES E., *The Life of John Dryden* (1961).

WEDGWOOD, C. V., *Poetry and Politics under the Stuarts* (Cambridge, 1960).

WHITFORD, ROBERT C., 'Satire's View of Sentimentalism in the Days of George III', *JEGP* xviii (1919), 155–204.

—— 'Juvenal in England, 1750–1802', *PQ* vii (1928), 9–16.

WILKINSON, ANDREW M., 'The Decline of English Verse Satire in the Middle Years of the Eighteenth Century', *RES* N.S. iii (1952), 222–3.

—— 'The Rise of English Verse Satire in the Eighteenth Century', *English Studies*, xxxiv (1953), 97–108.

WILLEY, BASIL, *The Seventeenth-Century Background* (1934).

—— *The Eighteenth-Century Background* (1940).

WILLIAMS, EDWIN E., 'Dr. James Drake and the Restoration Theory of Comedy', *RES* xv (1939), 180–91.

WILLIAMS, HAROLD, *Dean Swift's Library* (Cambridge, 1932).

WILLMOTT, R. E. A., *Pleasures of Literature* (New York, 1907).

WIMSATT, W. K., JUN., 'The Augustan Mode in English Poetry', *ELH* xx (1953), 1–14.

—— *Hateful Contraries, Studies in Literature and Criticism* (Lexington, 1965).

WOLFE, HUMBERT, *Notes on English Verse Satire* (1929).

WOOD, PAUL SPENCER, 'Native Elements in English Neo-Classicism', *MP* xxiv (1926), 201–8.

—— 'The Opposition to Neo-Classicism in England between 1660 and 1700', *PMLA* xliii (1928), 182–97.

WOODBRIDGE, HOMER E., *Sir William Temple, The Man and His Work* (Oxford, 1940).

WORCESTER, DAVID, *The Art of Satire* (Harvard, 1940).

WRIGHT, THOMAS, *History of Caricature and Grotesque in Literature and Art* (1839).

YOST, C. D., *The Poetry of the Gentleman's Magazine* (Philadelphia, 1936).

Index